A2

General Studies

Andy Collins & Martyn Groucutt

Contents

Contents

Specification lists

AQA A General Studies

MODULE	SPECIFICATION TOPIC	CHAPTER REFERENCE	STUDIED IN CLASS	REVISED	PRACTICE QUESTIONS
Module 4 (M4) Culture, morality, arts and humanities	Beliefs, values and moral reasoning	4.1, 4.3, 6.1			
	Religious belief and experience	4,1, 4.2, 4.3, 9.1			
	The nature and importance of culture	4.2, 6.1, 6.2, 6.3			
	Creativity and innovation	5.1, 5.3, 6.2			
	Aesthetic evaluation	4.2, 6.1, 6.2, 6.3			
	Media and communication	5.4			
	Foreign language comprehension – see note in Chapter 6				
Module 5 (M5) Science, mathematics and technology	Characteristics of the sciences	8.1, 9.1			
	Scientific objectivity and progress	7.1–7.7, 9.1, 9.2			
	Scientific methods, principles, criteria	9.2			
	Social, ethical and environmental implications	8.1–8.5			
	Technology, science, culture and ideology	7.1–7.7, 9.2, 9.3			
	Spatial and mechanical relations – see note at end of Chapter 7				
Module 6 (M6) Society, politics and the economy	Ideologies and values in society	2.3, 4.3, 5.2, 6.2			
	Political processes and goals	2.1–2.4			
	Objectivity in social science	1.3			
	Law, culture and ethics	1.2, 6.2			
	Social and economic trends and constraints	3.3, 3.4			

Examination analysis

Unit 4	Multiple choice questions – European language; one essay	1 hr 30 min test	15%
Unit 5	Multiple choice questions – spatial and mechanical relations; one essay	1 hr 30 min test	15%
Unit 6	Case study: with short **and** extended written responses	1 hr 30 min test	20%

AQA B General Studies

MODULE	SPECIFICATION TOPIC	CHAPTER REFERENCE	STUDIED IN CLASS	REVISED	PRACTICE QUESTIONS
Module 4 (M4) Conflict – resolutions (with coursework option)	*Understanding of science*	8.1–8.5, 9.1			
	Sustainability	7.2–7.4			
	Politics and the social contract	2.2, 2.3			
	Decoding arts and media	5.1–5.3, 6.1–6.3			
	Industrial relations	3.1, 3.2			
	Personal finance	3.4			
	Equal opportunities	1.1			
	Rights and responsibilities	1.3, 1.4, 4.1			
Module 5 (M5) Power – regulation	*Science – its use and abuse*	7.1–7.7, 8.1–8.5			
	Political accountability	2.2			
	Artistic standards and media ownership	5.1–5.3, 6.2, 6.3			
	Consumerism	3.4			
	Free trade	3.4			
	Changing norms and values	1.3, 6.1–6.3			
Module 6 (M6) Space – time	*Space research and measurement*	8.4			
	The idea of progress	1.3, 7.1–7.7, 8.1			
	Cultural diversity	4.2, 6.2, 6.3			
	Social change and reform	1.3			
	New arts, new media, music and literature	5.1–5.3			
	Heritage, tourism and new patterns of working	3.2, 6.2, 6.3			
	History, culture and secularism	4.2, 4.3, 6.1–6.3			

Examination analysis

The specification comprises three unit tests.

Unit 4 (with coursework option)

Either:	Problem solving exercise	1 hr test	15%
or:	Coursework – a problem solving assignment (1000 words)		15%
Unit 5	Five short–answer questions on source materials	1 hr 15 min test	15%
Unit 6	Two essays based on source materials	1 hr 45 min test	20%

Edexcel General Studies

MODULE	SPECIFICATION TOPIC	CHAPTER REFERENCE	STUDIED IN CLASS	REVISED	PRACTICE QUESTIONS
Module 4 (M4) Cultural expressions	***Culture, morality, arts and humanities***				
	The nature and importance of culture	6.1–6.3			
	Beliefs, values and moral reasoning	4.1–4.3, 9.1			
	Religious belief and experience	4.1, 4.3, 9.1			
	Creativity and innovation	4.2, 5.1–5.3			
	Aesthetic evaluation	6.1–6.3			
	Media and communication	5.1–5.3			
Module 5 (M5) Modern society	***Society, politics and the economy***				
	The ideologies and values in society	2.2, 4.1, 4.3			
	Political processes and goals	2.1, 2.3			
	Objectivity in social sciences	1.3			
	An evaluation of human behaviour	6.2			
	Law, culture and ethics	1.2, 6.2			
	Social and economic trends and constraints	3.3, 3.4			
Module 6 (M6) The contemporary world	***Science, culture and society***				
	Science and culture	4.1, 4.3, 5.1, 5.3, 9.1–9.3			
	Culture and society	4.2, 5.1–5.3, 6.1–6.3			
	Science and society	7.1–7.7, 8.1–8.5			

Examination analysis

Unit 4	(with coursework option)		
<u>Either:</u>	2 sections of short answers – 1 on subject areas, 1 on stimulus material	1 hr 30 min test	15%
<u>or:</u>	Coursework, approx 2000 words from the area of culture, morality, arts and humanities		15%
Unit 5	2 sections of short answers – 1 on subject areas, 1 on stimulus material	1 hr 30 min test	15%
Unit 6	Two structured pieces of extended writing from a choice of four	1 hr 30 min test	20%

OCR General Studies

MODULE	SPECIFICATION TOPIC	CHAPTER REFERENCE	STUDIED IN CLASS	REVISED	PRACTICE QUESTIONS
Module 4 (M4) The scientific and cultural domains	Scientific objectivity and the question of progress	7.1–7.7, 9.1			
	Social, ethical and environmental implications of science and technology	8.1–8.5			
	Technology, science, culture and ideology	6.1–6.3, 9.2–9.3			
Module 5 (M5) The social domain (with coursework option)	Ideologies and values	2.2, 4.1–4.3, 6.2			
	Explanation and evaluation of human behaviour	4.1–4.3, 5.1–5.3			
	Relationships between law, culture and ethics	1.2, 6.2, 7.1, 7.5, 8.1, 8.5			
Module 6 (M6) Culture, science and society: making connections	Topics covered in questions will seek to pull together all chapters and are relevant topics from the scientific, cultural and social domains.				

Examination analysis

Unit 4	Two essays	1 hr 30 min test	15%
Unit 5	(with coursework option)		
	<u>Either:</u> One question based on stimulus material and one essay	1 hr 30 min test	15%
	<u>or:</u> Coursework assignment		15%
Unit 6	Responses to resource material; one essay based on stimulus material	1 hr 30 min test	20%

AS/A2 Level General Studies courses

AS and A2

All General Studies A Level courses being studied from September 2000 are in two parts, with three separate modules in each part. Students first study the AS (Advanced Subsidiary) course. Some will then go on to study the second part of the A Level course, called A2. Advanced Subsidiary is assessed at the standard expected halfway through an A Level course: i.e., between GCSE and Advanced GCE. This means that new AS and A2 courses are designed so that difficulty steadily increases:

- A2 General Studies builds from AS General Studies.

How will you be tested?

Assessment units

For AS General Studies, you will be tested by three assessment units. For the full A Level in General Studies, you will take a further three units. AS General Studies forms 50% of the assessment weighting for the full A Level.

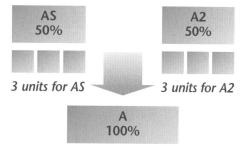

Each unit can normally be taken in either January or June. Alternatively, you can study the whole course before taking any of the unit tests. There is a lot of flexibility about when exams can be taken and the diagram below shows just some of the ways that the assessment units may be taken for AS and A Level General Studies.

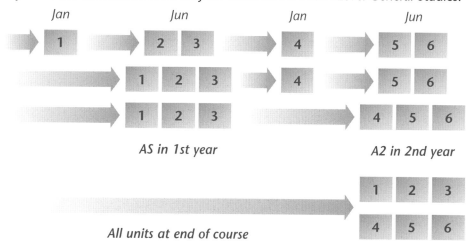

If you are disappointed with a module result, you can resit each module once. You will need to be very careful about when you take up a resit opportunity because you will have only one chance to improve your mark. The higher mark counts.

A2 and Synoptic assessment

After having studied AS General Studies, you may wish to continue studying General Studies to A Level. For this you will need to take three further units of General Studies at A2. Similar assessment arrangements apply except for the final unit, which draws together different parts of the course in a synoptic assessment.

Coursework

Coursework may form part of your AS or A2 General Studies course depending on the specification. However, it is optional in all specifications.

Key skills

It is important that you develop your key skills throughout your AS and A2 courses. These are important skills that you need whatever you do beyond AS and A Levels. To gain the key skills qualification you will need to collect evidence together in a 'portfolio' to show that you have attained Level 3 in Communication, Application of number and Information technology. You will also need to take a formal test in each key skill. You will have many opportunities during A2 General Studies to develop your key skills.

It is a worthwhile qualification, as it demonstrates your ability to put your ideas across to other people, collect data and use up-to-date technology in your work.

What skills will I need?

For A2 General Studies, you will be tested by assessment objectives: these are the skills and abilities that you should have acquired by studying the course. The assessment objectives for A2 General Studies are shown below.

Knowledge with understanding

- Skills gained from different disciplines

Communicate clearly

- Quality of language
- Able to use language in a concise, logical and relevant way

Marshal evidence and draw conclusions

- Select, interpret, evaluate and interpret data and written information
- Be able to use information provided to develop arguments
- Understand the difference between fact and assertion

Demonstrate understanding of different types of knowledge

- Show an understanding of different types of knowledge
- Be able to see the relationship between them
- Be able to appreciate their limitations

Different types of questions in A2 examinations

In A2 General Studies examinations, different types of questions are used to assess your abilities and skills. There are also some differences in the types of questions set in the different examinations.

Short-answer questions

These take the form of asking you to analyse and respond to questions or to short pieces of stimulus material (for example, a newspaper headline, some data or an advert). This can be either a written or a data-response answer. They are found in the AQA specifications A and B, and the Edexcel and OCR specifications.

Multiple choice objective questions

These take the form of questions with several possible answers and you have to choose which one is correct. Such questions feature in the AQA specification A and Edexcel papers.

Extended writing

This takes two main forms:

(i) the traditional essay written in response to a question

(ii) the creation of an argument to put forward based on stimulus material provided with the paper.

All of the specifications use both types of extended writing to some extent. The quality of your writing forms part of the assessment, as does your ability to examine a variety of sources and use them efficiently.

Four steps to successful revision

Step 1: Understand

- Study the topic to be learned slowly. Make sure you understand the logic or important concepts
- Mark up the text if necessary – underline, highlight and make notes
- Re-read each paragraph slowly.

GO TO STEP 2

Step 2: Summarise

- Now make your own revision note summary:
  What is the main idea, theme or concept to be learned?
  What are the main points? How does the logic develop?
  Ask questions: Why? How? What next?
- Use bullet points, mind maps, patterned notes
- Link ideas with mnemonics, mind maps, crazy stories
- Note the title and date of the revision notes
  (e.g. General Studies: Social class, 3rd March)
- Organise your notes carefully and keep them in a file.

This is now in **short term memory**. You will forget 80% of it if you do not go to Step 3.
GO TO STEP 3, but first take a 10 minute break.

Step 3: Memorise

- Take 25 minute learning 'bites' with 5 minute breaks
- After each 5 minute break test yourself:
  Cover the original revision note summary
  Write down the main points
  Speak out loud (record on tape)
  Tell someone else
  Repeat many times.

The material is well on its way to **long term memory**.
You will forget 40% if you do not do step 4. **GO TO STEP 4**

Step 4: Track/Review

- Create a Revision Diary (one A4 page per day)
- Make a revision plan for the topic, e.g. 1 day later, 1 week later, 1 month later.
- Record your revision in your Revision Diary, e.g.
  General Studies: Social class, 3rd March 25 minutes
  General Studies: Social class, 5th March 15 minutes
  General Studies: Social class, 3rd April 15 minutes
  ... and then at monthly intervals.

Chapter 1

Modern society

The following topics are covered in this chapter:

- *Equal opportunities*
- *Law and its enforcement*
- *Social change*
- *Dependency on the state*

1.1 Equal opportunities

After studying this section you should be able to:

- *define equal opportunities*
- *describe what it means in relation to gender, employment and race*

Defining equal opportunities

AQA A	M6
AQA B	M4
EDEXCEL	M3
OCR	M4

> Both the Equal Pay Act and the Sexual Discrimination Acts were passed in the 1970s.

Key points from AS

- **Social class**
  Revise AS pages 16–19
- **Gender roles**
  Revise AS pages 14–15
- **Employment and unemployment**
  Revise AS pages 40–43

Everyone thinks they know what the term equal opportunities means. How would *you* define it? Do we have it in the United Kingdom? Is it a worldwide phenomenon?

The answer to the second question would probably be in the affirmative, the response to the third question would probably be in the negative.

We know we have equal opportunities in the UK because there are various Acts of Parliament that have been passed to ensure equality in areas such as gender, race and employment. But does this always mean that 'equality' exists in practice?

The aim of this section is to explore the concept of equal opportunities within the areas of gender, employment and race.

Peter Saunders, in his book *Social Class and Stratification,* (1990) distinguished two types of equality relevant to our analysis.

- Formal or legal authority involves all members of society being subject to the same laws or rules – individuals being judged on what they do, not who they are. This legal equality is an integral part of Western capitalist society.
- Equality of opportunity means that people have an equal chance to become unequal. They compete for success and those with greater merit achieve more. This can be seen in areas such as the education system with its increasing reliance on outcomes (i.e. examination results at Key Stage 4 (16) or Key Stage 5 (18) which in all probability will determine employment prospects.

Merit, referred to earlier, may involve the ability to work harder or the possession of attributes or characteristics that are valued in a society.

> This concept is known as 'meritocracy'.

The UK (or anywhere else) is not a perfect society in which everyone has genuinely equal opportunities to use their talents to gain success. Even at this stage of our study it is relevant to point out that people with parents from higher social-class backgrounds have more chance of ending up in higher-class jobs themselves, than people from lower social-class backgrounds.

> This concept is known as 'social mobility'.

It also needs to be emphasised that opportunities for all social groups to move up the social strata, have increased radically in the second half of the 20th century because of the decline in lower-class manual jobs and because of the increase in higher-class non-manual work (e.g. in tertiary service industries such as education).

> **KEY POINT**
>
> Equality of opportunity can be seen as a pre-condition of a fair society. (NB Equality of opportunity does not guarantee equality of *outcome* – it means that people will achieve jobs suitable to their intelligence and talents, regardless of social background.)

Gender

Historically there have been two great eras of 'feminism' – or demands made for equality by women. The first of these coincides with the start of the 20th century and was associated with the right to vote. The suffragette movement played a very prominent role in the emancipation of women; by 1928 all women in the UK had the right to vote at 21 (the same age as men). This was reduced to 18 in 1969.

> The first moves for demanding the right to vote at 16 are just beginning. What are your views about this?
>
> (Bear in mind that the subject 'Citizenship' is to be made compulsory in school in 2002 and GCSE courses in it will be available at that time.)
>
> **KEY POINT**

The second era of feminism was linked to the late 1960s–1970s. There were several reasons for this.

- Women had developed political confidence in an era of demonstrations (such as those against the Vietnam War) and in mainstream politics. They therefore resented the patronising attitudes of many men.
- They had new sexual freedom. The introduction of the contraceptive pill in the early 1960s had freed many women from the fear of unwanted pregnancy. However, many women felt they were still being treated as sexual objects. Also, in spite of joining the workforce, there was still a prevalent feeling that a woman's place was in the home.
- Far more women were gaining degrees, embarking on careers, postponing the advent of their families. Consequently they felt that there should be more opportunities available to them.

Liberal feminists sought equal rights with men, stressing the need to compete freely with men and to have the same opportunities. Hence they campaigned for the removal of social, political, economic or legal obstacles that discriminated against women. The Equal Opportunities Commission has been a success here, as has legislation such as the Equal Pay Act 1975. Some, however, argued that this did not go far enough and **radical feminists** stressed the basic conflict between all men and all women. They argued that men use their power to ensure that society is run in their interests and that men's control over cultural attitudes ensures that people think that the status quo is natural. For these reasons radical feminists did not want equal rights, but freedom from male domination.

By the 1980s the women's movement had become more fragmented. Many believed that the legal, political and economic battles had been won (they could point to Margaret Thatcher as Prime Minister, a far greater proportion of female high-profile executives, and so on). The move by the Labour Party to have more 'all female' shortlists before the 1997 General Election led to a situation post-May 1997 of 101 new female MPs ('Blair's Babes'). Ironically all-women shortlists have now been ruled unlawful on sexual discrimination grounds.

You may wish to think about the greater attainment of girls compared with boys in GCSE. Why does this happen? Is it possibly a result of the introduction of coursework that girls handle better than boys?

- Men are often still perceived as being more capable of carrying out higher-level positions in work (e.g. women experience a 'glass ceiling' in relation to their opportunities for promotion).

However, even this is changing. Arguably girls are now portrayed by the media as strong-minded, independent and assertive (for example, characters in soap operas such as *Eastenders*, *Brookside*).

Similarly, boys are now depicted as being capable of having 'feelings'. However, this can be countered by the influence of 'lads' magazines (such as *FHM* or *Loaded*), which seem to portray females predominantly as sex objects.

The whole range of advertising also comes into this, with controversies over such items as Wonderbra adverts; the emphasis of the fashion industry on glamour and sexuality; the portrayal of young supermodels leading to claims of anorexia and bulimia. In other words, women's pictures displayed everywhere indicate a perfect being who is used to sell a variety of objects.

Hence, at the start of the 21st century we need to consider whether women are still exploited or are exploiting their opportunities by using their sexuality. (The answer is probably a combination of both!)

Progress check

1 Give three reasons for women in the 1970s feeling a need for greater equality with men.

2 Which of the following terms would you place under the heading of 'masculine traits or ideals' or 'feminine traits or ideals'?
i) aggressive ii) ambitious iii) affectionate iv) compassionate v) competitive vi) conciliatory vii) forceful viii) sensitive ix) shy x) self-reliant.

i) m ii) m iii) f iv) f v) m vi) f vii) m viii) f ix) f x) m.

greater self-confidence in their rights; new sexual freedom; higher levels achieved in qualifications.

Employment

Less than 20 years ago a major survey of female employment in the UK found that most married women regarded their real job as that of running the home and caring for children.

Paid work was not seen as being as pivotal to their lives as it was for men. It can be argued that this attitude and the employment patterns, by which women occupy different positions in the labour market, are changing.

By 1993, 44% of the workforce was female. 71% of women of working age were economically active compared with 91% of men. The increase in the female workforce is partly due to the growth of the service sector (where shift work and twilight hours employment are typified in the caring industry. However it is largely due to the increased economic activity of married women.

The proportion of married women in paid employment increased from 47% in 1971 to 68% in 1993. There is every reason to suppose that this trend will continue. In spite of all of this, certain points need to be remembered.

- The vast majority of part-time work is done by women (this is due to their major domestic and child-care responsibilities).
- Some part-time jobs have been specifically designed for married women.

There are several reasons for this.

- On the one hand certain factors restrict the quality of female labour. The state still seems to expect women to shoulder the main burdens of child-care and domestic responsibilities, thus reducing women's opportunities to obtain satisfactory employment. When they do find employment they usually work a 'double day', managing the dual responsibilities of employment and housework.
- From another perspective, there are features of the labour market that determine the demand for female labour. These factors include:
  - changing technology (for example a diminution of the requirements for dexterity amongst women in the traditional office environment or as telephone operators)
  - the attitudes of male employers (for example, if the 'top' jobs require long hours, then this handicaps women).

The figures in this section are a good example of the famous comment attributed to Mark Twain that 'there are three kinds of lies: lies, damned lies and statistics' – i.e. whilst they are accurate, statistics only reflect a particular moment in time, and incorrect assumptions can be drawn from them.

It must be remembered that the term 'women and the workplace' contains many great generalisations, which can in itself lead to a lack of precision in comments. There is a great deal of variation regarding women and employment (for example, factory work, secretarial work, and professional work). Each profession or area of work will tell a different story and in some there is more converging of the opportunities for men and women.

Progress check

Give some reasons why women have been able to penetrate the 'glass ceiling'.

Answers could include: higher educational qualifications; better child-care facilities; greater control of when family begins; greater support from 'new men'.

Race

It is important in this area of discussion to be clear about terminology. **Ethnic groups** are identified according to their distinctive **cultural** features. Members of ethnic groups often have a strong sense of belonging based on their shared culture and regular social interaction. A House of Lords judgement (1983) specified some legal requirements to qualify as an ethnic group:

- a long shared history
- a cultural tradition of its own
- a common geographic origin
- a common language
- a common literature
- a common religion.

It is not easy, however, to allocate people to ethnic groups: culture is sprawling and blurs at the edges. It is also complicated by the history of immigration in the UK.

However, it is vital to put the concept of immigration into perspective. The 1991 Census showed the ethnic population to be as shown in Table 1.1.

> How many of these requirements would the Welsh, or the Cornish fulfil? Yet one is perceived as a race and the other is not.

The UK has had successive waves of immigrants: Romans, Anglo-Saxons, Vikings, Normans, Jews, Huguenots, Irish. After World War II migration from the New Commonwealth countries increased:

1940s–50s – West Indies
1960s – Asia (India/Pakistan)
1970s – East African/Asian

Table 1.1 *The composition of the UK by ethnic group according to the 1991 Census*

Ethnic Group	Numbers (000's)	Percentage
White	51 843	94.5
Black Caribbean	499	0.9
Black African	207	0.4
Black other	178	0.3
Indian	840	1.5
Pakistani	475	0.9
Bangladeshi	160	0.3
Chinese	157	0.3
Other – Asian	196	0.4
Other – other	290	0.5
All minorities	3006	5.5

There are two areas where ethnicity is relevant to the idea of equal opportunity.

Education

Success in education is a vital pre-requisite to success in one's career. The stereotypical belief is that ethnic minorities do less well in terms of examination results. A Commission for Racial Equality analysis (1992), entitled *Set to Fail*, backs up this assertion, showing that Asian pupils of similar ability to whites were less likely to be entered for GCSE examinations. However, there could be a whole range of reasons for this, such as attendance and completion of coursework. It also needs to be borne in mind that statistics are merely a 'snapshot' at one point in time.

Evidence from surveys is often dated and as second or third generation of ethnic-minority families go through the education system, there are perhaps other factors, rather than ethnicity, that are relevant.

Employment

Table 1.2 Economic activity rates 1993 in percentage terms
(Source: Social Trends 1994, National Statistics © Crown Copyright 2001)

	Males	**Females**
White	86	72
Afro-Caribbean	80	66
Indian	81	61
Pakistani/Bangladeshi	72	25

Table 1.2 can generate certain conclusions:

- the Afro-Caribbean group has quite high rates when compared with whites
- rates are much lower for the Pakistani/Bangladeshi group, especially amongst women.

Not shown in this table but also true is the fact that among the younger age groups the ethnic minority economic activity rates are 20% lower than the equivalent white population. This is largely explained because the minority groups have a larger proportion of young people in further education.

Ethnic minorities are generally still concentrated in those sectors of the economy that they joined in the 1950s–60s. Hence there are significant differences with whites in such areas as construction, metal-goods manufacturing, transport and health services. The differences between whites and minorities are markedly less amongst women because women are generally concentrated in certain areas of the labour market.

Therefore there is not an even playing field in the labour market for minorities, who are more likely to work in the sections of the economy with greater risk of low pay, doing shift work with longer hours of work and with less access to training. Arguably events such as the decline of manufacturing as the basis of the economy and the use of 'new' technological industries located away from town centres (where most ethnic minorities live) in the last decade have made this worse.

There is, of course, the possibility that the minimum wage will become the maximum wage i.e. employers will automatically not pay more than the Government decrees.

This situation should in theory be countered by the Minimum Wage Act 1999 which is expected to have given a boost to ethnic minority wages – in spite of the dire warnings of job losses by Conservative opposition to this legislation.

Despite these comments, there are indications of good upward social mobility on the part of some ethnic minority groups, such as Indian and Chinese.

Progress check

Why do you think role models of successful, educated business people are important for ethnic minority groups?

Answers could include: to ensure a stereotypical life style is not accepted as the norm; to indicate that educational attainment can lead to success; to show that employment opportunities can be used as a way of climbing the social ladder.

1.2 Law and its enforcement

After studying this section you should be able to:

- explain what the terms 'law' and 'crime' mean and describe how they are continually changing
- describe how society attempts to control criminal activity and the ways in which crime is punished

LEARNING SUMMARY

What is the law?

AQA A	M7
AQA B	M5
EDEXCEL	M5
OCR	M5

Key points from AS

- **Power and influence of the press**
  Revise AS pages 90–93
- **Changes to family life**
  Revise AS pages 13–14

Weber, in his book *Economy and society: an outline of interpretative sociology* (1978), defined a state as 'a human community that successfully claims the monopoly of the legitimate use of physical force within a given territory'. In other words, a country, such as the UK, has authority over those who live in a defined geographical area and can use force (the force of law) to back up this authority. Thus, rules govern everyone's lives. It is what happens when these rules get broken that forms the main part of this section.

Consider a typical day in your life; you leave the house to go to college or work; when you return you expect that it will still be your home and that another family will not have moved in and taken over all of your property (i.e. the law protects you). If people had moved in, they would be guilty of trespass ('passing across'). Having passed across without permission they can be asked to leave and if they refuse to go, force could be used (i.e. legal force).

This is just one example of a crime that is basically a social act that offends the law of a society. It needs to be borne in mind that different societies have different laws; hence what is criminal in one society need not be so in another.

Progress check

Give some examples from the recent past where differing societies have differing laws.

Answers could include: race laws – under the Apartheid Regime in South Africa; Nazi repression and persecution of the Jews in World War II; the age limit for drinking is 18 in the UK and 21 in USA.

Crime

AQA A	M7
AQA B	M5
EDEXCEL	M5
OCR	M5

You should now be able to start to appreciate how difficult it is to obtain a conviction for a crime. You may be aware of the merits of the Scottish system, which allows three verdicts: Guilty, Not Guilty and Not Proven.

There are two definitions of a crime: it is a physical action (known in law as *Actus reus*) and a guilty mind (*Mens rea*). Hence the typical definition of theft as 'the dishonest appropriation of property (i.e. *Actus reus*) belonging to another, with the intention (*Mens rea*) to permanently deprive the owner of it'. This means that if I take sweets from someone, the prosecution would need to prove 'beyond a reasonable doubt' that I intended to deprive that person permanently!

Whenever crime figures are reported they need to be viewed with caution. They only indicate known crimes, not those actually committed (i.e. if I drive over the speed limit I have committed a crime. However, unless that is reported it is not registered as a **known crime**). Crimes are normally divided into **indictable** and **non-indictable** offences. The latter are the less serious ones that can be dealt with in a magistrate's court.

A definition of crime requires there to be a physical action (*Actus reus*) and a guilty mind (*Mens rea*).

KEY POINT

When people are asked to define crimes by example, they inevitably refer to murder, rape, assaults, muggings, etc. In all probability the reasons for this lie in the portrayal of crime by the media, in which newspapers and television focus on the brutal. For example: 'At the Old Bailey, a teenager was branded "dangerously evil" after stamping an 88 year old woman to death'. (*Today* 28.9.94)

This view of crime is boosted by political opposition parties who always attempt to make political capital from any rise in violent crime, even if overall crime rates are falling. The actual statistics show that 5 365 000 crimes were recorded in 1993–94, with 93% of these being crimes against property. However, it is crimes against the person that create media interest and therefore newspaper coverage – this enhances the perception that crime against the person is statistically very high.

This leads to great fears, particularly on the part of the elderly. The Home Office found that 58% of people who felt 'very unsafe' in their neighbourhood had not spent one evening outside their home in the week before they were interviewed. Of these, 81% said it was because they never went out alone or at night on foot.

In spite of this, the Home Office states that statistically each individual can expect to be injured in an assault once in every hundred years and robbed once every five centuries and burglary is once every 40 years. Hence while violent crime is increasing, it is doing so only slowly and there may be other reasons for this.

These figures show that, statistically, the people of the UK live in a non-threatening society. However, bear in mind that these figures are the norm or average, and there will be some areas of the country where the statistics will be far lower, i.e. where recorded crime against the person is far higher.

Reported crime

There are a number of reasons why official statistics for crime paint a rather incomplete picture.

- Although 80% of recorded crime results from reports by the public (bear in mind that the use of mobile phones will inevitably make reporting of crimes easier), there are many occasions when the crime will not be reported. For example, vandalism may seem too trivial; if a fraud has taken place then people may not even be aware of it, or it could be viewed as a 'domestic' (i.e. something which has happened inside the home and is therefore no-one else's business).
- The number of offences depends on how the counting rules work – for example, if several offences take place then only the most serious is counted.
- Only about 40% of offences reported to the police are actually recorded. In other words, the police have the power of discretion as to whether or not a particular offence is serious enough to warrant attention. If the police are being pressurised into improving their 'clear up' rate, they will target their efforts in certain areas and may not even record crimes in the first place.
- The official statistics do not even cover summary offences (that is, those tried in magistrate's courts or those dealt with administratively by organisations such as Customs and Excise).

Consequently, the hard figures presented to us by the police and media need to be interpreted with extreme caution. They are certainly not meaningless, yet how true a picture they paint is open to discussion.

Trends in crime

On the surface there would appear, at least, to be some kind of agreement regarding the trends in crime. Most statisticians will tell you that until the 1930s there had been little real rise in crime since the 1870s; there was then a gradual rise until the 1950s and then a sharp and sustained increase with a doubling in numbers each decade.

Public perception is quite interesting in this. It seems that the public has a 'rose-coloured' spectacled view of the 'good old days', when everyone left their doors unlocked, trusted their neighbours and everything was fine! Yet if the media of past generations is to be believed at that time the country was in the middle of a crime wave! For example, the following periods each suffered from different kinds of troublemakers.

- 1860s   the garotters
- 1890s   the 'hooligans' who fought pitched street battles
- 1930s   the Razor gangs
- 1950s   the Teddy boys
- 1960s   Mods and Rockers
- 1980s   Black street gangs

These are good examples of how, over the decades the media, principally the newspapers, have had a great effect on the public's perceptions.

Although by the 1990s it was becoming accepted that there was more crime, reasons could also be put forward for this:

- increased telephone ownership
- increased affluence in the home, i.e. more to steal
- a feeling that if items are insured then no-one is losing out
- a break-up of traditional communities that would have previously dealt with incidents, has led to people being more willing to bring in the police
- more laws to break due to increased legislation – one in every three crimes is linked to motor cars and the legislation that goes with them; an understandable reason for an increase in crime compared with the 1900s.

Table 1.3 Crimes committed by outcome in England and Wales (as a percentage of offences committed)

Year	Reported to the Police (%)	Recorded by the Police (%)
1981	36	22
1991	49	30
1993	47	26
1995	46	23
1997	44	24

Progress check

What can you deduce from the above statistics?

Answers could include: the proportion of crimes, both reported to, and recorded by, the police has changed over time; the proportion reported to the police increased during the 1980s, but has been falling during the 1990s; only just over half of the crimes reported to the police in England and Wales were recorded by them; non-recording could be due to the perception that the crime is too trivial; there is insufficient evidence or the victim may not want the police to succeed.

Punishment of crime

The percentage of those convicted who were first-time offenders varies with the type of offence. For example, in 1996 only 21% of males convicted of burglary had no previous convictions, as compared with 49% of males convicted of sexual offences. Following an arrest in England and Wales the police can:

- release the suspect without further action
- caution them, either formally or informally
- charge them.

Once an offender is charged and found guilty, the court will impose a sentence. These sentences range from immediate discharge to immediate custody. As you would expect, the form of sentence varies according to the type of offence committed. For example, motoring offenders are most likely to be fined, offenders sentenced for robbery are most likely to get immediate custody, whilst those sentenced for burglary are most likely to receive a community sentence. Again, as you would expect, those offenders who commit serious crimes or are persistent offenders are the most likely to receive custodial sentences.

Changes to the Law

AQA A	M7
AQA B	M5
EDEXCEL	M5
OCR	M5

These rights can be seen as the basic rights for everyone at the start of the 21st century. It may be worthwhile comparing them with those in the American Constitution, or even the rules stated in the UK before this time. (These latter can be found in the various statutes and laws passed by parliament over the centuries, as well as by 'conventions of the constitution' which lead to legal challenges if infringed, e.g. driving on the wrong side of the road.)

On 2 October 2000 the Human Rights Act came into force. This is considered by some to be the most important change to our legal system for a century, because it brings into UK law much of the European Convention of Human Rights and enables people to use the Convention in UK court proceedings, rather than taking their case to Strasbourg.

The Act introduces a 'new way of thinking' in that existing legislation, rules and laws are to be interpreted in a way that is compatible with the Convention rights.

The Human Rights act distinguishes three types of rights:

- **Absolute rights**: the right to life, prohibition of torture or of inhuman or degrading treatment and slavery and servitude. These cannot be restricted in any circumstance.
- **Limited Rights** cover liberty and security and the right to a fair trial. These may be curtailed by the state in certain circumstances (e.g. the arrest of criminals, conviction and imprisonment).
- **Qualified Rights** encompass private and family life, freedom of thought, conscience and religion, freedom of expression and freedom of assembly and association. These are subject to clauses and conditions that enable a balance to be struck between the rights of the individual and the interests of a democratic society.

Thus you can see how rapidly and radically the law can and does change. It will be worth your while keeping a vigilant eye on the ramifications of this Act. Although specific questions on this are unlikely, it will serve as a good example of how and why the law does change and therefore why it is difficult to compare the law over a period of time.

1.3 Social change

After studying this section you should be able to:

- *describe the great alterations to all aspects of society that are continually taking place*
- *explain how alterations in one element of society automatically cause ripple effects in others*

LEARNING SUMMARY

What do we mean by 'social change'?

AQA A	M6
AQA B	M6
EDEXCEL	M5
OCR	M5

The famous American sociologist Talcott Parsons argued that no social system is ever in a perfect state of equilibrium (that is, with all of its various parts contributing towards order and stability). He saw the process of social change as a

> It is mainly for this reason that the largest Catholic congregations are now found in Third World countries.

'moving equilibrium'. In other words, the various elements of a social system are interrelated and hence a change in one will produce responses in the others. To be able to appreciate this, it is useful to take certain examples and indicate where (or even if) social change has occurred in that example.

Religion

This is often seen as a factor that impedes social change – which was certainly the view of the Marxists, who believed that religion acted as a conservative force (maintaining the status quo and preventing change). Religion normally provides shared beliefs, norms and values and helps individuals to cope with stress that might disrupt the social order. The maintenance of the status quo will also include traditional customs and beliefs (for example, successive Popes' views about the use of contraception has resulted in the restriction in the growth of using artificial methods of contraception in countries where Roman Catholicism has a strong influence).

However, in some circumstances religion can support social change. This often occurs when there is a revival of fundamentalist religious belief which (in Christianity, for example) would usually be caused by a reaction against the authority of the established church.

Donald Taylor, in his book *Incipient fundamentalism: religion and politics among Sri Lankan Hindus in Britain* (1987), sees fundamentalism as:

- a group of people who believe **in the infallibility of an ultimate authority** (usually a god) and perceive a challenge to that ultimate authority
- a decision by this group that the challenge cannot be tolerated
- a reaffirmation of their belief in the authority that is being challenged
- opposition to those who have challenged the established beliefs and often the use of political means to further their cause.

There are various examples that support this viewpoint such as the 1979 revolution in Iran which was partly inspired by Islamic fundamentalists and led to immense social change, including the de-liberalisation of women.

Thus it can be seen in some situations religion has promoted social change. Further examples include:

- the role of Rev. Martin Luther King in establishing civil rights in the USA
- the role of Archbishop Desmond Tutu in the struggles against apartheid in South Africa
- the link between the Roman Catholic Church in Northern Ireland and Irish Republicanism
- the Roman Catholic Church opposing the Communist State in Poland and supporting the attempts of the free trade union Solidarity, to achieve changes in Polish society with final success in 1989
- in the 1960s radical and revolutionary groups emerging in the Roman Catholic Church in South America.

Family

> The idea of multi-generational families is, in fact, something of a myth.

Consideration of changing family roles can be enlarged upon by looking at examples of the family and elderly people. Although it is something of a myth that in the past the family provided more care for elderly relatives, this perception certainly exists. It is not statistically valid, however, because in the 19th century far fewer people lived to an age where they became economically or physically dependent on other family members. During the second half of the 20th century increasing employment for women, less opportunity to stay at home and look after elderly relatives, and the building of smaller houses have led to potential problems in the area of care for the elderly and the consequent growth of Old People's Homes.

In fact, only a small minority of elderly people live in institutions, while around 30% live alone.

Recent governments have emphasised the concept of 'care in the community' which attempts to avoid the institutionalisation of the elderly in homes and hospitals. This has only been partly successful because policies of community care which rely on the family will only be successful if families are given adequate support by the agencies of the Welfare State. Arguably, resources are insufficient and create an enormous burden on the mainly female family carers.

> A major factor involved in the Care in the Community Policy has been financial. The cost of long-term care for the elderly in homes has been deemed prohibitive – particularly bearing in mind that we are an ageing population.

In the last 50 years a smaller proportion of single elderly people have been living with relatives. This is largely a result of demographic trends:
* the rise in life expectancy has led to fewer orphans and more elderly people in the population
* as average family size has gone down, there are fewer children with whom the rising number of elderly might live.

KEY POINT

Employment

The most important change affecting family life has been the rise in the proportion of wives taking paid employment. Many have argued that women have increasingly been taking on a dual burden: retaining primary responsibility for household tasks whilst also being expected to undertake paid employment. Table 1.4 shows current and projected employment figures.

Table 1.4 Current and projected employment figures (in millions)

Year	Male	Female
1986	13.9	10.0
1998	14.6	11.5
2001	16.3	13.1 (projected)
2011	16.5	14.1 (projected)

Progress check

What can we deduce from the figures in Table 1.4?

Answers could include:
increasingly important role of women in paid employment; increasing number of women will move into the labour market, partly linked to the number of children being born per family and the later age at which the first child is being born.

> Do you feel that this situation reflects a truly equal sharing of roles, or is it linked to an overall desire for affluence, i.e. the husband wants his partner to work and is therefore willing to make some contribution?

Although women are without question more economically active and their dual burden still exists, research has shown that men do appear to be making more effort to do housework when their wives/partners are in paid work. (However, the more mundane household tasks continue to be a primarily female responsibility!)

Education

One great social change in the last two or three decades has been the increasing likelihood that young people will proceed to A Levels, vocational courses or to undertake government-supported training.

> This all links in with the greater public perception of education, with high levels of accountability (e.g. Ofsted) and the greater involvement of parents.

In 1997 about 75% of 16–18-year-olds were in further education or training, with 65% of 16–17-year-olds staying on in full-time education. Between 1991–97 the number of students enrolling in full-time higher education in the UK increased by 55% and the number in full-time further education increased by 71%.

Progress check

1 What are the reasons for the growth of students enrolling in full-time higher education?
2 What have been the results of this growth?

Answers could include:
1 qualifications are now needed for careers; greater concentration in the media on results (e.g. school league tables; lack of employment opportunities (and reduced opportunities for those without qualifications).
2 a better qualified workforce; graduate unemployment; employment/careers beginning at a later age; later 'settling down', living with partners/spouses and fewer children.

1.4 Dependency on the state

After studying this section you should be able to:

- explain how and why the state has taken on its present role
- describe the problems inherent within attempts to reduce social inequalities
- analyse the benefits and drawbacks of state intervention

LEARNING SUMMARY

The position of the Welfare State

AQA A	M7
AQA B	M5
EDEXCEL	M5

Key points from AS

- **Pressure groups**
  Revise AS pages 34–37

The Welfare State emanated from the lack of state care in the 19th century. Old Age Pensions were first given before World War I, free education came in with the Butler Act 1944, and the National Health Service began in 1948.

The Welfare State, which was to a large extent constructed during the Labour Government of 1945–50, has until recently been taken for granted. It has been assumed that it is a good idea – because of the concept of care 'from cradle to grave' – and that it would always remain. However, increasingly, questions are being asked about its effectiveness in areas such as health, housing and poverty. This, of course, leads on to questions about the role of the state itself – does it cushion people too much? Is it the 'nanny' state that the Conservatives portray as being Blair's Britain?

Inevitably, many of the theories linked to welfare and to the Welfare State are political and lead on to political ideas about how the state should be run. A social-democratic approach to welfare is based on the belief that a certain degree of collective welfare provision, organised by the state, is necessary to counterbalance some of the more undesirable features of a free market society. Take, for example, unemployment and low wages: the Labour government's introduction of the minimum wage in 1999, which in spite of political opposition (claiming that it would lead to more unemployment) has been a great success.

Social democrats usually favour **universal benefits**; the alternative is a **selective system** by way of a means test.

> Universal benefits are available to all; selective benefits are targeted at those in the greatest need.

KEY POINT

Progress check

Give examples of health service provision which are universal and ones that are selective.

Answers could include:
Universal *– use of GPs, hospitals, emergency ambulances, etc.*
Selective *– charges for prescriptions, eye tests, dental treatment, etc.*

Many 'market liberals' are opposed to state intervention in social policy. George and Wilding, in their book *Ideology and Social Welfare*, 1985, suggest that market liberals do not wish for anything above a bare minimum because they believe:

- The Welfare State interferes with individual freedom – people have to contribute to benefits and services they do not want (for example, senior citizens may not wish to contribute towards schools).
- Central planning of the use of resources can be inefficient – services through the market can give consumers choice. This was the basis of the argument relating to the Grant Maintained Schools coming out of local education authority control in the 1990s.
- The government can find itself overloaded by pressure groups that are competing for a bigger share of government resources.
- Arguably, state-run services are inefficient and inflexible, being concerned less with efficiency and value for money, and sometimes those who do not have the greatest need gain the most.
- A dependency culture is created, which undermines people's capacities and willingness to take responsibility for their own welfare. In other words, citizens have responsibilities as well as rights – which many do not seem to recognise.

Many of these ideas were typified by Margaret Thatcher (Conservative prime minister, 1979–90). They have not all been reversed by New Labour, e.g. though grant maintained schools no longer exist (they are now called Foundation Schools), all schools now have far more control of where they purchase their services from.

Types of welfare provision

AQA A — M7
AQA B — M5
EDEXCEL — M5

There are four providers of welfare provision within the UK today. We will look at each one in turn.

The state

This is by far the largest provider. Central government welfare services include:

- **Department of Social Security** – benefits include old age pension and child benefits
- **Department of Health** – NHS, including general and psychiatric hospitals, GP services, etc.
- **Department for Education and Employment** – co-ordinates local education authority provision, further education and higher education sectors, job centres, training schemes, etc.
- **Department for the Environment** – co-ordinating town and country planning, environmental protection
- **Department for Transport** – motorways, roads, subsidies to rail services, transport safety
- **Home Office** – prisons, metropolitan police, probation service, co-ordination of police forces nationally.

The informal sector

This comprises family, friends, neighbours. Some argue that this has been replaced by the Welfare State. However, there is a lot of evidence that for many, nuclear and extended families continue to provide help and support in coping with daily life.

The voluntary sector

This is made up of organisations such as the NSPCC, MIND and Barnado's. It also includes such things as parents helping out in classrooms. Some voluntary organisations provide services that the state does not, some supplement statutory services. Many of these voluntary organisations are cost effective because of the use of unpaid volunteers and because they can sometimes react more quickly to new problems than the state.

The Conservative Governments of the 1980s–90s gave a greater priority to the voluntary sector. This, of course, coincided with their market-force philosophy, referred to earlier in the chapter.

It is almost a truism that voluntary organisations could play a more important role if they received more financial support. However, the allocation of that support could become a bureaucratic nightmare and could be perceived as being counter-productive.

The private sector

It may be necessary to question some of the motives of subscribers to private health-care schemes. In an emergency the NHS is as good (or better) than private medicine. Possibly the major reason is speed of access to treatment when required.

This includes private hospitals, schools, pensions, medical insurance. These services are usually paid for by individuals rather than being funded by taxation. Evidence within the UK indicates that this sector is increasing. In 1997 six million people were covered by annual subscriptions to private health-care schemes. Between 1986–1996 the overall number of private hospitals and clinics increased by around 10% per year and the number of registered beds rose by a similar amount (see Table 1.5).

Table 1.5 Households covered by private health insurance 1996–7
(Source: Association of British Insurers)

	%
Professional, employed and managers	17.2
Intermediate non-manual	15.1
Junior non-manual	7.7
Skilled manual	6.7
Semi-skilled/Unskilled manual	4.8
Self-employed	13.6
Retired	7.0

Progress check

What conclusions can you draw from Table 1.5?

In relation to the figures in Table 1.5 it is worth noting that: the higher elements of social class are more likely to be covered by private health schemes; the self-employed who need it, as they will receive no compensation from work, can't always afford it; other less well-off groups cannot afford private health contributions either.

Arguably, welfare pluralism (that is, the use of all the above sectors) is the most likely direction for social policy in the future. As the state struggles to provide an increasingly wide range of services and benefits, one solution can be to pass more responsibility to other sectors.

The outlook for the Welfare State and its provision is rather bleak, with an ageing population making extra demands on the National Health Service and on the Treasury to pay for state pensions. While spending on the Welfare State has increased, much of it has been used to pay for unemployment benefit. A reduction in unemployment could lead to increased spending on the Welfare State, hence Mr Blair's priority 'Education, education, education'. It is possible that the pressures regarding senior citizens' pensions (that occurred in October 2000) could result in a re-alignment of priorities by the Labour Government before the next General Election.

Sample question and model answer

1

'There is a "glass ceiling" which prevents women obtaining equal promotional opportunities to men.' How far do you agree with this statement?

It needs to be borne in mind at all times that this needs an A2 response (that is, at a higher level than that of AS). Certainly mark schemes and examiners will be looking for this in the response of candidates.

Step 1:
Provide introduction.

- The question asks you to analyse why women do not obtain as much promotion as men and to decide whether, if this is the case, the reason is that of the glass ceiling.

- Arguments here could include such comments as:

Step 2:
Give arguments why women now have equal promotional opportunities.

- Equal Pay Act
- Equal Opportunities Act
- greater success of females in the examination area (e.g. GCSE/A Levels)
- larger proportion of females going on to higher education.

- Arguments here could include:

Step 3:
Reasons why the glass ceiling exists.

- Promotion within a career takes time. Women have more time off (to have children, for example) than men do. Therefore men stay on the promotion ladder.
- Many women do not want extra promotion after returning to work because of 'the dual burden'.
- The exception still proves the rule – e.g. Cherie Blair (the main breadwinner in the Blair household) and Margaret Thatcher.

Step 4:
Well-argued conclusion.

- Points here should include a resumé of previous information as well as an analysis of why and how things are changing and improving.

The following is a response by a Year 13 student who has tried to weigh up the issues involved in the above question. This is not the student's full response but it gives a good flavour of how the student was thinking and the ways in which the arguments were constructed.

It could be argued that there is a glass ceiling in operation relating to the way in which women generally find it difficult to achieve promotion. In my own school there is a male headteacher and two male deputy heads, most heads of department are male yet there are more female staff than male. I know that in the local education authority where I live that 50% of primary heads are male, yet they are, on occasions, the only male member of staff. So, certainly there seems to be something blocking women's promotion.

One of the main reasons why this happens is down to human biology. Women have the babies. Therefore they take time off work. Their male rivals for promotion keep on working and when promotion comes up they are more likely to get it because they are there. The question really is, do employers give promotion to men because they are there!

Legally, of course, women are equal, there is the Equal Opportunities Act and the Equal Pay Act and there are now more role models for women (e.g. Cherie Blair) who recently went back to work as a judge after having a fourth baby.

There is paternity leave now for men but they don't have to take it, so possibly there is not equality and for that reason the glass ceiling exists.

Sample question and model answer (continued)

Altogether this is a reasonable response.

On the plus side the student has:

- tried to explain (relatively successfully) what the situation is
- given some pertinent examples of apparent male commandeering of promotion opportunities
- provided a sensible example of a role model
- given a major reason why the glass ceiling exists.

To get a top grade the student would really need to:

- wrestle with a definition of 'glass ceiling'
- give more examples from different walks of life
- try not to use 'first person' terminology
- give other reasons in addition to biology.

In spite of this, this answer is very much on the right lines.

Practice examination questions

1 To what extent is political correctness likely to contribute to a fairer, more just society? *(Assessment and Qualifications Alliance B Specimen)*

2 What do you understand by the phrase 'equality of opportunity'? Why is it a concept that has received so much attention in Britain during the last 30–40 years? What measures have been taken to eliminate discrimination and how effective do you consider them to have been? *(Assessment and Qualifications Alliance A Specimen)*

3 To what extent do attitudes to obeying the law vary between people of different age groups within one of the following groups:

- people from different residential areas;
- people from different ethnic groups;
- people from different social classes. *(OCR Specimen)*

4 Using your own knowledge and evidence, examine the assertion that 'all men are created equal'. *(Edexcel Specimen)*

Chapter 2

Politics – continuity and change

The following topics are covered in this chapter:

- *The House of Lords*
- *The House of Commons*

- *The Monarchy*
- *Political reform*

2.1 The House of Lords

After studying this section you should be able to:

- *describe the role of the House of Lords in the year 2000*
- *explain why there are pressures for reform*
- *outline the difficulties inherent in organising these changes*

LEARNING SUMMARY

The historical background of the Lords

AQA A	M4
EDEXCEL	M5
OCR	M5

Historically, the House of Lords grew up based on the hereditary principle (that is, a seat in the House of Lords was guaranteed because of an accident of birth).

> **KEY POINT**
>
> Members of the House of Lords have never been subject to election.

Key points from AS

- **Political parties**
  Revise AS pages 30–31

Historically, Labour representing the 'working class' would be more likely to be against the House of Lords.

This chapter shows how the political system within the UK, although on the surface rigid and unchanging, is in fact continually changing and modifying its role. Students should consider how they can use the information in these topics and apply it to any question on political change.

The fact that its members are not representative has led to the House of Lords occupying a position of both political and legal inferiority to the House of Commons. However, this was not confirmed by law until the Parliament Act of 1911, which gave the House of Lords only a suspensive veto over legislation. In other words, they could not prohibit laws, only delay them.

Before the 1997 General Election, Labour made some noises about changing the format of the House of Lords and in January 2000 a Royal Commission on the Reform of the House of Lords was presented to Parliament.

As it stands today, the House of Lords has four different kinds of members:
- two-thirds are hereditary peers (that is, they inherited the right to be members along with their titles)
- one-quarter are life peers
- 26 Church of England bishops
- 12 Law Lords.

The role of the Lords

AQA A	M4
EDEXCEL	M5
OCR	M5

There are various arguments both for and against the House of Lords and we will look at each of them in terms of their pros and cons.

Hereditary principle

For
They are answerable to no-one and are truly independent.
Their services are given cheaply.

Accountability is one of the major concepts of the age – everyone needs to give reasons why they make decisions.

Against
It is indefensible in a democracy that people who make laws should be accountable to society as a whole. It certainly represents outdated values such as inherited privilege and wealth.

Constitutional function

For

The argument is that the Lords' power of amendment and delay provides a useful check against ill-thought out legislation.

Against

Why should a body of non-elected peers frustrate the will of the elected chamber? Also, there is a permanent Conservative majority over Labour in the Lords, which therefore gives the Conservatives greater control than is necessary during Labour periods of office.

Useful for the Prime Minister

For

A useful way for a prime minister to recruit ministers without an election. It can be used as an appropriate 'dumping ground' for those who need to be marginalised.

Against

Ministers should be accountable to the House of Commons and the Prime Minister has too much power.

Deliberative function

For

The Lords represent a mix of wisdom and experience. Televising debates there has generally been judged a success.

Against

Few people bother to read reports of debates in the Lords.

> One could ask how many people watch these broadcasts!

Legislative function

For

The Lords does play a key role in non-controversial legislation, relieving the work of the overloaded Commons. They also revise and improve Bills on the route to Royal assent. In its Select Committee work there are over 100 peers involved whose role includes consulting expert opinions.

Judicial function

For

The highest court in the land – a role performed by the Law Lords. They do not pass judgements, but rather clarify the law and give their opinion upon appeals.

Against

This function could be performed by a separate institution altogether.

The future of the Lords

AQA A ▸ M4
EDEXCEL ▸ M5
OCR ▸ M5

The new Labour Government in 1997 had to decide whether to reform or abolish. The Labour Party has had a long and difficult relationship with the House of Lords. As late as 1990, ex-Leader Michael Foot said: 'It (the House of Lords) really can do very little. It performs a minor useful function of looking at matters in detail which the Commons has not got the time to do, but that is no satisfactory bi-cameral system.'

> A bi-cameral system is one where there are two separate Houses who rule the country.
>
> **KEY POINT**

There were party-conference decisions in the 1970s calling for abolition and this was part of the 1983 Labour election manifesto. By 1989 Labour was preparing a reformed second chamber. When Tony Blair became leader in 1994 he remained cautious about wholesale Lords reform. However, by 1996 he had pledged that a Labour Government would act to end the system under which individuals wielded power simply by right of birth. *The Times* commented that this placed hereditary peers on 'notice to quit.'

Once in power, early in 1999 the Government published a paper 'Modernising Parliament: Reforming the House of Lords', outlining the following step-by-step approach to reform.

* Removal of the right of hereditary peers to sit and vote in the House of Lords.
* A transitional House of Lords by which a small number of hereditary peers would be allowed to sit temporarily as members. No one party would be allowed to dominate this transitional House.
* Appointment of a Royal Commission to examine a range of alternatives (see earlier).
* These recommendations would be considered by a joint committee of both Houses of Parliament.
* Legislation to implement the proposals designed to 'renew the House of Lords as a modern, fit and effective second chamber of Parliament for the 21st century'.

Moves to a transitional House are underway. *The Guardian* (13.10.00) reported that 191 people have already been formally nominated or completed application forms since adverts for 'people's peers' were placed in mid-September. An appointments commission is touring cities trying to drum up applications from voluntary groups, businessmen and public-sector employees.

Progress check

Why do you think that the UK needs a second chamber?

Answers could include the following: acts as a form of check and balance against the House of Commons; can act as a source of challenge when there is a large majority in the Commons as at present; it allows greater time and thought on contentious events; as MPs become more 'clone-like' it gives a greater degree of variety of opinion.

2.2 The House of Commons

After studying this section you should be able to:

* *explain the basic functions of the Commons*
* *describe how it operates*
* *identify why and how it may need to be reformed*

LEARNING SUMMARY

The role of the Commons

AQA A	M4
EDEXCEL	M5
OCR	M5

In other words, to make it clear how well a policy is supported.

The basic role of the House of Commons has not changed in well over a hundred years. In his book *Parliament* (1969), Jennings described its purpose as '...to question and debate the policy of the Government and in doing so to bring home the unpopularity (or popularity) of a particular line of policy.'

MPs in the House of Commons are representatives in two quite different senses.

* When an analysis of educational and occupational backgrounds of MPs is carried out it is found that a large proportion come from professional occupations and comparatively few from working-class backgrounds. This

Key points from AS

• **Political parties**
  Revise AS pages 30–31

demonstrates the growing 'embourgeoisement' of the House of Commons, with the vast majority coming from middle-class backgrounds. Over 75% of MPs have also experienced higher education.

> Embourgeoisement is the process by which members of the working class seem to be adopting middle-class lifestyles and living standards.
>
> **KEY POINT**

Arguably MPs in the UK can be seen as something of an élite in educational and occupational terms. However, possibly they are also beginning to mirror society with a decline in the size of the 'working class', the corresponding rise of the 'middle class' and a larger percentage of the population receiving higher education.

• If UK MPs are analysed on the basis of reflecting the composition of the electorate as a whole the assessment fails. Women make up 52% of the population, but only 18% of MPs.

> Do you think that there should be positive discrimination in favour of women candidates? (Refer back to the Equal Opportunities section of Chapter 1.)
>
> **KEY POINT**

The power of the Commons

AQA A	M4
EDEXCEL	M5
OCR	M5

In many ways the power of the House of Commons has been subsumed into the power of the government of the day. At present with a very large Labour majority it is difficult for the Commons to have any control. It is therefore necessary for the Government party to control its MPs and in that area it is mainly influence on individual MPs that ensures that the boat is not 'rocked' too severely.

Party 'whips' control the MPs and indicate where and when they are required to vote.

The Commons itself has certain traditions that perpetuate even into the 21st century. One example of this is the party conflict being organised by party whips 'through the usual channels'. This means that there is a recognition by both sides that:
• the Government must get its legislation passed
• the Opposition must have full opportunities to oppose.

Another tradition is that of 'pairing' – MPs from different political parties to agree to miss certain votes so that the overall result of the vote is not affected.

The functions of the Commons

AQA A	M4
EDEXCEL	M5
OCR	M5

It is possible to argue that there are four main functions of the House of Commons.

Representation and redress

An MP represents the interests of his or her constituents and seeks redress for constituents' grievances. This can include such actions as writing a letter to a Minister, leading a delegation to lobby a Minister and putting down a Parliamentary Question for either a written or oral answer. If MPs did not intervene on behalf of their constituents, people might be even more cynical about the role and value of MPs.

The party battle

This continues all the time and has the benefit of encouraging the voters to take an interest in politics between elections as well as to consider two sides of every political argument. Evidence over a long period suggests that the opposition parties' counter proposals have a cumulative effect on public opinion.

The legislative process

This has absorbed an increasing proportion of Parliamentary time over recent decades. It has several stages:

1 **First reading** – the formal stage at which printed copies of a Bill are made available for all MPs and other interested parties.

2 **Second reading** – (usually two weeks later) a wide-ranging debate at which the purpose of the Bill is discussed and at the end of which a vote is usually taken to see whether or not the House approves of the Bill in principle. On all Government Bills the votes are whipped.

> 'Whipping' means that MPs are expected to support the position of their own party unless they have overwhelming reasons for doing otherwise, e.g. conscientious objections to a Bill.

KEY POINT

3 **Committee stage** – the Bill is referred to a Committee of between 16–50 MPs where it is debated in detail and at length, clause by clause, line by line. This can be very time consuming – many involve a committee stage of 100 hours or more.

4 **Report stage and third reading** – this is the stage when the House as a whole has a chance to speak and vote on any new amendments, etc. The Third Reading follows immediately and is a brief debate on the merits or otherwise of the Bill as it stands.

5 **The Bill then moves to the House of Lords.** Certain amendments can be made here, but if they are not acceptable to the Commons, then eventually the Commons would get their own way under the Parliament Acts of 1911 and 1949.

6 **The Royal assent** by the Queen is the final formality which changes the Bill into law.

> This is the 'suspensive veto' – in other words, they cannot refuse legislation indefinitely.

The whole process normally takes between six and twelve months. However, emergency legislation (for example, Bills to deal with terrorism) can be put through all the stages in 24 hours if necessary.

Parliamentary scrutiny and control

This is the function, referred to earlier, by which the Commons is supposed to seek to control the Government. This palpably does not happen today, although in theory Ministerial and Prime Ministerial Question Time are supposed to enable this. Many Parliamentarians now try to use the Select Committees to carry out this function. They have the explicit aim of scrutinising and controlling the activities of the Government in given policy areas. They have tended to be more powerful when the Government of the day has a small majority (for example, in the last few years of Major's administration – 1992–1997). In recent years their influence has increased because their hearings are often televised and attract media interest. However, in the final analysis select committees and Parliament are likely to remain weak when forced by a strong or dominant government.

Progress check

What controls are there on the Government?

Answers could include the following: public opinion; loss of seats at by-elections; negative media coverage; the knowledge that it has to face the electorate in a maximum of five years.

2.3 The Monarchy

After studying this section you should be able to:

- *explain the rationale for the existence of the Royal Family*
- *analyse the role of the Royal Family in the 21st century*
- *outline arguments both for and against its continuation*

LEARNING SUMMARY

Key points from AS

- **The political system**
  Revise AS page 28

Any person from abroad, asked to cite something that represents what the UK stands for, would probably say 'the Queen', 'the Royal Family' or 'the Monarchy'.

The role of the Monarchy

AQA A ▶ M4
EDEXCEL ▶ M5
OCR ▶ M5

The Royal Family and its role has changed dramatically over the centuries. It was the English Civil War that decided who would rule this country – King or Parliament. In the 19th century various Reform Acts gave the electorate the ultimate decision in the wielding of power and Queen Victoria was slowly eased towards a position of influence but no real power.

What, then, is the role of the Monarch in 2001?

- **Symbolic** – She represents the UK at home or abroad, which is, in fact, a task ascribed to any head of state. However because she has no political agenda the Monarch, in representing the UK, stays above the fray, as opposed to the President of the USA who has the role of both head of state and head of government.
- A spin-off from this is that the Queen has accumulated considerable experience by virtue of the fact of how long she has been on the throne. Hence she is able to **offer prime ministers detached and informal advice**. This has been attested by several former prime ministers, including Harold Wilson and James Callaghan.
- This experience can also be seen in the international arena. For example, in the 1980s when the UK's Government had poor relations with several Commonwealth countries over sanctions against South Africa, the Queen acted as a **unifying influence on the Commonwealth**.
- In the symbolic role, the Monarchy can also be **good for British trade** – the Royal Family is a continual source of media and public interest abroad.
- It is interesting that the armed forces give their allegiance to the Crown, rather than to the government. This is emphasised by the close links maintained by the Royal Family with the various services. The Queen takes a **particular interest in military matters**, including awards for service.
- The monarchy also symbolises **continuity in affairs of state**, such as the state opening of Parliament, the ceremony of Trooping of the Colour, royal garden parties and the investiture of honours.
- The Monarch is **supreme governor of the Church of England** and links between the Monarch and the church are close and visible. Bishops are appointed by the Crown, albeit acting on advice. The Monarch is looked to, largely by way of example, as a symbol of basic Christian morality and the Royal Family made some notable sacrifices in the 20th century to preserve that morality. A prime example is that of Edward VIII's abdication in 1936 because of his insistence on marrying a twice-married and twice-divorced woman. In 1955 Princess Margaret decided not to marry Group Captain Peter Townsend because he was divorced. However, the various divorces within the Royal family in the last 20 years – Charles and Diana, Anne and Captain Mark Phillips, Princess Margaret and Antony Armstrong-Jones, have raised questions about the Monarchy's ability to uphold Christian morality.

You may think that the Royal Family's behaviour is simply mirroring society as it is today. However, many still believe that since the Monarch is the Supreme Governor of the Church of England the Royal Family are in a position of higher responsibility than the rest of society and should therefore set an example.

Formal political powers of the Monarch

Major powers still, in theory, remain with the Monarch:

- choice of prime minister
- right to withhold assent to legislation
- the dissolution of Parliament
- the declaration of war.

All of these are, however, governed by convention.

> 'Convention' means that nowadays, the Monarch agrees to all legislation and she asks the leader of the party with an overall majority to form a government. She does not make decisions herself.

It can be argued that this convention is a waste of time. However, by keeping this apparently residual power, the Monarch can act as a safeguard for the constitution. There are two reasons for saying this.

- If, for example, there was to be an attempted military coup, the Monarch as Head of State and Commander-in-Chief of the Armed Forces could stop it – or, at the very least, make it illegal.
- Holding these powers reminds ministers that they owe a responsibility to a higher authority than a prime minister, who could be voted out of office at any time.

There is still, therefore, a fair degree of truth in **Bagehot's** famous 19th-century assertion that the Monarch had 'the right to warn'. She can still stand as the ultimate deterrent as, for example, in 1993 when John Major sought a vote of confidence in the House of Commons, following the loss of an important vote the previous evening. Major made it clear that in the event of the Government losing the vote, the result would be a general election, but the Government took the precaution first of checking that the Queen would agree to the dissolution of Parliament.

Progress check

Does the Monarch have any real powers and if so what are they?

Answers could include:
She does have the following powers: • representing the UK • uniting people • maintaining continuity • 'encouraging, advising and warning', • holding the allegiance of the armed forces

In spite of what has been said so far, there are various arguments that can be put forward against a continuation of the Royal Family.

- Heads of state should be elected – the vast majority of developed countries have popularly elected heads of state and our system is archaic.
- Conservative values and maintenance of the status quo are bound to be emphasised by the monarchy.
- The cost – a great subject of criticism in the 1990s. The Monarch is paid a Civil List – an annual sum to cover the cost of staff, upkeep of royal residences, holding official functions and for public duties undertaken by other members of the Royal Family. (The Civil List was set at £7.9 million for 10 years in 1991.) Many felt that Royal 'hangers on' should not be paid and after the fire at Windsor Castle in 1992 and the government announcing it would pay for repairs (estimated at £50 million) the Queen announced that she would now

Has the proliferation of awards to entertainers, etc. demeaned the system? You may wish to think about that.

pay income tax. She also opened Buckingham Palace to the public, the money that was raised being used to defray some of the cost of the repair of Windsor.

- The honours system (one of the main roles of the Monarch) is archaic – elevating some people above their equals.
- Most of the supposed powers either do not exist or are meaningless:
  - the opening of Parliament is ceremonial only – the Queen's opening speech is written by the Prime Minister.
  - the Queen has not selected (in the true meaning of the word) a Prime Minister since she accepted the advice of Harold Macmillan in 1963 and chose Lord Hume
  - the appointments at her disposal are, in practice, prime-ministerial nominations
  - no monarch has seriously attempted to delay legislation for over 200 years.
- Since all of the Royal power has been taken over by the government one could question why we still have a monarchy?

Faced with that daunting list, let us now rehearse arguments in favour of the Monarchy (some of which were touched on earlier).

- The Queen has great experience and can give her prime minister non-partisan advice.
- Would a transient president have as much history, glamour, etc. as the Royal Family?
- The Queen is good value for money, is no more expensive than a president and is a tourist attraction.
- Arguably the Royal family is very much in touch with the realities of life, through its activities and work for charity.
- Quite importantly, the Monarchy does take the ceremonial role off the prime minister, allowing him to concentrate on running the country. The comparison with the USA is quite illuminating here, where the US President is expected to fulfil both roles – with always a chance that he will somewhat slip between two stools!

Progress check

In what ways would you say that the Royal Family is an anachronism?
(NB In any question such as this, make sure you define the main word – i.e. 'out of touch', 'not relevant', etc.)

Answers could include: it is isolated from real life and mixing with ordinary people (e.g. William and Harry go to Eton); it fulfils an idea that is now out of date – e.g. the Opening of Parliament; it typifies a backward-looking state – we need to be looking forward to a technological age; everything is done by the Government anyway, so why continue with the sham?

2.4 Political reform

After studying this section you should be able to:

- *describe how reform in politics is continual and continuous*
- *explain how reforms have, on occasion, a short 'shelf life' (that is, the reform can itself be reformed quite quickly)*
- *outline why reforms can take a great deal of time to achieve in reality.*

LEARNING SUMMARY

Reform of the Houses of Parliament

AQA A	M4
AQA B	M6
EDEXCEL	M5
OCR	M5

Key points from AS

- **Recent changes to main parties**
  Revise AS page 31

Any student who is taking A Level History will probably be aware of the huge volume of reform legislation that took place in the 19th and 20th centuries on a matter as basic as the right to vote (known as 'suffrage').

1832	– saw the vote being given to some middle class (3–5%) of the whole population (wealthy and upper middle class)
1867	– the vote was granted to wealthier workmen in towns
1884	– extension of the franchise in towns and the vote given to agricultural labourers
1919	– full suffrage to men
1928	– the vote given to women over 21 (i.e. equality with men)
1969	– age for suffrage reduced to 18

Note how long it took to obtain the system everyone takes for granted today. In the light of this, it is necessary to be aware of the danger of assuming that such reforms were inevitable. Hindsight is a wonderful thing (and can be dangerous).

'Jim Crow' laws were pieces of petty legislation that made it virtually impossible for blacks to register to vote: e.g. literacy laws were imposed to ensure that blacks who had been given poor levels of education would fail them and become disenfranchised.

> The same argument applies to the extension of the suffrage for blacks in the USA where various pieces of legislation, including 'Jim Crow' laws, needed to be reformed before the Civil Rights Act of 1964 could be made into law.

KEY POINT

While any law that is passed in the UK can be viewed as a 'reform' and is certainly portrayed this way by its sponsor (whether that be the Government or a private member) in order to concentrate the mind it seems sensible to look at reforms to the Houses of Parliament itself and the effect these have had on the electorate. In doing this, we need to ask ourselves the following questions.

- Why is a significant minority of the electorate so disillusioned with the political process?
- Why do so many young people appear so apathetic to the political process?
- In what respect is Parliament now an outmoded concept with an executive (a government) ruling through Parliament?

The Executive is concerned with making government decisions and policies rather than with passing laws. In the UK the political executive is the Prime Minister and the Cabinet. The Legislature is the law-making branch of government, i.e. the House of Commons, the House of Lords and the Monarch.

It is certainly valid to say that Parliamentary reform has been limited – partly because of the third point made above and also because of the tensions between the Executive and the Legislature (in other words, between ministers and back-benchers). It is almost a truism that if a government with an overall majority in the House of Commons agrees to a reform that strengthens the power of the Commons, this is likely to mean a relative weakening of the power of Government. In spite of this it *is* possible to achieve reform, partly because of the changing composition and outlook of the political parties. This is particularly true of the 'new' generation of Labour and Liberal Democrat MPs. Since 1997, and the election of over 100 women MPs, MPs have generally been very critical of the unsocial hours and outdated procedures of Parliament, which makes a normal family life difficult.

Progress check

What procedures of the House of Commons make family life very difficult?

Answers could include: very late sittings (all night on occasions) of the House of Commons; the necessity to be present to cast your vote under three-line whips; the beginning of the Parliamentary day at 2.30 p.m.

After the 1997 election a select committee on modernising the House of Commons was established under Ann Taylor, Leader of the House. This had the remit to:

- allow more effective consultations and scrutiny
- review the structure of the Parliamentary year
- overhaul the process for scrutinising European law
- strengthen the ability of MPs to call Ministers to account.

> Far more heat than light seems to have been generated over this issue so far. It will be interesting to see whether a reforming New Labour government actually achieves more progress than has been achieved so far.

The first report of the Committee recommended:

- a more open and formal approach to timetabling
- increased consultations on draft Bills
- more effective use of Standing Committees
- the carry-over of Bills from one Parliamentary session to another.

There has subsequently been little impact by these recommendations and one questions how serious many MPs are in their efforts for procedural change.

The impact of radio and television

Proceedings at Westminster have now been broadcast for over ten years. The idea of broadcasting had been discussed since the 1960s and had received growing support from MPs in all parties. On the radio, producers use edited extracts from the tapes of the proceedings as the raw materials for programmes usually broadcast after the event (for example, in 'The Week at Westminster'). On television it has been possible for the public, at home and abroad (courtesy of the C Span Channel on satellite television), to watch coverage in the Chamber. It is inconceivable that television will ever be withdrawn now.

> One can ask whether television highlights the antiquated nature of much of the rest of Parliamentary custom and practice.

There are various effects of allowing television into the House of Commons. These can perhaps be seen in a positive and/or negative light.

Positive

- It brings Parliament closer to the public, thereby creating greater public understanding and support of democracy.
- With 55 million TV sets in the UK in the year 2000, a failure to have cameras inside Westminster could have led to a condemnation of Parliament seeming irrelevant to most of the population.

Negative

- It trivialises and sensationalises proceedings – MPs 'play to the gallery'. However, it can be argued that this is what MPs have always done, and this is just a larger stage or gallery!
- MPs are more and more aware of the 'sound bite' issue – that is, the telling phrase that can be used on national news.
- Will MPs and cabinet Ministers be judged on their TV persona in future because of the ability to perform in that form of the media? (Again, in real life this has happened for the past 40 years – MPs with a good TV image have been far more likely to gain promotion within their parties: for example, Neil Kinnock, Mo Mowlem, Tony Blair.)

Youth and politics

AQA A	M4
AQA B	M6
EDEXCEL	M5
OCR	M5

In the 1997 General Election, New Labour targetted first-time voters by sending them a video explaining the advantages of voting for them.

We are continually being told that young people are 'turned off' by politics, see no relevance in it for them and even when given the chance to vote do not do so in any great numbers.

Arguably, it has been like this for a long time and certainly the reduction of the voting age to 18 in 1969 did not automatically lead to greater youth involvement in politics. There were exceptions to this of course – the young William Hague's intervention at the Conservative Party conference in 1977 brought him to national attention at the age of 15 and certainly some MPs are elected in their late twenties.

There is slowly beginning a movement towards reducing the age of voting to 16. What arguments can be put forward in favour of this?

- In many other spheres of life, sixteen is seen as the age of adult responsibility. For example, at 16 people can leave home, get married with parental consent, have a full-time job, have sexual intercourse, etc.
- It would mean that younger people would have to confront the political system.
- It would force the political system to be more relevant to young people.
- With the introduction of the subject of Citizenship into the school curriculum from 2002, it seems a logical extension for young people at 16 to be enfranchised.

Against this it can be stated that:

This could form the basis of a typical General Studies question, with no right or wrong answer. The examiner will decide the validity of your response by the balance of your arguments.

- more young people than ever before stay in full-time education post-16, so they are not yet totally standing on their own feet
- the younger the vote is given, the more chance there is of trivialising and simplifying the political system to appeal to them
- there is little evidence that people at 16 actually want the vote – for example, many Young Conservatives groups have folded through lack of support.

Having said all this, although statistically many young people seem apathetic to the current political system, this does not mean that young people do not have political views. Issues such as environmentalism, 'green politics', protests about involvement in wars (such as Vietnam) have always played a part in young people's political psyche. In the year 2000 perceived apathy by young people could simply be because they feel excluded, or, to quote a famous rock 'n' roll record of 1958 ('Summertime Blues' by Eddie Cochran): 'I called my Congressman and he said "Woah, I'd like to help you son, but you're too young to vote"'.

Sample question and model answer

1

Discuss factors that limit the rights of individuals to act entirely as they please within a democracy.

(AEB 1999)

To tackle this question, first provide a sensible definition (or definitions) of democracy – for example, 'Democracy comes from the Greek words "demos" (people) and "krator" (power) and means "power to the people"'. Having analysed what democracy means, you then need to explain what rights individuals have. From there, you should then describe how the one impinges on the other.

Here is an example of an answer to the question from a year-13 student. This is possibly a typical response. However, it just scratches the surface. It has some good points but it screams out to be amplified, to give examples. The first section sets the scene *but* is only a paraphrase (done very badly) of the question itself.

The discussion about the government is very thin – how does that government get there (through a democratic process called election); by 'person' I assume the candidate means MP!

A valid point is made about the police – but it also needs to say that their role is to uphold the law *whether they disagree with it or not.*

The rest of the paragraph is accurate and relevant but needs examples – if the majority do not like the laws which are passed, the government that is passing them can be voted out of power at the next election.

The last paragraph also needs to be expanded. What does the student mean by 'to an extent'? If the answer had said freedom of speech is allowed as long as libel or slander does not occur then the point becomes more creditworthy. For example, a comment such as 'Mr Blair's a bad prime minister' is allowed but a comment such as 'Mr Blair killed my dog' (if factually inaccurate) is not allowed under free speech and Mr Blair could take action against such a statement!

You can see why this candidate would not have scored highly on this question although it contained one or two relevant ideas – these could and should have been developed.

Although we live in a democracy, there are factors that limit the rights of individuals to act entirely as they please within a democracy.

Firstly, we have a strong government that enacts the law and makes the decisions. No person can commit an act without passing it through the government. Similarly we have a police force to keep order and peace. People are different and may feel things should be run differently while the next person may disagree. Therefore you need a system which works for everybody with people in power who will make decisions that hopefully the majority of people would like. If everybody could do and say what they liked then it would lead to chaos and alarm, people would get violent which is dangerous to everyone.

That's why although we live in a democracy, we also have a government that works for the best of the nation, so that we put our trust in them to make the right decisions.

As individuals we have the right of freedom and free speech which to an extent we can voice in a democracy though with limitations as well.

Practice examination questions

1 Outline the various factors and considerations which contribute to our notion of 'right' and 'wrong' and the way we behave individually or in groups. To what extent is it possible to tolerate differences of opinion about such matters?

(Assessment and Qualifications Alliance A Specimen)

2 Vandalism is a growing and complex problem in your community... Among those involved in trying to solve the problem are councillors, the police and young people. Illustrate the main issues involved. *(OCR Specimen Coursework Project)*

3 Examine the main issues and dilemmas raised in plans to build a second runway for Manchester Airport. *(OCR Specimen)*

4 Young people are as a group less likely to register as electors. Does this mean that they are less likely to be interested in politics than older people? *(AEB 2000)*

Chapter 3

The economy today

The following topics are covered in this chapter:

- *Industrial relations*
- *Work*
- *Global economic issues*
- *Consumerism in the UK*

3.1 Industrial relations

After studying this section you should be able to:

- *identify the range and different types of trade union*
- *describe changes that have taken place within industrial relations*
- *explain the complexities of industrial relations in the 21st century*

A brief history of UK industrial relations

AQA A	M6, M4
AQA B	M4
EDEXCEL	M5
OCR	M5

Key points from AS

- **Employment and unemployment**
  Revise AS pages 40–41

Put basically, the term 'industrial relations' refers to the relationship between employees and employers – also called 'labour relations' or 'trade union relations'. There has, of course, always been a relationship between employer and employee – from the 'master and servant' relationship which led in the 19th century to the growth of organised labour, through such events as the Tolpuddle Martyrs (1834), the Bryant and May Match Strike (1889) to the General Strike of 1926.

The Tolpuddle Martyrs were a group of farm-workers from Dorset, who were sentenced to transportation for swearing an oath to a union; the Bryant and May Match Strike was the first example of successful industrial action by a non-skilled workforce; the General Strike of 1926 was an attempt by the mineworkers and their allies to paralyse the country to obtain their demands.

> A trade union is an organisation of workers that has been established to represent their interests.
>
> **KEY POINT**

'Closed shop' meant that a union would not allow a non-union person to work in their particular establishment.

By the early 1980s trade-union membership in the UK was over 12 million. This was linked to elements such as 'the closed shop'.

The 'winter of discontent' of 1978, when many public service workers (e.g. dustbin men, grave-diggers, etc.) went on strike, after they refused to accept James Callaghan's wish for a 5% limit to wage claims, was one of the main reasons for the defeat of the Labour Government in 1979 and Mrs Thatcher's Conservative administration coming to power. As a result of attacks by the Tory administrations of the 1980s upon the power of the trade unions, by 1993 union membership had declined to 8 million – only 37% of the workforce in 1993 was in a union compared with 53% in 1979.

Amongst the legislation passed by the Thatcher Conservative governments was:

Secondary action – e.g. picketing – means that union members not directly involved in a dispute are used to persuade other members not to cross over picket lines.

- Employment Acts 1980, 1982, 1988 and 1990. These required secret ballots to be held to get approval for strike action and elections to union posts; they also
  - allowed a member to prevent the union from strike action if no other ballot had been held
  - protected members from disciplinary action if they refused to strike
  - made closed shops (see earlier) and all forms of secondary action, illegal
  - allowed damages to be awarded against union members who were not involved in a dispute, but who took secondary actions.

- The Trade Union Act 1984 – this made a union liable for damages if it has not carried out a secret ballot to get approval from its members for strike action.
- The Trade Union Reform and Employment Rights Act 1992 made it unlawful for employers to collect union dues without the written consent of workers.

Progress check

Why do you think that the Conservative administration 1979–1997 devoted so much time to union legislation?

Answers could include: unions had dominated affairs in Britain in 1960s and '70s leading to the 'Winter of discontent' in 197; the miners, led by Arthur Scargill, had comprehensively defeated Conservative Governments in 1972 and 1974; there was a perception that many unions were led by 'left-wing' activists who did not represent true union feelings; support for the Conservatives came predominantly from middle-class workers who did not perceive themselves as trade unionists, hence anti-union legislation could count upon electoral support.

In 1998, for the first time, union density was higher in service industries (31.1%) than in production (30.9%). However, bear in mind that this only reflects the trend in employment anyway.

Factors that have affected union membership in recent years

We have already considered changes in the trade unions over the last two decades, primarily linked to power and membership. So what affects union membership?

- **The state of the economy** – in periods of recession and high unemployment union membership falls. The recession of the early 1990s, for example, may have contributed to a fall in membership. Relatively low inflation rates in the 1990s could also be a factor, because in periods of inflation people may join unions to protect their living standards.
- **Government** – legislation certainly made it easier for employees to 'opt out' of union membership. The encouragement of union participation in business since the late 1990s (see later) and the growth of legislation to protect workers' rights (e.g. the Minimum Wage Act 1999) may persuade workers to join unions.
- **Flexible workforce** – part-time workers, temporary staff, etc. are less likely to be covered by employee legislation. The workers themselves may feel 'why bother to join a union?'
- **Growth of small independent businesses** – those employing less than ten workers are not affected by certain employee-protection legislation.
- **Economic, technological and labour market changes** – the decline of certain staple industries like ship building or coal mining, which by tradition were heavily unionised, has led to a fall in membership that has not been totally reflected by a rise in membership in service industries.
- **Privatisation** – this could have affected membership because areas such as rail and gas had large memberships and splitting them after privatisation is likely to have reduced union influence.
- **Demographic trends** – the UK has a falling number of school leavers and an ageing population (many of whom retire early). Hence there are fewer recruits for unions in the first place.

The changing role of trade unions

AQA A	M6, M4
AQA B	M4
EDEXCEL	M5
OCR	M5

During the 1990s four significant new practices became part of union activities. We will consider each of these in turn.

Single-union and no-strike agreements

Single-union agreements enable a business to recognise and negotiate with one union over pay and conditions. The benefits of these agreements for employers are that they:

- reduce time and complexity of negotiations
- provide a single job status that removes differentials in salaries, conditions, etc.
- allow for job flexibility – which may mean that workers agree to annual hours rather than a number of hours per week
- provide union acceptance of training and retraining of employees
- facilitate the use of negotiation or arbitration rather than industrial action.

Business and union partnership

This means both sides working together for a common goal. The main benefit is that unions have a 'stake' in the business. Examples of partnership have included an agreement between Tesco and USDAW, the shop workers union, allowing consultation through workplace, regional and national forums and improved facilities for recruitment.

Negotiations

Unions are now far more likely to negotiate on aspects other than pay. This could include facilities for women members or for older or disabled workers, reflecting the changing nature of the workforce.

Services

Unions increasingly offer a wide range of services to employees including insurance schemes, pension schemes, financial and legal advice, education courses, etc.

The TUC

AQA A	M6, M4
AQA B	M4
EDEXCEL	M5
OCR	M5

The Trade Union Congress is the organisation that represents trade unions in the UK. In the late 1990s its 74 affiliated unions had 6.6 million members. The main activities of the TUC are to:

- act as a pressure group to influence government policy on labour and union issues
- decide on the rules and regulations for member unions, but not to interfere with their everyday running.

Progress check

Why do you think that the TUC has had less influence in the last 20 years?

Answers could include:
There was little or no consultation with governments between 1979 and 1997. Before that time in Labour administrations there was a perception that the unions 'controlled' the Government. It is noticeable that the Blair administration has not re-introduced the 'beer and sandwiches' negotiations of the 1970s.
Legislation has ensured that the TUC's voice has been weakened.
General increase in affluence means that unionists (and the population as a whole) are far less militant.
Co-operation between both sides is palpably working; hence the TUC has less of a role to play.

The CBI

AQA A	M6, M4
AQA B	M4
EDEXCEL	M5
OCR	M5

The Confederation of British Industry was formed in 1965 and voices employers' views. Its membership is drawn from private-sector industry, service and commercial enterprises, public-sector employers, and so on. Its role can be seen as:

- seeking to influence government policy
- providing legal, financial and economic advice to its members
- giving support and advice to local businesses and, through its Brussels office, acting in the interests of British Industry in the European Union.

Conflicts between employer and employee

AQA A — M6, M4
AQA B — M4
EDEXCEL — M5
OCR — M5

Inevitably there are occasions when conflict can arise in the workplace between employer and employee. It could be over such diverse issues as:

- rates of pay
- introduction of new machinery or technology
- flexible working procedures
- work conditions.

Industrial relations procedures aim to make sure that each party finds an acceptable solution to the conflict. One way of minimising conflict is through 'collective bargaining'.

> **KEY POINT**
>
> Collective bargaining is a method of determining conditions of work and terms of employment through negotiation between employers and employee representatives.
>
> For this to work:
> - employees must be free to join trade unions
> - employers must recognise unions and agree to negotiate with them
> - such bodies must be independent of employers and the state
> - bodies should negotiate in good faith in their members' interests
> - employers and employees should agree to be bound by agreements without having to use the law to enforce them.
>
> Negotiations can take place at a number of levels – international, national, local, plant or individual – depending on the structure of the organisation.

The extent to which consultation takes place before agreement is reached depends on a number of factors:

- **legislation** – for example, the Employment Relations Act 1999 stated that employers must consult with unions on training plans
- **corporate culture** – some businesses have developed a culture that recognises the importance of consultation when decisions are made, valuing the contribution that employees can make to effective decision-making
- **tradition** – normally happened in state-run industries (for example, the railways before privatisation)
- **ICT introduction** (information and communications technology) – the internet for example, has helped to speed up and extend the process of consultation
- **use of quality standards** – schemes such as Investors in People (IIP) have ensured that consultation must take place.

IIP is a business standard ensuring that all employees are fully trained and valued. Consultation through dialogues with senior staff members is an integral part of this process.

Sometimes parties fail to reach agreements after consultation and negotiation. In this situation the Advisory, Conciliation and Arbitration Service (ACAS) can be brought into action. ACAS seeks to:

- prevent and resolve employment disputes
- conciliate in actual or potential complaints to industrial tribunals
- provide information and advice
- promote good practice.

Before acting, ACAS will want to see that union officials are involved and that the organisation's disputes procedure has been followed. If conciliation is unsuccessful, ACAS can offer arbitration by providing an independent arbitrator who can examine the case for both sides and then judge the right outcome. If both sides agree in advance, the arbitrator's decision can be legally binding. ACAS is also a great source of advice and operates a number of information centres that can deal with queries on virtually all employment law matters. It's main weakness, however, is that both sides have to agree to accept its outcomes. A failure on this count means that the whole system collapses.

There has been a great reduction in the number of working days lost through stoppages in the last 20 years. For example, in 1980 there were 1300 separate stoppages, in 1997 the number was 250.

Industrial action

Many students assume that industrial action merely means striking. However, there are various weapons that both sides use when industrial action erupts.

From the employer's side, the following tactics can be used:

- withdrawal of overtime
- lock-outs (i.e. the employer closes the place of work for a period of time, with wages not being paid during this period)
- closure – the right of management to shut down uneconomic enterprises, this may not even be seen as industrial action
- dismissal – the Employment Relations Act 1999 (referred to earlier) stated that employees are protected from dismissal for taking industrial action for the first eight weeks of a strike, after that, dismissal can be judged to be fair.

In the employees' point of view organised action can take a number of different forms.

- **'Work to rule' or 'go slow'.** A work to rule means that employees do not carry out duties that are not in their contract. A go slow, as the term implies, is where employees deliberately attempt to slow down production whilst still working within the terms of their contract.
- **Overtime ban.** Used by unions to demonstrate to management that the workforce is determined to take further action if their demands are not met.
- **'Sit ins' and 'work ins'.** Mass occupation of premises by workers (i.e. the employers have lost control of the premises); in the former, production does not take place, in the latter, it does.
- **Strikes.** This is the ultimate sanction used against employers. Official strikes are where a union officially supports its members in accordance with union rules during a dispute, after a ballot for action has been carried out and agreed by union members. Unofficial, or 'wildcat', strikes were common in the 1960s and '70s when union convenors could call out a factory workforce over apparently trivial issues. These have now been halted by the Conservative Government's union legislation of the 1980s. A study of strikes by the Department of Employment discovered that:
  - strikes appear to be over major issues
  - strikes are concentrated in a very small proportion of plants
  - industries and regions that have large factories on average tend to experience a relatively high numbers of strikes.

It is necessary to bear in mind that striking is the ultimate weapon of a workforce – the last resort. Always be aware of the other tactics that can be used.

A final area to analyse is that of the problems that arise for both sides from industrial action. From the employees' side industrial action can lead to:

- loss of earnings
- closure of the business – and hence redundancy
- stress for the workforce
- the employees being in a weaker position in the future if the action fails
- public support may dwindle if the action affects their everyday lives.

From the employer's viewpoint, industrial action can lead to:

- lost production for the business
- non-utilisation of resources, many of which (such as machinery) may have fixed costs (i.e. the hiring or leasing of the equipment)
- poor future relationships within the business
- the directing of managers' attention away from planning
- a loss of output and delays in production which can harm the firm's reputation.

3.2 Work

After studying this section you should be able to:

- describe the different types of work
- explain motivational attitudes behind work
- outline changes that have occurred in the world of work

Defining work

AQA A	M6
AQA B	M5, M6
EDEXCEL	M5
OCR	M5

Key points from AS

- **Employment and unemployment**
  Revise AS pages 40–41

Everyone purports to know what work is, everyone says they do it and yet there are still confusions in understanding what the term means. If by work we mean paid employment, that limits the workforce within the economy to those aged between 16–60. However, as students, you would probably state that you work at your studies although you might wish to qualify this by pointing out that you do 'temporary' work to augment your income.

As far as the economy of this country is concerned there are three main forms of work:

- primary – the extractive industries such as forestry, fishing, farming, mining and quarrying
- secondary – the manufacturing and construction industries
- tertiary – the service sector of work, such as banking, retailing, education, leisure, etc.

There has been a decline in primary-production employment figures in the last 20 years, and in the early 1990s they contributed only 6.2% of the workforce.

Progress check

Why do you think that there has been a decline in employment in primary industry?

Answers could include: over-fishing of some areas and the introduction of quotas has led to less fishing; the demise of coal-mining through competition from abroad and through the effects of the Conservative administration in the 1980s; the way in which agriculture has become very labour intensive, ensuring a smaller workforce, coupled with rural economic deprivation in the late 1990s.

This will be enlarged upon in the next section on global economic issues.

There has also been a similar decline in the relative importance of the manufacturing industry in the same period. This 'de-industrialisation' reflects a long-term trend towards tertiary production. The reasons for this can be found in our relative uncompetitiveness in producing manufactured goods compared with newly industrialised countries such as Taiwan and Malaysia. The improvements in global communications now make it efficient to import worldwide, particularly from the countries of the Pacific Rim. Their labour costs are far lower than ours and consequently the overall cost of the item is cheaper. Thus, the UK manufacturing industry is suffering a decline (certainly as far as employment figures go).

> It is worth emphasising that de-industrialisation is a global phenomenon. In other words, in our Industrial Revolution we moved from primary to secondary production. This is now happening in the Far East where a number of countries are experiencing the move from primary to manufacturing employment.

KEY POINT

Work and motivation

Most people tend to say that they work to earn money to buy goods or services (they have a need to ensure that they have a particular lifestyle). Every Saturday evening millions of us probably say 'if the lottery numbers come up I'll stop work!'

Yet in research published in November 2000 by the Industrial Society, over 50% of the respondents to a nationwide survey agreed with the statement 'If I had enough money to live as comfortably as I would like, I would still work.' These figures are actually backed up by the Lottery, which stated that 51% of all lottery winners who won £50 000 or more have returned to work in spite of their win.

Therefore we begin to appreciate that the needs of individuals that are satisfied by working are not always linked to wages or salaries. Satisfaction through work could relate to such issues as variety in the workplace and feeling appreciated for the work one does.

All members of a workforce are individuals and it is important for the employers to find out what satisfies the needs of each individual employee – because a lack of satisfaction leads to a lack of efficiency on the part of the worker.

In the traditional area of financial reward, it is always assumed that the workforce will become/remain motivated by this incentive. A workforce can be rewarded for its labour in a variety of ways:

- time rates (weekly wages)
- annualised hours (salaries divided normally into monthly tranches)
- piece rate (payment by result system)
- fees (paid for 'one off' tasks)
- fringe benefits (such as private medical insurance, company car, etc.).

> The problem with financial reward as a motivational tool is that it might not work! We might find it difficult to appreciate why the successful pop-group ABBA would not re-form for a £1 million concert tour – money is obviously not everything!

Progress check

Why do you think that financial rewards for employment are not always successful?

Answers could include: more money in itself may not motivate; financial incentive schemes can be difficult to operate; other factors can have more importance; staff become accustomed to a certain level of financial remuneration (i.e. it becomes the 'norm', and is therefore no longer an incentive).

If finance is not necessarily a motivational factor, what else might be? A list of possibilities could include:

- interesting and stimulating tasks
- a sense of achievement
- opportunities to show flair and initiative
- chances to take responsibility
- chances of promotion
- prestige and recognition of achievement.

However, actually applying these is quite difficult, and motivational problems which can result in high labour turnover, increased absenteeism or sickness, poor time-keeping, etc. are not easily overcome. There are however some strategies that can be used in an effort to do so:

- **changing leadership styles** – for example, a more democratic and consultative style can give benefits if it has not been used before
- **establishing teamwork** to develop a team spirit and a sense of common purpose
- **improving communication** – both in quantity and quality within the organisation; in other words, ensuring that the workforce understands what is happening and why it is happening

Quality circles are small groups of workers in the same area of production who meet regularly to study and solve production problems.

- introducing greater employee involvement, through the setting up of suggestion schemes, quality circles and other formal or informal groups
- allowing job rotation and developing job enrichment
- setting up training and staff-development schemes.

Types of employment

AQA A	M6
AQA B	M5, M6
EDEXCEL	M5
OCR	M5

Self-employment

If an employer pays tax and national insurance contributions for the worker, then the worker is an employee. A self-employed person is someone who pays their own national insurance contributions and income tax, and is in business on his or her own account.

Working from home does not necessarily mean self-employment – see 'homeworkers and teleworkers' below.

Permanent and temporary employment

The former is employed for an indefinite period, the latter for a limited period.

In the UK 10% of the workforce is temporary. Obvious examples are casual employees employed at busy times – post office workers at Christmas, for example. Some may not be so obvious – for example, temporary 'supply' teachers or nurses who do not wish to take on the full-time responsibility of a particular role.

Progress check

What are the perceived advantages to employers of employing temporary workers?

Answers could include: lower costs – temporary workers may not receive the same benefits as permanent staff; can be hired for 'one off' tasks after which they leave; some firms use temporary positions to try out workers who may later become permanent.

Part-time employment

Part-time workers are defined as 'people normally working for not more than 30 hours a week except where otherwise stated' (*Labour Market Trends*).

There has been a large increase in part-time workers in the UK in recent years because:

- they provide flexibility for a business – such as employing twilight shift workers to stack supermarket shelves
- they allow job-sharing. This happens, for example, in teaching where two staff can share a primary school class – one working mornings, the other afternoons
- it benefits the employees – for example, single parents can be employed; students can supplement their wages, etc.

Homeworkers and teleworkers

The former can include farmers, shop owners, representatives, telesales people, hotel owners. For an employer, the use of homeworkers has a number of advantages:

- less space is needed
- fewer problems with absenteeism and transport delays.

Teleworkers are people who work from their own home or use it as a base and who could not do so without a telephone or computer. Much of the 'cold selling' (which many find so irritating) probably emanates from homeworkers.

3.3 Global economic issues

After studying this section you should be able to:

LEARNING SUMMARY

- explain why there is, today, a global market
- list the advantages and disadvantages of being involved in this market, particularly in relation to the European Union affairs
- describe how the globalisation of our economy will have effects on life within the UK

The global village

AQA A	M4
AQA B	M5
EDEXCEL	M5
OCR	M5

Key points from AS

- **Locations of industry**
  Revise AS pages 48–49

The phrase 'the world's a global village' is commonly used today and a moment's thought will allow us to appreciate what this means. When we go shopping in the middle of winter we are no longer surprised that fresh fruit and vegetables are available in our supermarkets. In fact, we no longer (usually) question the country of origin of the product. Similarly when we travel abroad to the most exotic locations it is no longer surprising to find there 'McDonald's' or 'Hard Rock Café' logos. So how and why has this happened? Put simply, countries specialise in producing particular products as a result of such disparate factors as:

- the nature of the land
- the climate
- the availability of raw materials
- the level of training and experience of the labour force.

Specialisation leads to mass production, which in turn leads to a surplus that can be exported. The profits from this can be used to buy the products that the country cannot produce – for example see Table 3.1.

Table 3.1 UK exports (Jan–June 1998)

January – June 1998	UK exports
Machinery and transport	£38 888 m
Other manufacturing	£20 862 m
Fuels & Chemicals	£14 579 m
Food & Drink	£5 283 m
Other	£2 117 m

Progress check

1 What conclusions can you draw from the figures in Table 3.1?
2 What do you think is not shown here?

Answers could include:
1 Machinery, vehicles and chemicals are the important categories – for example, cars are important, as are Scotch whisky, North Sea oil, marmalade, etc.
2 Export of services (e.g. 40% of Virgin Atlantic's customers originate outside the UK. Americans pays dollars to the travel agent who changes it to sterling to pay Virgin).

KEY POINT

> An invisible export is invisible because it is a service and is an export because it earns foreign currency.

Forms of global trade

AQA A   M4
AQA B   M5
EDEXCEL M5
OCR   M5

Free trade

This occurs when the movement of goods and services between countries is not restricted in any way. The benefits of this are that countries' specialisation leads to mass production and economies of scale can take place. Also, consumers can gain (in lower prices) from the efficient use of resources through mass production. In theory, free trade encourages co-operation and goodwill between countries. In spite of this, many countries do not follow free-trade principles.

Protectionism

This occurs when restrictions are placed on free trade to:

*   improve the country's balance of payments by increasing exports and reducing imports
*   protect the country's exchange rate
*   raise revenues (from customs duties, etc.)
*   restrict the 'dumping' of goods from overseas competitors who export at low prices to establish a position in the market
*   safeguard domestic employment and industries, particularly 'infant' industries not yet strong enough to compete with established overseas firms.

The main methods of protectionism include:

*   **Tariffs** – taxes placed on imports to make them comparatively more expensive than home-produced products
*   **Embargoes** – where a country refuses to trade with another, often for political reasons (for example, our attitude to Iraq over the last decade)
*   **Subsidies** – a country's government may give support to one of its own industries, thereby improving its competitive position at home. (For example, farming subsidies are always requested by the beleaguered rural community.)
*   **Quotas** – physical limits can be put on the amount of a product or service that is imported, the car market is a case in point here
*   **Government procurement policies** – this means a country could 'buy from within' using its own industries to supply goods. It was the refusal to do this by the Thatcher Government of the mid-1980s (i.e. they wanted to buy the cheapest coal from anywhere) which was the root cause of the Miners' Strike of 1984.

In other words, it may seem logical to protect your industries but it does not always work out.

When protectionism takes place it can lead to less choice, higher prices for consumers and also inefficiency because of reduced competition. More importantly, there is always the danger that one country adopting protectionist measures can lead to other countries following suit – to the eventual detriment of all.

The European Community

AQA A   M4
AQA B   M5
EDEXCEL M5
OCR   M5

When referring to global trade it is necessary to remember that although the USA and Japan are the world's two largest industrial economies, the European Community as a whole is larger than either – containing 350 million people and 15 states. These belong to a Customs Union, which means that a common external tariff is placed on all imports, but that there is free trade within its borders.

The EEC started in 1957, the UK joined in 1973.

Advantages for the UK operating within the European Union include:
*   free access to the members' market
*   free access to factors of production (such as land)
*   large markets to sell to
*   the area inside the EU will be protected from other states because of the common external tariff.

It is fair to say that preference buying from the commonwealth (e.g. Australia and New Zealand) was coming to an end anyway.

However, there are also disadvantages:

- before joining the EU, the UK could buy goods from lowest cost producers around the world (e.g. New Zealand and USA), this is no longer true
- EU businesses will also have free access to UK markets
- protection, even of a very vast area, can lead to inefficiency.

In 1999 a single European currency (Euro) was introduced as a physical demonstration of European Monetary Union. Eleven of the fifteen member states signed up to the Euro; the UK, Denmark, Sweden and Greece did not. In 2002 Euro notes and coins will be made available. Some analysts saw the introduction of the Euro as a significant move towards the creation of a European trading area, that will be able to compete with Japan and the USA. The argument in favour of a European Monetary Union for businesses within the EU include such factors as:

- reduction in transactions costs (i.e. for the changing in currencies)
- reduction of uncertainty of trading within the Eurozone. If exchange rates are fixed, businesses will not experience a sudden change in exchange rates which could, for example, increase the price of their imported components
- transparent prices – using one currency makes price differentials more obvious. Nothing is hidden by exchange rates.

There is a major argument against the use of the Euro, however, and that is cost:

- initial conversions will be costly
- accounting systems will need to be changed
- staff training will be needed
- dual pricing can lead to redesigned packaging, advertising, etc.
- competition will increase, which could force down profits.

Progress check

What do you think could be the effects for the UK of staying outside the Euro?

Answers could include: it would not incur the costs of entry into the Euro; it would not gain from the benefits; businesses will need to quote prices in euros; uncertainties connected with dealing with different EU states with different currencies would be reduced.

The effects of globalisation

AQA A	M4
AQA B	M5
EDEXCEL	M5
OCR	M5

This is the term used to describe the growing integration of the world's economy.

> **KEY POINT**
>
> As globalisation takes place, national economies become integrated into a single 'global economy', with similar characteristics. In other words, decisions taken in one part of the world affect other parts.

Evidence for this can be seen in the fact that large companies selling branded consumer goods and services now think globally and do not simply set out to dominate their domestic market. Transnational companies (such as the Marriott Hotel chain) treat the global marketplace as their domestic market.

There are three major results of globalisation:

- the growing importance of international trade – this doubled between 1980–90 and is also partly explained by increasing sophistication of communications technology in every sense (i.e. computer technology, aircraft technology, etc.)
- the rise of the multi-national business – they operate worldwide, with familiar names such as Coca-Cola being commonplace in many different countries.

- the emergence of businesses that think globally about their strategy – for example, a business may make parts for a product in several different countries and assemble them in another because this is the most cost-effective and efficient method to get the product to its consumer.

There are various factors that have contributed to the growth of globalisation:

- technological change – computers and the internet allow for the easy transfer of data
- the cost of transportation has fallen
- the deregulation of business (i.e. the privatisation of many formerly state-owned businesses in many countries worldwide) – this allowed more competition and with the removal of restrictions on businesses operating in former communist states a further opportunity for global expansion became evident
- the liberalisation of trade (see earlier)
- a change in consumer tastes – people are now quite willing to buy things like Korean cars and it can also be argued that consumers worldwide have increasingly similar tastes
- growth of emerging markets (such as in the Pacific Rim) – as businesses in these countries have become more successful, they have been able to compete in Western economies.

Globalisation has had many effects upon business throughout the world, some of which are opportunities and some of which can be viewed as threats.

- **Competition has radically increased because of globalisation:**
  - foreign competition now enters markets previously the domain of domestic business
  - deregulation has meant that many previously monopoly-type businesses are now opened up to the forces of global competition
  - it has provided opportunities for innovative businesses to enter the market to compete effectively against market leaders such as IBM.
- **Consumer expectations and tastes have increased.** Businesses must now meet ever increasing consumer demands about quality, service and price. Globalisation has also made predicting consumer preferences more difficult, (e.g. few businesses predicted the huge rise in the popularity of mobile phones).
- **Economies of scale** – a global presence implies a larger scale of operations. This allows them to spread their fixed costs over a larger volume of output and thus reduce unit output costs. (For example, global hotel chains like Marriott are in a position to benefit from volume discounts from catering supply companies.)
- **Choice of location** – a global business can choose locations for a variety of reasons. Nike's decision, for example, to locate in Vietnam was probably cost-based, whereas Microsoft's decision to locate in Cambridge was probably research-based.
- **Mergers and joint ventures** – these happen increasingly with firms in other countries in order to provide a business's goods or services to a global market. For example, a manufacturer may merge with another in order to make products in the country in which they will be sold.

Progress check

Which of the factors in the last bullet list above would you identify as being opportunities to a firm and which as threats? (NB they might be both at the same time.)

Answers could include:
Opportunities: competition has increased – can get into foreign markets; choice of location – a worldwide concern can locate anywhere; merger and joint ventures – can ensure further growth of a firm.
Threats: competition has increased – cheap imports could overwhelm us; consumer expectations and demands – need to keep up or go out of business; economies of scale – small is no longer beautiful.

3.4 Consumerism in the UK

After studying this section you should be able to:

- explain why we are such a consumer-oriented society
- describe the drawbacks of such a situation
- suggest what the future holds in this area

LEARNING SUMMARY

Consumer sovereignty – the consumer as king

AQA B M5
OCR   M5

In many respects this section is closely linked to that of the previous one. Globalisation has meant that we now expect to get products from anywhere in the world, both quickly and cheaply and there is total consumer sovereignty.

> Consumer sovereignty is the process by which consumer choice signals to businesses what they should be producing.
>
> KEY POINT

In other words the 'customer is king'. Businesses are very aware of this and go to great lengths to make sure they obtain a clear picture of their customer (young? old? affluent?). This 'consumer profile' is a statistical breakdown of the people who buy a particular product or brand.

The main uses of this profile are for:

- setting quotas for research surveys (i.e. to ensure that all the categories above are covered)
- segmenting a market (i.e. dividing up a potential market to find which area of it might be the most profitable for the company concerned)
- deciding in which media to advertise.

> It may be worth considering how much advertising drives consumers and *vice versa*.

All business activity results in the production of a good or service. Consumer goods are those that are sold to the general public. They fall into two categories, durable and non-durable. The former, such as cookers, televisions, etc. can be used repeatedly for a long period of time; the latter such as food, newspapers, etc. are used very soon after purchase.

There are also, of course, consumer services such as hairdressing and plumbing which are used more frequently as income grows and are associated with satisfying physical needs (for example, personal appearance and safety – e.g. house repair needs).

Mankind has always been a consumer but the vast increase in consumerism within the UK in the last half century can be put down to several factors:

> The 'underclass' is the marginalised group at the 'bottom' of society.

- affluence – the general UK public is better off than at any time in the past
- although there is an underclass, the vast majority of people have higher standards of living than fifty years ago and hence have more disposable income to spend on consumer goods
- the lack of a major war since 1945 has ensured that this affluence has not been affected (i.e. in wartime much of the state's energy would be concentrated on war production and luxuries that are part of our affluent society would not be produced)

> This was dealt with in the Dependency on the State section in Chapter 1.

- the use of the Welfare State to provide a safety net 'from cradle to grave' has ensured that the population is protected (the safety net means that more of the family's wage can go on luxuries).

Consumer protection

The growth of this consumerism has been recognised by various UK governments in laws relating to consumer protection. There are also consumer organisations that assist in consumer protection.

- **The Advertising Standards Authority (ASA).** This oversees much of the advertising in the UK and aims to ensure that advertisements are 'legal, decent, honest and truthful'
- **The Consumer Association.** Best known for its '*Which?*' magazines, this researches into the quality and standards of consumer products and services
- **The British Standards Institute (BSI).** This organisation sets standards for a wide variety of goods and services. It is best known for its 'Kitemark' which indicates that an item conforms to British standards
- **Citizens Advice Bureaux (CAB).** These help with a range of consumer problems
- **Consumer councils and regulating agencies.** Privatised firms are regulated by authorised agencies such as Ofgas and Oftel. These agencies are empowered by law to ensure that the privatised firms meet their obligations.

The effects of increasing consumerism

- **Increases in costs.** Improving the safety of a product can increase costs for a firm – for example, an electrical firm producing table lamps, may find that its product contravenes legislation. The re-designing of the lamp or its components would raise the firms costs.
- **Quality control.** This has had to be improved in all areas such as hygiene regulations in the production of food.
- **Dealing with customer complaints.** Most firms now have departments to deal with customers' problems – to 'nip them in the bud'.
- **Changes in business practice.** Attempts to ensure that customers are treated fairly by a firm may place pressure on it to become more market oriented and possibly lead to a greater use of market research.

There is, however, another cost arising from this growth in consumerism – a cost to the planet itself. Consumption is often promoted as the defining human characteristic and at present 30% of the world's population consume 80% of the world's resources. This is not only unfair, it is unsustainable in the long term. We are already seeing environmental costs such as climate change, a decline in the number of plant and animal species and an increase in toxic pollutants.

> Consumerism is very much enhanced by the advertising industry.
> - £13 billion was spent on advertising in the UK in 1999.
> - Most people will have seen two million sales messages by the time they are 30.
> - Advertising sells a lifestyle in an effort to make luxuries look like essentials.

KEY POINT

In trying to focus on the drawbacks of consumerism, it is worth concentrating on the following five areas.

Commerce and industry

Many products such as cars and light bulbs are designed with a limited lifespan, even though manufacturers now have the technical expertise to make them last longer. This is known as 'built-in obsolescence' and leads to greater profits for manufacturers. Computer manufacturers, for example, upgrade their products for the same reasons. Each year 15 million working PCs are thrown away in the USA.

Governments of developed nations

Forty-eight of the world's least-developed countries account for only 0.4% of world trade. Stringent quota systems, high tariffs and export subsidies put in place by developed nations undermine the efforts of under-developed countries to develop.

Communities

If the amount of food wasted in the USA each day was reduced by 30% it could feed a further 26 million people. North Korea is gripped by famine and has 25 million people. As much as 12% of products bought are never used.

Consumption

Thirty-three percent of apples eaten in the UK come from abroad as do 80% of pears. In addition to putting strains on agricultural practices in developing countries, there are also environmental impacts. Annual imports of bread-making wheat are currently 800 000 tonnes. If all of these came, for example, from Europe (which they don't) transporting them would generate 11 250 000 kg of carbon dioxide, 45 000 kg of carbon monoxide and 150 000 kg of nitrous oxide. The questions thus arises 'why don't we produce more of this wheat ourselves?

Waste

Every week we produce enough rubbish to fill Wembley Stadium – over half of this could be recycled. Over 80% of paper thrown away is from packaging. Table 3.2 shows this in numerical form.

Table 3.2

Kg of waste generated per person per year		% waste landfilled
USA	1,410	61
Holland	547	13
England & Wales	525	85
Spain	439	73
Sweden	409	31

Progress check

What conclusions can you draw from these two sets of figures?

Answers could include: USA is the most profligate country; even 'clean' countries like Sweden produce 25% of the amount of waste produced by the USA; very little of England and Wales' waste is recycled; Holland possibly does not have the room for landfill – arguably England and Wales do not either!

Natural resources

The problems facing fisheries now are as serious as those that threatened rainforests ten years ago. In one study of the North Sea up to 4 kg of fish were being discarded for every 1 kg of fish landed. Shrimp trawling, for example, impacts on other species – for every 1 kg of prawns trawled between 5 kg and 10 kg of other species are caught and discarded.

Production

It is estimated that if 30% of the thermoplastics consumed in the UK were recycled to replace virgin raw materials, substantial energy savings could be made and carbon dioxide emissions could be reduced by about 3 million tonnes a year.

Sample question and model answer

1

In what circumstances could it be argued that it is right for the government to become involved in industrial disputes?

(AEB 2000)

In answering this question it is important to be able to define 'industrial dispute'. A simple definition could be 'an industrial dispute is a disagreement between employers and employees over working practices, recruitment, retention or remuneration'. An analysis of the different sorts of industrial disputes should then be made. After this analysis, a good candidate will give reasons for increasing government involvement as the industrial dispute escalates.

Below is an example of a student's response to this question. This is a good response, but it could have been even better. The candidate has given arguments for and against the assertion that intervention is good. However, with better planning he could have included his last point about Rover/BMW earlier on in the essay, so that it does not appear to be so much of an addendum.

The candidate certainly identified several cogent reasons for intervention:
- national interest
- public services
- knock-on effect of one group
- against the law.

For each of these he gave reasonable examples – although some of them could have been given extra elaboration.

The counter argument is much thinner. Some detail on ACAS' role, for example, would have been useful, as well as an explanation about the comment 'capitalist society'.

Although the answer appears to have a lot of merit it could have been improved with closer analysis and more thought.

There are two viewpoints to a question such as this – whether and when to be involved, or never to be involved. I shall deal with the former of these first. I suppose that the most obvious reason why a government should get involved in any form of industrial dispute, whether it be go slow, lock in or strike, is when the country itself is threatened. In times of war the government would not want people not producing for the war effort and a great effort was made to ensure that production flowed during World War Two.

A second point would be if public services are affected. In other words, if nurses or police went on strike, it could have a catastrophic effect on the country. Policemen are not allowed to go on strike and if nurses or firemen take industrial action, then the government soon draft in ancillary workers to fill their place – using troops on occasions, with their 'green goddesses' for ambulance or fire strikes.

Another reason for the government intervening could be if a small group take industrial action and effectively hold the country to ransom by doing so. This happened with the miners in the 1970s, though in those days they could hardly be classed as a 'small group'.

As I have touched on earlier, obviously if a strike occurred which was illegal, e.g. the police, then we would expect the government to step in.

Sample question and model answer (continued)

It can also be argued that a government should never intervene. An industrial dispute is, at baseline level, a dispute between employer and employee. It is up to them to sort out a compromise or deal. After all there are organisations like ACAS whose job it is to do that sort of thing. So it is possible to argue that the industrial processes will resolve things more effectively than the government in the long run.

So, possibly state intervention is wrong. We live in a capitalist society and it is better for businesses and unions to come to agreements rather than expecting the government to get involved. Having said that, there are occasions when the dispute spreads over the country's boundaries that the government should be 'involved', e.g. the dispute between BMW and Rover in the summer of 2000.

Practice examination questions

1 To what extent would you agree with the proposition that the world would be a better place without designer gear?

(OCR Specimen)

2 It is stated that one in seven of us is now obese and that the problem is worsening. Define a balanced diet. What advice can you offer regarding the integration of both a healthy diet and exercise into a person's lifestyle? To what extent do you consider that attention to these two factors enhances the quality of life?

(Assessment and Qualifications Alliance A Specimen)

3 To what extent do you think that people of high ability deserve higher rates of pay? Should there be a maximum as well as a minimum wage? What overall principles should determine the financial rewards for the work that people do?

(Assessment and Qualifications Alliance A Specimen)

Chapter 4

Belief, non-belief and values

The following topics are covered in this chapter:

- Belief
- Religion in society
- Alternatives to religion

4.1 Belief

After studying this section you should be able to:

- *put belief into a cultural setting*

Defining religion

AQA A	M4
AQA B	M4, M5, M6
EDEXCEL	M4
OCR	M4, M5

The word 'religion' comes from the Latin 'religare', meaning 'to bind' – binding humans to God, in other words. Hence it is a belief, or a philosophy that often involves the worship of a god, or gods. Belief in a supernatural power is not essential (it is absent in Buddhism, for example), but more usually a faithful adherence to God is considered to be rewarded.

A 'religious' person can be described as someone who obeys the rules of their religion in a very careful and often devout way. Being 'religious' is not tied to the observance of any one religion – Christians, Muslims, Jews and others can all equally well be 'religious'. Virtually all religious people believe that there is a life of the spirit (i.e. an existence beyond the purely physical) and in the existence of one or more gods who have a powerful effect on the people of the world – often with the power to bestow an eternal life on earthly mortals once their physical bodies die.

Key points from AS

- **The influence of religion in the UK**
  Revise AS pages 67–69
- **Major faiths in the UK**
  Revise AS pages 69–74
- **Religious, political and social values**
  Revise AS pages 75–77

Religious belief in Britain

AQA A	M4
AQA B	M4, M5, M6
EDEXCEL	M4
OCR	M4, M5

A comparison between religious and scientific belief can be found in Chapter 9.

Many people, if asked whether or not they believe in a God, will still say that they believe in some form of deity, although the percentage of the British people who attend Christian worship (the principal form of religious observance in Britain for the past one and a half millennia) has shown a marked decline in recent years. This is in part a result of an increase in the percentage of adherents to other religions (Islam and Hinduism have both grown over the last half century, for example, as Britain becomes a more multi-faith society). It is also partly a result of the absolute decline in numbers who attend Christian churches on a regular basis, even if non-attenders stick to some vague concept of a God (one who does not demand their absolute obedience and regular attendance at worship).

Religion and the State

For many, religion has always been a pragmatic, not a dogmatic, philosophy of life.

However, although religion once played a far more direct role in the life of many people, the part it played in directing the thoughts and actions of ordinary people can be over-stressed. For example, during the reign of the early Tudors a Protestant state religion (the Church of England) was created with the Monarch as Supreme Head and people were expected to adhere to the Protestant faith. Then in the reign of Queen Mary, England and Wales (Scotland was then a separate country) reverted to adherence to the Roman Catholic faith. When Elizabeth I took over from Mary, the English Prayer Book once again took over from the Latin Mass, and the clergy had to swear an oath of allegiance to the new Protestant order. Out of 8000 parish priests only 200 were deprived of their living because they weren't prepared to take the oath of allegiance. There are also more modern examples that might be quoted to show followers of Christianity being prepared to make their beliefs fit the prevailing political viewpoint – Christianity thriving in the midst of Nazi atrocities in Fascist Germany in the 1930s and 1940s, for example.

Followers of major faiths in Britain:	
Christianity	1 833 022 000
Islam	1 025 585 000
Hinduism	732 812 000
Buddhism	314 939 000
Sikhism	18 000 000
Judaism	17 822 000
(1992 figures)	

KEY POINT

Source: Microsoft Encarta '98

Is religion a matter of geography?

The 18th-century French writer and philosopher Rousseau claimed that religion was geographical. In other words, your perception of a divine truth was based on where in the world you were born. This is echoed by the 19th-century Irish writer and socialist, George Bernard Shaw, who wrote, 'There is only one religion, though there are a hundred versions of it' in his preface to *Arms and the Man* (1898).

It is true that religion and politics can easily get entwined. However, with the world increasingly becoming a 'global village' the idea of a local geographical character is perhaps harder to sustain. Over the last half century Britain has become much more of a multi-faith community. The extent to which this will undermine adherence to the traditional Christian perspective of the UK can easily become a matter of political controversy. The far-right wing of British politics talk of 'threats to the British way of life', while many others (in large part supported by the law) talk of the creation of a multi-cultural and multi-ethnic society as being a positive experience for all the people who live in Britain.

Religion and politics can easily get entwined.

Progress check

1 What are the two things that virtually all religious people believe, irrespective of religion?

2 For how long has Christianity been the dominant religion in Britain?

3 Who declared, 'There is only one religion, though there are a hundred versions of it'?

3 George Bernard Shaw, in the preface to *Arms and the Man.*
2 Approximately one and a half millennia (1,500 years).
1 A belief in a life beyond the physical and in a divine being, or beings.

4.2 Religion in society

After studying this section you should be able to:

- comment on links between religion and politics
- discuss the impact of religion on art
- describe something of the complexity of a multi-faith and pluralistic society

LEARNING SUMMARY

Politics in religion

AQA A	M4
AQA B	M4, M5, M6
EDEXCEL	M4
OCR	M4, M5

Key points from AS

- **Major factors in the UK**
  Revise AS pages 69–74
- **Values**
  Revise AS pages 75–77

A very good example of the impact that religion can have on the politics of a nation is provided by the spread of what some political commentators came to call 'radical Islam'. The effects of this were that the governments of countries concerned introduced strict laws based firmly on the Qur'an (the Islamic holy book) and were dominated by the clergy.

The impact of radical Islam

The best example might be the popular overthrow of the Shah of Iran in 1979, who had been given strong support by Western governments and oil companies. In a 'bloodless coup' the Shah flew out, and an elderly Muslim cleric, Ayatollah Khomeini, who had been in exile in Paris for many years, flew in to an ecstatic welcome. What had been a superficially Westernised country reverted to traditional Islamic social structures, codes of dress, legal codes and theocracy (government in the name of God).

The introduction of Islamic law has not always been so peaceful. The military overthrow of the democratically elected government of Benazir Bhutto by the Pakistani military in 1990 led to the introduction of Islamic law in that country. In Afghanistan years of internal war against Soviet forces, and later between rival factions internally, was ended by the military campaign of the Taliban – a military force of predominantly young, religiously inspired males who sought to unify the country under their religious and military leadership. This group, perhaps more than others, have aroused Western criticism since their strict interpretation of the Qur'an has, for example, seen women not only having to cover their bodies from head to toe in public, but also to withdraw from public places – including, for example, girls being forced to withdraw from the education system. The West believed that the regime harboured Islamic revolutionaries, and the US invaded the country after the September 11th atrocities against that country.

As the impact of Western colonialisation has reduced across Africa and Asia, there have been examples of Islam replacing Christianity as the dominant religion. This is particularly true in the parts of Africa where Islam and Christianity came into contact with each other – Christianity having been introduced by missionaries on the back of the military and commercial exploitation by European powers during the eighteenth and nineteenth centuries. Nigeria provides a good illustration of this when, in the closing years of the 20th century (in itself a Christian concept based on the passage of time since the estimated birth of Jesus), the northern areas of the country introduced Muslim law by popular demand.

The Established Church means the Church of England, which has formal links with the Monarchy and the Government, in that its head is chosen by the Prime Minister, who in turn crowns successive Monarchs.

Religion in Western politics

There used to be a popular description of the Church of England as 'the Conservative Party at prayer'. Although this could only be claimed in very general terms, there has been a traditional tendency for the followers of the Established

Church in England to vote Conservative, while Roman Catholics and those attending chapels vote for other parties. This divide in voting is particularly striking in Northern Ireland, where the Protestant community tends to vote for the Unionist parties who wish to remain part of the UK and the Catholic community tends to vote for the Nationalist parties which wish to see a united Ireland.

It is interesting that at a time when a smaller percentage of the population attend Christian worship or believe in God than for 1000 years or more, the Labour leader Tony Blair has turned to Christian priests as advisers, and made this very public. He clearly believes that Christianity still has a relevance to political decision-making.

Should religion influence political decisions?

We need look no further than the United States to see the increasing influence of Christianity in the political process. In the Presidential election campaign of 2000, both the Democratic Party candidate, Al Gore, and the Republican Party candidate, George Bush, played the 'religious card' for all it was worth. Both candidates insisted that God was on their side – and this in a country whose tradition and constitution separates politics and religion. For example, Gore told one rally that he was 'a child of the Kingdom and a person of strong faith', while for his part, Bush spoke about how his 'heart belonged to Jesus' and when asked who was his favourite philosopher answered, 'Jesus Christ'.

> Religion can be a key factor in binding a community together. However, it can also be a cause of dispute and tension when such a community comes into contact with another which holds different views or beliefs.
>
> **KEY POINT**

Progress check

1 On what book is Muslim law firmly based?
2 The Taliban introduced strict Muslim law in which country?
3 What was once called 'the Conservative Party at prayer'?
4 What enabled Christianity to make great inroads into Africa in the nineteenth century?
5 Who did President George Bush declare to be his favourite philosopher?

5 Jesus Christ.
4 Military conquest and economic domination by European powers.
3 The Church of England.
2 Afghanistan.
1 The Qur'an.

Art in religion

AQA A	M4
AQA B	M4, M5, M6
EDEXCEL	M4
OCR	M4, M5

All of the A2 specifications in General Studies contain elements on art. This could come under a variety of headings, such as aesthetic experiences, or beliefs and values. The AQA A specification is the most explicit, clearly stating that A2 candidates should be able to discuss 'spiritual experience and religious belief manifest through works of art'.

> The role of art is different in different religions. You must try to appreciate the role from the perspective of adherents to each religion.
>
> **KEY POINT**

Islamic art

Humans are not portrayed in Islamic art.

It is important to appreciate that for Muslims art has traditionally served very definite purposes in helping bring people to God. One central and powerful view is that since the power of creation of all things belongs only to God, to try to copy that creation by painting or sculpting human beings is to usurp the power of God.

Islamic art tends therefore to be ornamental and there has been a tradition going right back to the foundation of Islam in the 7th century (this is discussed in the AS Revision Guide) of the role of the artist as a skilled and devout craftsman.

For example, since sculpture was not allowed, carvers turned to the production of exquisite inlay and fretwork – particularly on doors and screens.

Art and the Qur'an

To Muslims their holy book, the Qur'an, is the word of God himself – the very words themselves are sacred. Islamic art developed around ornamental styles based on plants and flowers, geometrical shapes and actual Arabic scripts, particularly in illustrating the Qur'an.

Calligraphy

The art of beautiful writing is called 'calligraphy' and this is central to the development of Islamic art. Writing became ever more ornate and decorative – by the 10th century there were six classical scripts. Calligraphy also developed in architecture and by the time that is known in the Christian world as the Middle Ages, entire surfaces within some of the grander buildings, particularly mosques and palaces, were covered with words from the Qur'an or from the Prophet Mohammed. We can see here a very clear and direct link between art and religious devotion.

> The concept of 'art for art's sake' is alien to Islamic thought. The artist has a clear role in bringing the faithful to God.

Other Islamic arts

Calligraphy extended to the decoration of pottery, textiles and metalwork. Most notably, it also extended into the illustration, as well as the production of ornate script – of books. From this developed the tradition of the painting of miniatures, which reached a peak under the Moguls of India.

Because Islam would not allow artists to reproduce the human figure there were also developments in other craft areas. Islamic weavers have for many centuries produced fine silk brocades (heavy fabrics with elaborate raised patterns in gold and silver thread) and carpets of unprecedented fineness and beauty, which have been much admired and sought after in Christian Europe since the Renaissance in the 16th century.

Art in the religions of Southern Asia

In the AS Revision Guide we saw that some of the world's oldest religions originated in, and still dominate, Southern Asia. Hinduism and Buddhism are the largest examples.

Art and religion intertwined

The framework of religious art was in place by the 1st century BC and has shown a remarkable continuity. As far back as the 3rd century BC there are examples of sculptures from the Indus Valley in marble and alabaster which include naked goddesses.

Hinduism

In Hinduism, art is a medium through which spiritual ideas can be expressed. Sculpture in particular was important, and often showed the family of Hindu gods. The aesthetic experience is seen as having three related elements – the senses, the emotions and the spirit. Representations of the gods can appear ornate, sensuous and voluptuous. In a religion which believes in reincarnation, death does not have the finality of the Christian view. Within this context of birth, death and rebirth the form of a Hindu temple and of the gods and goddesses portrayed are intended to glorify, and to help people meditate on the mysteries of life and death, of time and eternity.

It is not only in painting and sculpture that the relationships between humans and the gods is portrayed – this runs through all forms of Hindu arts and is seen as a form of worship in its own right. For example, dance troupes tour India performing ritualised and traditional dances that not only tell stories of the gods, but are also seen as honouring them. There are also many sculpted dancing figures and the creator-god Shiva is often portrayed dancing.

Buddhism

Buddhism is the other great religion of Southern Asia – again, the nature of the religion itself is described in the AS Revision Guide.

From the origins of Buddhism in the 6th century BC, the Buddha was represented by symbols and reflected in scenes of his life. However, over time, images of the Buddha himself became more prevalent and from the 4th century AD these were sometimes in the form of statues which were often on a very grand scale.

Much old Buddhist art failed to survive the coming of the Moguls, who were Muslims, to India from the north. However, murals survive in cave temples, such as the frescoes in the Ajanta Caves near Hyderabad in India. These are marvellous examples of work painted for religious purposes, but which are erotic and secular (earthly) in style.

> **KEY POINT**
>
> The religions of Southern Asia stress contemplation and meditation. Against a backcloth of reincarnation, the sacred mysteries of life, death and rebirth are reflected in the Arts in all their forms.

Christian art

Any look at the role of art in Christianity has to acknowledge that there are three distinct strands, each of which has affected the arts in different ways. These are:

* the Orthodox tradition
* the Catholic tradition
* the Protestant tradition.

The Orthodox tradition

The Orthodox churches are most commonly found in Greece, Russia, eastern Europe and Asia. In their artistic tradition art is seen as a pictorial confession of faith. They believe since God came to Earth in the form of Jesus and was therefore clearly visible and had a human form, to create representations of this is seen as a channel for religious experiences. This tradition differs from the Protestant and Roman Catholic ones in stressing the importance of icons – the face of God rather than an image of the divine appearing in wider painting.

Icons

The most noteworthy contribution of Orthodox Christianity to the history of art has been the painting of icons.

> **KEY POINT**
>
> Icons are images of Christ as man. They confirm God's coming to Earth and his direct personal contact with people, so they are seen as worthy of veneration.

Icons are usually in the form of small painted panels. The painting of an icon is seen as a religious act in itself. They are stylised in nature, and the tradition of icon painting has been passed on, often in the same families, for many centuries. This even continued in the Soviet Union in what was, in theory, the world's first atheistic state. However, there has been a revival in Orthodox Christianity and in icon painting since the re-emergence of separate countries like Russia following the demise of the Soviet Union.

Other Orthodox art

Another form of Orthodox art that sought to glorify God was that of mosaics – the creation of pictures using small cubes of coloured glass, or of glass overlaid with gold leaf. These had an almost luminous effect on the walls of churches and often contained images that showed the mystical nature of Orthodox Christianity. However, as the centuries progressed the cost of producing mosaics became too great and by the 14th century they had largely been replaced by wall paintings, often showing huge narrative scenes.

Orthodox monks also produced beautiful and richly illustrated manuscripts from the 9th and 10th centuries onwards.

The Catholic tradition

The Christian church of Western Europe was based in Rome under the authority of the Pope, until the Reformation saw the creation of new Protestant churches in the 16th century.

Early art

The earliest religious art was strongly affected by the art of the Roman Empire, the style and medium, e.g. mosaics and frescos, that had been popular in the earlier empire, started to reflect Christian motifs. Since the early Christians feared persecution, their ideas were often expressed in an almost coded way. Jesus was symbolised, for example, as the Good Shepherd, or in the form of a cross, or a fish. However, once Christianity became the accepted religion of Rome and of Europe as a whole, we see the emergence of richly decorated buildings with marble floors, frescos (wall paintings), mosaics and altar furnishings such as gold and silver goblets. One famous piece of Anglo-Saxon art that still survives is the Lindisfarne Gospels (690–700 AD) with its abstract, highly patterned and interlaced ornamentation – see Table 4.1. At the same period in Europe, similar beautiful manuscripts of the Bible and other religious texts were being produced, many with beautiful covers inlaid with ivory and jewels.

Durham Cathedral

Romanesque to Renaissance

The 11th and 12th centuries were called 'Romanesque' because many of the great churches being built had a grandeur unmatched since Roman times – Durham Cathedral is an excellent British example. In terms of religious art there was a major trade in the creation of manuscripts and sculptures that were used in church services or for private devotions. The Winchester Bible (1170–80) is a good example, which is still on view – see Table 4.1. A popular form of artwork was the 'illuminated scroll' which featured humans and animals amongst foliage. These were produced in large numbers.

In the 13th century (sometimes known as the Gothic period, referring to the Germanic style (pointed arches, etc.) that originally belonged to the Goths) there was a trend towards greater realism in the portrayal of the human form. A good example is Giotto's 'Saint Francis Receiving Stigmata', which shows an angel giving the saint the same wounds as those given to Jesus at his crucifixion (the stigmata). Such paintings often had a gold or similar background – it was felt this helped the observer to concentrate on the storytelling aspect of the picture.

Artists began to have an increased social status in Western Europe at this time, particularly those who had the backing of a patron. The Church, as well as wealthy individuals, guilds and city governments, was an important patron and major decorative schemes were commissioned. One very good example would be the paintings in the church of St Francis in Assisi that was so seriously damaged by earthquake in 1999, but subsequently rebuilt.

Renaissance

The period from the late 14th century through the 16th century was noted for the revival of interest in classical literature and art. It was a 'rebirth', which is what the word 'renaissance' means. It was a period of fabulously rich patrons, such as the Medici family in Florence, or successive Popes in Rome. Starting in Florence and spreading to Padua, Venice and Rome, and after 1500 to northern Europe, Renaissance art brought a realistic depiction of space and form, in which perspective became important.

Leonardo da Vinci and Michaelangelo

Religious scenes in paintings became set in contemporary settings (sometimes including portraits of the artist's patron and his family in the picture).

Two names in particular are well known to this day – Leonardo da Vinci (1452–1519) and Michaelangelo (1475–1564). Leonardo da Vinci was famous even in his own lifetime as a painter and sculptor, but also as an architect, engineer and scientist. His painting influenced the course of Italian and European art. He was the personification of 'Renaissance Man' – the person who is not merely skilled in one area, but who has talents in a range of disciplines. His religious painting 'The Annunciation' shows the angel Gabriel appearing to the Virgin Mary in a very formal Italian setting.

Michaelangelo was a sculptor, painter and architect. By the age of 25 he was the predominant sculptor of his age, producing, for example, the 'Pieta', a young Mary holding the body of the dead Jesus, which is still on view in St Peter's Cathedral in Rome. His most magnificent achievement was the painting of the Sistine Chapel as a commission from the Pope. He worked on this single-handed for four years from 1508–12 and the result can be seen as a high point of Renaissance art.

Religious art since the Renaissance

Europe changed dramatically in the centuries after the Renaissance. The Church in Western Europe was split by the emergence of the Protestant churches, which came to be dominant in northern Europe, while Catholicism largely retained its pre-eminence to the south. The rise of industry and capitalism, again more predominant in northern Europe and then in North America, created new wealth and new goals. The Earth was no longer the 'vale of tears' of Mediaeval times in which eternal life was a positive thing to look forward to because life on Earth was so hard. Art in general became increasingly decorative, rather than serving an illustrative or teaching function.

Catholic artists continued to paint altar pieces, and paintings of Jesus and the saints, but the Church was no longer so powerful and threatening with the fear of eternal damnation for those who failed to obtain entry to the Kingdom of Heaven. From the 18th century, even in Catholic states like France, the power of humanist philosophy was growing.

The Protestant tradition

The emerging Protestant groups rejected the artistic decoration, paintings and statues that adorned Catholic churches. In England and Wales, Henry VIII's break with the Pope resulted in the disappearance of much religious painting and patronage. From the mid-1500s many painters moved to the increasingly wealthy

England to look for work, but by the time of James I much of this involved painting the portraits of those who could afford it, such as courtiers and the gentry.

Protestant churches were plain and simple, unadorned by the artistry so much a part of Catholic tradition. However, this has mellowed over the years, so that cathedrals and churches in Britain again contain sometimes inspirational examples of sculpture (Coventry, for example), painting and stained glass.

In philosophical terms, Protestants saw the way to heaven through the words of the Bible and by prayer. The attempts to glorify God through art formed no part of such a philosophy – nor did the idea that the creation of statues and paintings could be used for veneration to bring people nearer to God. That is not to say that Protestantism was against art – indeed the arts flourished in Britain after the religious break with Rome. However, art was not seen as devotional. 'Art for art's sake', an idea rejected by Islamic art was actually a powerful motivation for the creation of paintings, sculptures and the other forms of the arts in the Protestant world.

Table 4.1 shows key works of art in the development of religious art in Europe, and you can still see them today.

> **KEY POINT**
>
> In Orthodox and Catholic Christianity, particularly until about the 17th century, art was seen as being closely linked with worship and prayer. It was not 'beauty for its own sake', but a tool to enable humans to form a link with their creator. Prayer, spirituality and worship were the driving forces.

Table 4.1 Some key artistic works in the religious tradition of Western Europe**

Type	Artist	Date	Name*	Location
Manuscript	Anglo-Saxon Monks	c698	Lindisfarne Gospels	British Library, London
Manuscript	Celtic Monks	mid C8th	The Book of Kells	Library of Trinity College, Dublin
Manuscript	Unknown	C12th	The Winchester Bible	Cathedral Library, Winchester
Pulpit panel	Giovanni Pisano	1301	Massacre of the Innocents	St Andrea's Church, Pistoria, Italy
Painting	Giotto	1310	St Francis receiving the stigmata	The Louvre, Paris
Manuscript	Jean Pucelle	c1325	Belleville Breviary	Bibliothèque Nationale, Paris
Manuscript	Limbourg Brothers	c1416	Très Riches Heures	Musée Condé, Chantilly
Painting	Gentile da Fabriano	1423	Adoration of the Magi	Uffizi Gallery, Florence
Altar piece	Jan & Hubert van Eyck	1432	The Ghent Altarpiece	Ghent Cathedral
Painting	Leonardo da Vinci	1481	St Jerome	The Vatican, Rome
Wall painting	Leonardo da Vinci	1498–97	The Last Supper (fresco)	Monastery of Santa Maria delle Grazie, Milan
Painting	Hieronymous Bosch	c1500	The Temptation of St Anthony	Gemaldegalerie, Berlin
Painting	Raphael	1507	La Belle Jardinière	Uffizi Gallery, Florence
Fresco	Michaelangelo	1508–12	–	Sistine Chapel roof, The Vatican, Rome
Fresco	Michaelangelo	1536–41	–	Altar wall, Sistine Chapel, The Vatican
Painting	El Greco	1612–14	The Adoration of the Shepherds	Prado Gallery, Madrid

* These works are all on public display.

** These works were motivated primarily by ideals of the service of God and of helping others to worship.

Progress check

1 Why are no human figures painted in classical Islamic art?
2 What artistic form of writing has been seen as the ultimate form of Islamic art?
3 What performing art is seen as a form of worship and honour of the gods in Hindu communities?
4 Murals depicting scenes belonging to which religion were found in the Ajanta Caves?
5 What has been the principal contribution of Orthodox Christianity to styles of painting?
6 Who was responsible for painting the ceiling and altar walls of the Sistine Chapel?

1 Because it usurps a power of creation belonging only to God. 2 Calligraphy. 3 Dance. 4 Buddhism. 5 The painting of icons. 6 Michaelangelo.

4.3 Alternatives to religion

After studying this section you should be able to:

- assess the possibility of a world without religious belief
- discuss some philosophies that are put forward as alternatives to traditional religious belief

LEARNING SUMMARY

Could there be a world without religion?

AQA A	M4
AQA B	M4, M5, M6
EDEXCEL	M4
OCR	M4, M5

Key points from AS

- **Values**
  Revise AS pages 75–77

Whatever your own views on religion, you cannot deny the power of its influence throughout history.

Secularism – the belief that the world can be explained without the need for the supernatural.

Religion is one of the most universal activities in the world. It has been practised in some form in virtually all cultures throughout the whole of recorded history, right through to the present. Whether it is the simple concept of a spirit god present in the winds, earthquakes, eruptions and other natural phenomena, or the far more sophisticated concept of an unseen but omnipotent Creator who will share eternal life with His adherents, there have always been spiritual explanations for our mortal existence.

However, it is true that there has been a marked reduction in the percentage of people attending church regularly in the countries that make up the world's most advanced economies. This leads some people to argue that industrialisation, science and technology have led to a society in which it is believed that the physical world is self-contained and does not need the idea of a Creator god to explain it. The growth of secularism has seen thinking, social practice and institutions lose their religious significance. Marriage might be a good example – the Church of England wedding service stated that marriage reflected the relationship between God and His church, and that it stopped the sin of fornication. Few people who marry today – especially if they do not get married in a church – would regard these as the primary reasons for the ceremony.

Just because people have always adopted some kind of religious belief, this does not in itself mean that it is correct, or that it should continue into the future. It has been said that more has been discovered in the last century than in the rest of history added together. Could it, therefore, be claimed that the need for the concept of some kind of supernatural being to explain what would otherwise be incomprehensible has gone? This view would certainly not be shared by those scientists who are also practising members of a faith, or indeed by the majority of the population. In the United States, the world's richest and most advanced economy, over 80% of the people still believe there is a God.

Marx's view of religion

The idea that organised religion was not needed began to be discussed to any real degree in the 18th century, but many see Karl Marx's views on religion as the first popularisation of the ideas of atheism. He wrote:

'Man makes religion, religion does not make man. Religion is indeed man's self consciousness and self awareness as long as he has not found his feet in the universe. Religion is the sigh of the oppressed creature, the sentiment of a heartless world, and the soul of soulless conditions. It is the opium of the people. The abolition of religion, as the illusory happiness of men, is a demand for their real happiness.'

Was Marx right? Does religion exist primarily to give hope in a hopeless world? If so, then as our quality of life, our power over life and death, and our understanding of the universe and the cosmos increases, why do we any longer need religion? Has the need to explain the world in terms of its creation by an unseen supernatural force gone – or are people now trying to act like gods themselves and in so doing, risking catastrophe for the future.

These are important issues in A Level General Studies – you should be able to construct good arguments about them.

Some alternatives to traditional religions

AQA A M4
AQA B M4, M5, M6
EDEXCEL M4
OCR M4, M5

Atheism is from the Greek: 'a' – not; 'theos' – god.

Atheism

Atheism is the positive denial that there is a God. In a sense it is, therefore, a kind of faith in itself, since it is impossible to prove or disprove the absolute existence of a deity. The word was first used in the Roman Empire to describe Christians, since they denied the existence of the Roman gods. Today some people say that Buddhists are atheists, since they do not believe in a personal god. However, the term is more generally applied to the rejection of the Christian God. Having its philosophical origins in the Enlightenment period in the 18th century, and later spread by philosophers like Marx and Nietzche, atheism has become much more widely accepted in recent years.

Argument on the creation of evil in the world.

The strongest argument for atheism is that around the existence of evil, both human and natural – such as terrible natural disasters. Atheists argue that since 'total perfection' could not allow evil – which clearly exists – then there is no total perfection, i.e. God.

Agnosticism

Agnostic is from the Greek: 'agnostikos' – not knowing.

Agnosticism was a word coined in the 19th century by the biologist Thomas Huxley, who was a convinced supporter of the new Theory of Evolution, which did so much to shatter the prevailing view of the Creator god, and the absolute truth of the Biblical view of creation. The existence of a god is neither certain, nor impossible and agnosticism is a philosophy that claims that whether there is a Supreme Being or not, it is beyond human ability to find out, or understand, so we must therefore remain not knowing.

Materialism

Materialism is sometimes wrongly portrayed as a belief about greed and acquiring lots of possessions, but this is a very shallow perception of it. Essentially, it is the view that everything in the world is either made of matter, or caused to exist by matter. The philosophy goes back to Ancient Greece, but has become popularised over the last century and is now seen as being essentially anti-spiritual, and therefore anti-Christian or anti-Muslim, since both believe in a personal creator God.

Karl Marx developed the idea of materialism, not so much in explaining the

Marx's view of
materialism.

existence of human consciousness in terms of 'matter', but rather in seeking to explain social organisation in terms of the making and production of the material necessities of life. He said that it was the technological ability to make these necessities at any point in history that determined the economic system – farming moving to industrial manufacture, for example. This economic system will then determine the basis of social organisation, and the religious, political, ethical, intellectual and artistic history of that age.

Some biologists, who call themselves 'socio-biologists', believe that the natural process of evolution gives rise to humanity's views on matters such as morality, criminality and authority. The socio-biological approach reduces, or denies, the need for a God to act as the originator of 'good' and 'bad' in the world.

Hedonism

Hedonism is from the
Greek: 'hedone' –
pleasure.

Hedonism is a philosophy that has its origins in Ancient Greece, being based on the idea that pleasure is the sole, or chief good in life and that the pursuit of it is the ideal aim of conduct. In Greece there were two strands of thought:

- **Cyrenaics** (the egotistical hedonists) who believed in the gratification of one's own immediate desires
- **Epicureans** (the rational hedonists) who held that true pleasure is attainable only by reason being applied through self-control and prudence.

The idea was further developed in the 19th century by important thinkers and social reformers such as Jeremy Bentham and John Stuart Mill. They developed a philosophy that became known as Utilitarianism. In essence, this said that the essence of human life should be found in promoting things that would promote the greatest good for the greatest number. It then follows that it is the use of this yardstick that determines whether an action is good or bad, not the pre-determined creation of a Divine being.

Humanism

Humanism is a word sometimes used to embrace all these alternatives to formal and traditional religion. It can be summed up as an attitude that emphasises the ultimate dignity and value of the individual, without the need for a God. Underlying this is the view that people are rational beings, having the capacity for truth and goodness. Humanists would therefore flatly deny the Christian and Muslim view that morality comes from God and cannot exist without God as the root of goodness.

Progress check

1 How might you define 'secularism'?
2 What percentage of the population of the United States believe that there is a God?
3 Who claimed that religion 'is the opium of the people'?
4 What philosophy believes you can neither prove nor disprove the existence of a God?
5 What is the name given to a lifestyle based around the pursuit of pleasure?

1 The belief that the world can be explained in ways that do not need the supernatural.
2 80% (according to a 1999 survey). 3 Karl Marx. 4 Agnosticism. 5 Hedonism.

Sample question and model answer

1

How is humanity's concept of God, or gods, expressed through art?

Step 1
Introduction.

All that is needed here is a brief introduction to acknowledge that all cultures throughout history have sought to create images of deities for:

- worship
- trying to express the divine in terms that humans might understand
- forms of prayer – that what is expressed in artistic form might actually happen, for example.

Step 2
Description and analysis.

Do not let your answer be bound by the confines of the dominant religion of the community in which you live. For example:

- try to explain Islamic objections to trying to paint any representation of a deity and the importance given to art in calligraphy (i.e. art in the written word describing God)
- you could compare the austerity of much of the Christian representation of the Divine as opposed to much of the sensuous art produced in the Hindu tradition

All of this should be supported by examples of works of art wherever possible.

- within Christianity you could look at the abiding importance of icons within the Orthodox tradition, or the increasing realism in the depiction of images of Jesus and Mary, particularly after the Reformation.

You could look at the broader Arts beyond painting (e.g. sculpture, glass), not just at times when there was a need to try to explain the unexplainable and hence the need for a god.

You could look at some contemporary alternatives to traditional religion – atheism, agnosticism, humanism, materialism, hedonism. Could any of these provide an alternative philosophy of life?

Do not assume that the views that you personally hold are the only ones that might be seen to have validity.

Step 3
Conclusion.

Try to pull together, in a very succinct way, the main points you have made and come to a personal perspective. A conclusion to the essay might be like this.

Different religions express their view of their Gods in very different ways. However, our concept of the divine is always limited to our humanity. Whether it is the Muslim view that to try to create a direct image of God is to usurp his sole power of creation, or the Christian view that we can develop a limited ability to comprehend the wonder of creation, but never its full majesty, art and religion have been linked. For myself, when I am in one of our great cathedrals, and see a painting or a statue, the grandeur of the setting and the power of the piece of art combine to create a sense of awe which lifts my soul and strengthens my belief. Humanity's concept of the divine may be extremely limited, but through art it is expressed in a direct and uplifting way that can express our wonder in a way that words would not find possible.

Practice examination questions

Short answer questions

1 Name countries where revolutions have introduced radical islamic governments.

2 What are the three main strands within Christianity?

3 Name five alternatives to a traditional religious belief.

Essay question

4 As we enter a new Christian Millennium could we become a nation without religion?

Chapter 5

Artistic and social developments

The following topics are covered in this chapter:

- Architecture
- Painting, photography and sculpture
- Stage and screen

5.1 Architecture

After studying this section you should be able to:

- describe how architecture brings art and science together
- list some of the great motivations in architecture

LEARNING SUMMARY

What is architecture?

AQA A	M4
AQA B	M6
EDEXCEL	M4
OCR	M4, M6

Key points from AS

- **Twentieth century architecture**
  Revise AS pages 85–87

Architecture is a classic area in which important scientific principles from the world of physics combines with aspects of visual art – the practical and the beautiful.

This is not to say that all buildings are things of beauty – many are merely functional, and others are pre-fabricated kits that slot together. However, at their best, buildings of whatever age can make you stop and admire their beauty, or their power, or their ability to create a sense of awe.

Buildings are an essential part of our heritage – they help us to understand the people who lived or worked in them. They tell us a lot about the social and artistic circumstances in which they were built. Whether a modern block of flats or a castle, buildings help us to reflect on the spirit and culture of their age. A good example of this is by comparing two of Britain's designated World Heritage sites – on the one hand, Durham cathedral and castle, side by side and reflecting the enormous earthly and political power of the medieval Bishops and the City of Durham; on the other, is the most recently designated British site (designated in 2000), the Blaenavon Iron Works in the Welsh valleys, where visitors can look at industrial sites and the cramped housing in which the factory workers lived.

Architects have come to be involved not only in the design of buildings – industrial, commercial, religious or domestic – but also in many of the great feats of engineering that developed with the coming of the industrial age. They were used in designing many 'public faces' of projects including the building of canals, railways, huge bridges, tunnels and dams in conjunction with engineers. It was in their understanding of strains and load-bearing strengths that architects can be seen as technologists, and in the beauty of their designs as artists.

A brief history of the development of building construction

AQA A	M4
AQA B	M6
EDEXCEL	M4
OCR	M4, M6

In your exam, try to support description with examples.

- The 'post-and-lintel' technique was the earliest building style that can be seen as using architectural methods, and was a way of supporting roofs by having a series of pillars that supported horizontal lintels (beams). The Romans developed this with a way of spanning larger openings – the arch. This further developed with vaults and domes, examples of which can still be seen in many of our great cathedrals.
- In terms of domestic architecture, by about 1600 most town houses in Europe were built around a wooden frame that took the weight of the building. The frame was filled with various materials, the best known of which was wattle and daub – a mixture of inter-twined twigs all bound together and held firm with a filler of clay or mud. This box-like framed building was often

constructed with an overhanging upper storey which cast rainwater a safe distance from the lower storey. Stunning examples of streets built with houses in this style can still be seen in use in some of our ancient towns and cities, such as York, where The Shambles is a famous example.

- As a consequence of industrialisation, factories developed which needed large floor areas – which were provided by the use of pillars to support beams and floors in a way not dissimilar to the techniques used in the cathedrals. The Great Exhibition of 1851, which provided a showcase for Britain's rapidly expanding industrial and commercial might, was housed in a building that was revolutionary for its time. It had huge cast-iron frames, and a body made primarily of glass. This provided the inspiration for the great steel-framed buildings of the twentieth century, which allowed construction up to great heights. The earliest 'skyscrapers' were built in the USA, becoming more practical following the invention of the lift by Otis.

- Over the past 50 years skeleton-framed buildings have become increasingly popular, especially in offices. These are buildings constructed around a hard frame that takes all the strain. The gaps can be filled in with softer, flexible material. They allow for light and airy construction, with large open areas. Walls can be very thin, often using a lot of materials like glass, because the weight of the floors and of the building itself is taken by the frame.

> This is looked at in more detail in Revise AS.

> Architects can be seen as combining technology and art.

Styles in architecture

AQA A	M4
AQA B	M6
EDEXCEL	M4
OCR	M4, M6

Architectural styles reflect the values and needs of society – be it a huge cathedral with its pointed arches leading the eyes heavenward, or the contemporary airport hotel providing short-term comfort and service for long-distance travellers.

Travel has always led to the creation of buildings, many of them very fine. Good examples are the medieval buildings that acted as hostels for pilgrims on their way to the great centres of pilgrimage – which in Britain were Canterbury and Walsingham (now just a small Norfolk village, but in the Middle Ages a buzzing centre for pilgrims after reported sightings of the Virgin Mary and the appearance of a 'holy well' with healing water). Long-distance vehicular travel led to the development of a chain of coaching inns – providing accommodation, as well as refreshment and mail collection, while the horses were being changed. The Railway Age saw enormous rivalry between the different railway companies, reflected in the grandness of many of their buildings, particularly their terminal stations – the great 'cathedrals of steam' that are still in daily use by thousands of people – Victoria (named after the monarch), Waterloo (named after a great military victory) and King's Cross being good examples. Today, airport construction is a modern equivalent, but tends to be more functional than flamboyant.

> Effective architecture combines the aesthetic and the practical.

Religion has inspired many great buildings around the world – temples, mosques and churches. Few people in Britain live outside easy travelling range of such a building – where the use of stone, marble and glass can inspire whether you are religious or not. In the Middle Ages, when heaven and hell were very real places to virtually everybody, these huge buildings reaching heavenwards must have been truly inspiring. Some modern cathedrals, like those in Liverpool or Guildford, can be equally awe inspiring – go and have a look! Cathedrals (built using the techniques described earlier) demonstrate the power and enormous resources available to the church – being built at a time when most people lived in little more than huts built of primitive materials.

With many of us now travelling freely around Europe we are able to see classic examples of Islamic religious architecture – for example, in Spain. (Remember that much of Spain had been conquered by the Moors of north Africa and converted to Islam.) The great mosque at Córdoba is a classic example of Islamic architecture.

Rheims cathedral, built 1211–1300 during the peak of the High Gothic period.

The Mosque of Córdoba. Begun in AD 786 it became a Christian cathedral when the city was recaptured from the Moors in 1236.

You should take a view on styles of modern building – think of real examples from towns near your home.

Begun in AD 786, it later became a Christian cathedral after its recapture in 1236. (You might also get the chance to visit the fabulous Islamic palace, with its courts and fountains, called the Alhambra in Granada).

Defence has also provided the rationale for many of our great buildings. Many thousands still visit the Tower of London, started by William the Conqueror to assert his conquest of the capital and built on the same area as some of the major Roman defences from an even earlier period. In turbulent times castles provided safety, particularly for invaders imposing their will on a resistant people – the Normans on the Saxons, for example. The spectacular ring of castles built around the coast of north-west Wales by Edward I in the latter years of the 13th century show how conquest can be imposed by controlling communication and trading routes, and setting up an impregnable fortress containing soldiers with the latest military equipment. Not all military buildings belong to the period, put up by invaders to subdue the local population. In the 19th century, for example, a line of maritime forts were built along the south coast of England when there was concern about an attack from the French under Napoleon III.

Building materials have always been an important consideration in styles of architecture. In densely forested northern Europe it is not surprising that wood was used in building homes. Wood frames and infill provided Britain with its classic black and white beamed houses. In areas where there were extensive reed beds this provided a handy (and cheap) form of roofing thatch. Building was practical, using materials that were available locally.

Stone and marble were classic materials for grand buildings that required great strength (with the added bonus that they are fire proof). As the amount of timber declined, so the importance of clay baked into bricks began to increase and this transition from wood to brick can be seen in many of our historic stately homes.

In the 19th century the development of our huge industrial cities changed the face of Britain. In the cities, wealth and poverty were often near neighbours. Not more than a mile or so from appalling slums and tenements were built vast temples to civic pride. Fine examples are seen in many of our largest Town Halls – those of Manchester, Liverpool and Leeds, for example. In Birmingham the Town Hall was built to resemble an enormous Greek temple.

Today there is a battle between 'modernists' and 'traditionalists'. Should new buildings aim to be eye catching, like Sir Norman Foster's Pompidou Centre, or should they seek to blend in to existing townscapes? Traditionalists are often boosted by the support of prominent people like Prince Charles, who once famously described a proposed new extension to the National Gallery in Trafalgar Square as a 'monstrous carbuncle on the face of a well-loved friend'!

> You can learn a huge amount about a society and its culture by looking at its architecture. In some ways buildings are the 'soul' of any society. **KEY POINT**

Progress check

1 Which Welsh industrial town has become a World Heritage site?
2 What architectural technique was the first to be used for buildings with large roofs or an upper storey?
3 Who developed the arch?
4 Which cast-iron framed building was constructed for the Great Exhibition in 1851?

4 The Crystal Palace.
3 The Romans.
2 Post-and-lintel technique.
1 Blaenavon.

5.2 Painting, photography and sculpture

After studying this section you should be able to:

- describe key aspects in the development of these art forms
- discuss whether photography can be viewed as a form of 'pure' art

LEARNING SUMMARY

Painting

AQA A	M4
AQA B	M4
EDEXCEL	M4
OCR	M4, M6

Key points from AS

- **Culture and the arts**
  Revise AS pages 61–63

> Do not simply dismiss modern abstract just because you don't know much about it.

Painting is the earliest form of the Arts that we can still see in surviving form. In caves in southern France and Spain, most famously at Lascaux, can be seen primitive cave paintings of people and animals. We don't know exactly why these paintings were made, but they were probably playing a part in ritual magic or religion. Painting is certainly one way in which humans have tried to comprehend the divine and throughout history religion has been a powerful force behind painting. (Religious experience and belief in art is discussed earlier, in Chapter 4.)

Five thousand years ago the Egyptians were painting the inside walls of the tombs of their pharaohs and these paintings have provided a remarkable insight into everyday activities of Egyptian life, such as hunting and fishing. The earliest record of the brewing of beer comes from such a tomb.

Until the 20th century, painting was almost always based on drawing – i.e. it was based on 'real' images of people, things or places, or a human representation of the divine, such as gods or angels. The 20th century saw the rise of abstract art – which caused many observers to ask 'But what is it?' when confronted with an abstract work, as if a painting had to 'be' something.

Types of paint used throughout the history of art

- **Pigment based** – the most elementary form of paint, used by the cave painters. Made from products found in nature, powders made from plants, berries and animal matter.
- **Tempera** – paint made from powdered pigments mixed with egg yolk. This was often painted onto wood panels covered with linen.
- **Fresco painting** ('fresco' is Italian for 'fresh') was paint applied directly to wet, or fresh plaster on walls.
- **Oil paints** – this largely replaced tempera and fresco during the later Renaissance. This method was developed by artists such as the Van Eyck brothers.
- **Watercolours** – this became popular for landscapes and outdoor scenes. The English painter Turner toured England and Wales in the 18th and 19th centuries painting landscapes and everyday scenes, including the new technological marvel, the railway.
- **Acrylics** – these became popular in recent years. They have several advantages, they are water-based, dry quickly and do not darken with age.
- **Enamelling** – this technique involves a wire outline being filled in with coloured enamel of a variety of colours.

An example of a School of painting: Impressionism

A brief history of Impressionism

> In your exam you might be asked about styles of painting. Here is an example to help you.

- Impressionism is often regarded as being the first modern school because they were the first group of painters to move towards the 20th-century idea that 'art' wasn't about the formal re-creation of perceived reality. In reality it had no clearly defined programme and was simply a group of painters who got together to stage their own exhibitions rather than compromise their ideals by showing their work at the official government-sponsored Paris Salon – the traditional venue for getting work known.

- In the summer of 1869 Claude Monet and Pierre Auguste Renoir worked together at a popular bathing spot just outside Paris on the river Seine called Grenouillère, producing a series of paintings seen as the first works of Impressionism.
- One new trend was to complete the whole picture outdoors on site, rather than doing a sketch that was later finished in a studio – so these pictures were smaller and more intimate than the works traditionally shown at the Salon.
- In order to represent sunlight on the water they used the characteristic 'broken' brushstroke, with dabs of pure pigment laid side by side on the canvas rather than being smoothly modelled, as was the usual style. They also got rid of black from their palettes, concentrating on the primary colours of red, yellow and blue and their derivatives. They observed that the colours of objects were modified by their surroundings – light and shade, for example.
- Although these essential features of the Impressionist style had been formed by 1869 it was not until 1874 that there was a group exhibition that gave the group a kind of coherent identity. This was held in Paris at the studio of the photographer Nadar. Motivated in part by their persistent rejections at the Salon, and partly by a desire for sales, 39 artists displayed works. In addition to Monet and Renoir others included Cézanne, Degas, Morisot and Pissaro. At later exhibitions they were joined by Gaugin, Seurat, Cassatt and Signac. At the 1874 exhibition they formed themselves into a limited company, but didn't immediately call themselves the Impressionists.
- That name was first given to the group in a derogatory way by the art critic Louis Leroy, commenting on Monet's work 'Impression: Sunrise', which depicted boats in a port seen through mist. Leroy was angered by the work for its lack of sharp detail, failing to see that the whole point was the creation of the atmosphere.
- The group eventually held eight exhibitions between 1874 and 1896, although only Pissaro exhibited at them all. By the time of the last one their character had changed fundamentally. Monet, Sisley and Pissaro favoured landscapes, while Renoir produced a series of figure studies. Degas did not like working in the open, and reverted to working in a studio from sketches. He went on to produce a series of famous oil paintings specialising in ballet scenes, and also, along with others, took horse racing as a theme after the use of photography showed the movement of the horse in frozen form for the first time.

Photography

The technology of the camera is examined in Chapter 9. Here we consider whether photography can be seen as an art form (as well as having a range of technical and industrial uses, X-rays for example). Certainly the famous quote by French artist Paul Delaroche suggests it can be. He saw the photographic image created by Louis Daguerre and pronounced, 'Painting is dead'. He was saying that the camera had the ability to capture every detail of the world in a second and this would kill painting and drawing. One early use of photographs was to provide a reference for detail and composition for a painter. As mentioned above, Degas used photographs of galloping horses, so the detail could be got right for the first time.

A brief history of photography as an art form

In order to try to win approval from the artistic establishment many early photographs adopted the same high moral themes of much 19th-century painting, with highly posed pictures. However, with technical improvements so that a photograph could be taken in a fraction of a second, the camera later came to be used for its ability to 'capture the moment'.

By the early 20th century photography was gaining in status. The American Alfred Stieglitz displayed his work at his new Gallery 291 in New York. He also produced a magazine, *Camera Work*, which advocated photography as a pure art form with aesthetic value.

In the USA photography tended to be inspired by nature and the great outdoors, but in Europe some photographers worked with avant-garde artists, such as the Futurists in Italy, who looked to photography to celebrate the rhythm and speed of the machine age. The style of combining many images into one work, photomontage, brought different views of reality into conflict and created a tool that could be used for social and political satire.

The Surrealist movement found photography a shortcut to the unusual and bizarre, using the camera's ability to cast the ordinary in a strange light as a way of mystifying and confusing. The leading exponent of this was the American Man Ray.

An alternative way of looking at the world was also proposed by a 'new objectivity' from the Hungarian László Nagy, who led a group of photographers closely associated with the Bauhaus design group. This group of photographers found the unusual not in a surreal way, but in the choice of unusual angles.

> The Bauhaus movement is discussed in Revise AS.

Some photographers who are now regarded as masters of the form never saw themselves as artists. People like Eugene Atget and André Kertesz documented life as they saw it around them. Walker Evans and others recorded the lives of the rural poor, the sharecroppers and tenant farmers in the USA, providing a powerful witness to inequality and the struggle for survival. In the UK Bill Brandt was one photographer who produced memorable images of social life across the whole spectrum of society in the 1930s.

Since World War II photography has continued to innovate. In the 1950s and 60s came the new, seemingly informal style of 'street photography'. An early classic example of this is a photo of an unemployed miner begging from King George V when he visited Merthyr Tydfil in the 1930s. At the same time photography and art became more closely aligned, in the work of pop-artists like Andy Warhol, for example.

Sculpture

AQA A	M4
AQA B	M4
EDEXCEL	M4
OCR	M4, M6

There are two types of sculpture:
- carving
- modelling.

There are three main materials used for sculpting:
- stone (granite, marble, limestone and sandstone, in particular)
- wood (using mainly the wood available in the area)
- metal (unlike stone and wood this is 'built up' rather than being cut away).

Carving

The sculptor uses a series of specialist tools to produce the works. With stone these are:

- a mallet and point for knocking off big chips to produce the rough shape
- a square hammer to work rough edges
- chisels (flat, bullnosed, tooth and claw) for smoothing
- a drill, for defining detail like hair, or for undercutting
- rasps and files for polishing up the finished work.

With wood carving the same basic types of tools are used, but they are lighter and sharper.

Modelling

Another style of sculpting is modelling, using clay, wax or plaster to build up the shape. This is built up around a frame of metal or wood. If the work is to be flat on a board, the material being used is held to the board by studded nails that act as a key to grip the material. The material is modelled using fingers, knives and scrapers. Models in clay are fired in an oven to harden them, those in wax or plaster are left in their raw state.

Techniques for metal casting in sculpture

There are two different techniques used in the creation of metal sculptures, such as those produced by Rodin:

- the lost-wax process
- the sand-casting process.

The lost-wax process

In the lost-wax process the *exact shape* of the sculpture is originally made in wax and this is then melted off and the gap filled with metal. A wax layer of exactly the thickness required for the final bronze (or sometimes brass) shape is built up around an inner core of plaster. On top of the wax a further layer of plaster is built up to cover it, and rods are inserted through the plaster into the wax. The whole thing is then baked in an oven at 650°C, which hardens the inner and outer layers, but leads the wax to melt away. The molten metal being used for the sculpture is then poured through the rods to fill the gap left by the melted wax. When it has cooled the outer plaster is chipped off, and the inner core is chipped away, leaving your metal shape.

The sand-casting process

In sand casting a mould is made of a model using casting sand, which has the ability to retain a detailed impression even when it is inverted. The sand is dampened and put into two metal frames. The mould is created by packing the sand around each half of the model and the two are then clamped together. A cavity for the molten metal is made by suspending an inner sand core in the frames, held in place by metal rods. Channels are cut in the sand into which the molten metal will be poured. The whole clamped frame is then hardened in an oven and the molten metal is poured in. When cool, the mould is broken away and the core chipped out. There will be a line of raised metal left where the two halves were joined together. This is usually smoothed off, but some styles, like Chinese bronzes, leave this for decorative effect.

Modern, avant-garde sculptors have started to use the techniques of industrial metalwork, such as welding.

It is not the role of a revision guide to tell you what styles of sculpture you should like, that has got to be a personal thing. However, before your exam you should look up examples of famous works so that you can describe them, together with the style in which they were created.

> Painting, photography and sculpture can be seen as the 'pure arts', though some dispute whether photography can be regarded as an art form. In your General Studies exam you might be asked to discuss your favourite examples – so think about some examples that you particularly like. The details given in this section should help you to support your description with a more 'technical' background.
>
> **KEY POINT**

5.3 Stage and screen

After studying this section you should be able to:

- describe the development of the performing arts
- set your own personal favourites into a developmental framework

Theatre and stage

AQA A	M4
AQA B	M5
EDEXCEL	M4
OCR	M4, M6

Key points from AS

- **Culture in the arts**
  Revise AS pages 61–64
- **20th-century music**
  Revise AS pages 83–84

The traditions of western theatre go back to the Ancient Greeks – and some of their works are still performed today, such as 'The Frogs' by Aristophanes. Plays were performed in the open air, with the audience seated in steeply tiered rows so that they were as near as possible to the actors, although Greek theatres often had amazing acoustics. The Romans later developed this style across their empire, with the development of having a raised stage and less of an encirclement of the actors by the audience – they were more in front of the action.

In the Middle Ages in Europe we saw the development of plays that were a cycle, or a pageant, with religious themes. They were performed in churches, town squares and from moveable wagons, used by the actors to go from venue to venue. In time these pageant wagons developed into trestle platforms with the audience sitting in boxes in front of this, so there was a defined audience, rather than a group who could wander in and out of a performance. This style of trestle stage productions was most widely used by comedians, who had developed as a form of entertainment by the 18th century.

The first permanent theatre building was constructed in Vicenza in Italy in 1580 and was designed in the Classical style of the Renaissance that was then all the rage. The first theatre to use flat sets on the stage, and a proscenium arch (the front arch that frames the stage between the curtain and the orchestra – which is still the most common theatre design) was also in Italy, at Parma in 1618.

The Globe Theatre

In Britain by 1640 there were four playhouses at Bankside by the River Thames in London. They had a circular galleried section and a large, open, standing space in front of the stage – based very much on the design of the yards of large inns where plays had traditionally been performed. The Globe was the best known of these playhouses and was where Shakespeare's group of actors was based. It was, however, destroyed (together with many others) by the Puritans in the Civil War period. (It has now been re-created in the 1990s as an exact replica on the same site.)

A major development that came about in the 19th century was the theatre in which the whole audience was facing the stage so that they could see the increasingly sophisticated and technical productions. Multi-tiered theatres, and opera houses like La Scala in Milan, were built in this way, with the audience separated from the actors by an orchestra pit. Sophisticated lighting allowed the audience to be in very subdued light, with bright light on the stage helping to create the atmosphere needed for 'the suspension of disbelief' – i.e. the necessary quality for the play to become 'real life', not just a piece of entertainment.

In the 20th century some theatres broke free from the confines of the proscenium arch. The first was probably the Shakespeare Festival Theatre at Stratford, Ontario in Canada, where the stage bursts straight past the arch, enabling the actors to be surrounded by the audience on three sides once again. Recent years have seen the increasing popularity of 'theatre in the round' (a good example is the Royal Shakespeare Company's 'Swan Theatre' in Stratford, England) which re-creates the old playhouse atmosphere. 'Promenade' performances are also increasingly seen – with the actors walking among the audience to perform the scenes.

Theatrical productions

AQA A   M4
AQA B   M5
EDEXCEL   M4
OCR   M4, M6

'Production' refers to the way in which any form of theatre is presented to a live audience. Theatre is more than merely a way of entertaining those who pay to see it. It is also used for:

- artistic expression
- religious ritual
- political persuasion
- entertainment
- moral teaching
- to alter awareness.

Traditional theatre has become very expensive to perform and many traditional theatre companies now rely on sponsorship. Most countries have national theatres which receive government support, while many major theatres in provincial towns and cities are supported by their local councils. However, there is also commercial theatre, which aims to play to big audiences and make a profit – London's West End theatres, for example. Since these shows are very costly to produce, unknown writers – or experimental plays – are rarely seen in the West End in case they couldn't create a mass audience. This tends to make commercial theatre rather conservative and works against innovation.

There is another more non-commercial form of theatre, sometimes called the 'Fringe'. This often tries to meet a variety of purposes – political, literary, artistic and avant-garde, for example. It is here that the work of new playwrights, actors and directors is more likely to be seen. Such groups often operate with limited budgets, and the temptation for some of the more successful groups is to accept sponsorship – but this then puts pressure on them to become as commercial as the theatre they have rebelled against.

Community theatre groups, often supported by funding from the Arts Council, exist to write, produce and perform local works in communities – in village halls, community centres, schools and the like. On similar lines, there are Theatre in Education (TIE) groups working in schools on a variety of projects and workshops. However, since local education authorities now have to give most of their budgets directly to schools such groups are now rarer, since the authorities do not have the money to cover their costs.

Personnel in the theatre

AQA A   M4
AQA B   M5
EDEXCEL   M4
OCR   M4, M6

The functions of the personnel in the theatre is now described using the model of what happens in big national theatres.

The producer

This is the person responsible for the overall administration of a theatre – raising and allocating funds, hiring personnel and overseeing all aspects of production. For a commercial production the producer contracts a playwright for a script, raises funds from private investors (called 'angels'), hires the artistic and technical staff, rents a theatre and the necessary stage equipment and oversees publicity and ticket sales and all financial aspects of the production (although box-office operations are handled by a general manager, and there will be a house manager responsible for theatre maintenance and audience control). The producer might also arrange tours, subsidiary productions and the sale of subsidiary rights (including film, TV and amateur production rights).

The director

This is the person who makes all artistic and creative decisions about the play. Working with designers, the director will take decisions on the interpretation of the script, the selection of actors and rehearsals. Scenery, timing and effects are all determined by the director. In a musical show the director will be assisted by a musical director, and dancing will be arranged by a choreographer.

The performers

These include not only actors, but often musicians and dancers. A modern production will usually rehearse for 2–6 weeks before opening. There will be pressure to keep this time to the absolute minimum because the performers need to be paid during rehearsals even though there is nothing coming in from ticket sales. During this rehearsal period the actors learn the blocking (the movement of the performance), their lines from the script, the interpretation wanted by the director and, eventually, to polish the performance.

Virtually all professional actors belong to Equity, their trade union, and without an 'Equity card' they cannot get work. The union also negotiates with theatre managers the rates of pay, the length of rehearsals, the number of performances a week and basic working conditions. This makes it sound as if Equity has great power, and in terms of governing the acting profession it probably does. However, it should also be remembered that the basic rates of pay for 'ordinary' actors and dancers is far below that of most trade professions and that at any one time around 85% of Equity members will not be employed as actors (i.e. they will have other part-time jobs to keep them going between jobs).

Film

AQA A	M4
AQA B	M5
EDEXCEL	M4
OCR	M4, M6

The technical developments associated with film are discussed in Chapter 9. Here we consider various types of film and their artistic uses.

Early films

The earliest films showed just one scene, running for about one minute – the time taken for a standard roll of film of the time to run through the camera. Each roll was 20 or 25 metres long. From the start these short clips were specially staged and acted – one very early example being Edison's 'Barbershop' scene.

The year 1898 saw the first British example of a number of scenes being joined together into a longer story in the Robert Paul Company film 'Come Along Do'. However, most of the early multi-shot films were made in France by Georges Méliès, who told well-known stories, such as 'Cinderella' in 1899. These were commercially successful and prompted a general move to longer films.

By 1905 there were enough films lasting for 10–15 minutes each to enable the earliest public cinemas, called nickelodeons, to open in the United States. The name came from the nickname 'nickel' for a 10 cent coin – the cost of admission.

One early pioneer of film making who introduced dramatic storytelling and acting technique was D.W. Griffith, who was first employed by the Biograph Film Company. He remained a powerful figure for almost a generation.

The first Westerns were shot in California as early as 1912, and were interesting because they saw the final major developments in film construction – the use of the reverse-angle shot (that is, shots taken in the opposite direction to the preceding shot). This technique had a number of advantages, including showing the actor's facial expressions more closely, enabling a smoother continuity as actors moved about the set and drawing the audience into the action.

One popular early style of film was comedy, such as films with Charlie Chaplin and the Keystone Cops. The style was developed by D.W. Griffith and the master of comic effect was the director Mack Sennett. The effects were often intensified by deliberately speeding up the action at climaxes (done by turning the camera at a slower speed and then projecting at normal speed).

As films got longer script-writing became more important – although words were still displayed as camera shots in the action because they were still silent films. Films often contained a wide variety of styles – action, comedy, drama and romance often within moments of each other! As sophistication increased during World War I years there were many films that used symbolism, allegory and parable, and in the years up to 1925 a new generation of directors emerged, like Frank Borzage, although the early directors who kept up with technical and artistic developments, like Cecil B. DeMille, continued to be prominent.

In the years during and after World War I there were also important business developments in the industry. Large purpose-built cinemas holding more than a thousand people replaced the working-class nickleodeons. Vast new studios were built around Hollywood, replacing the previous centre of New York. Integrated companies like Universal and Paramount owned the cinemas, the studios and the distribution agencies. Ever bigger fees were earned by superstars like Charlie Chaplin and Mary Pickford and were passed on to audiences by making admission for their films more expensive – the age of the film star had arrived. Realising their own value to cinema, Charlie Chaplin, Mary Pickford, Douglas Fairbanks and D.W. Griffith joined together in 1919 to create their own company, United Artists.

New stars – a second generation – emerged during the 1920s – people like Rudolf Valentino, Gloria Swanson and Norma Talmadge. When Valentino died at the age of 31 some fans are said to have killed themselves from grief.

The advent of the 'talkies'

An immense step forward came with 'the talkies'. The first idea for sound was for canned sound to accompany films in cinemas that were too small to employ their own orchestras to accompany the silent films! However, when Al Jolson spoke a few lines in 'The Jazz Singer' (1927) people flocked to hear the actor's voice. Development in this area was rapid, but costly, but had been accomplished by 1930 in the USA and a couple of years later in Europe. The introduction of sound meant that plots could now become far more complex.

These themes were not always serious – the classic comedy 'Some Like It Hot' starts with a gangster mob massacre.

The introduction of sound brought three new genres into being – the musical (which remained popular until the 1960s when rising costs made them too expensive), gangster films and newspaper men films, these latter two reflecting public interests of the time.

The arrival of colour

Cinema in the 1930s was providing mass entertainment, so it rarely tackled unpleasant or challenging topics – although there were noble exceptions towards the end of the decade, for example, John Ford's 'They Won't Forget' (1937, about lynching) and 'The Grapes of Wrath' (1939, about rural working conditions in America).

A major development in the 1930s was Technicolor – full colour cinematography, which basically worked by taking three simultaneous negatives in the primary colours. This was used in live action filming from 1934, but due to the cost was only used in very special full length films like 'Gone With the Wind' (1939).

In the 1940s and '50s film became more prepared to tackle unpleasant topics – audiences had become used to seeing horrible images in the newsreels shown in cinemas during World War II. There was also a growing move to shoot outside scenes on location. During the war film production decreased, but audiences and profits grew. This trend continued, until spectacularly reversed by the arrival of television in virtually every home.

Film since the War

By the 1960s the older part of the cinema audiences had largely gone. Audiences were younger and better educated, so films became more complex in plot and technique. By the 1970s there was a definite art film section of the industry, with film makers like Robert Altman and Woody Allen directing distinctive films. Also by the 1970s the sales of videos of films and sales to TV companies accounted for around half of film income. It was possible to finance the making of a cheap film from these sources alone – the made-for-TV film had arrived.

In the years since the latter part of the 1970s there has been a stress on extremely expensive, all-action blockbuster films that have attracted huge audiences. A far higher proportion of the total financial expenditure on new films goes into a few really expensive productions, rather than making a large number of films. George Lucas, with the Star Wars trilogy that started in 1977, and Steven Spielberg, with films like 'Close Encounters of the Third Kind' in 1977 are good examples of contemporary film makers producing this type of film.

Today the huge and often architecturally striking cinemas of the 1930s are largely a thing of the past. They have been replaced by multi-screen complexes showing a range of films on the same day. Often they are built at strategic sites on the edge of town so that audiences can drive there, often from some distance from areas where the number of cinemas has severely reduced.

> Film is a good example of technological development leading to improvements throughout the 20th century. The new century will see the continuation of the recent process of concentrating on a few key expensive 'blockbuster' films, rather than the mass production of many films as in earlier times. The development of new cinema complexes seems to have reversed the decline in audiences, but it will be impossible to ever attract the huge weekly cinema attendances that were seen in the pre-television age.
>
> The technological advances in the theatre may not have been so striking, but nevertheless developments in lighting and sound – combined with a move by directors to break away from the confines of the proscenium arch – has seen the advent of some striking new styles such as 'theatre in the round' and 'promenade performance'.

KEY POINT

Progress check

1 What was the name given to part of the stage that provided a physical barrier between the audience and the actors, behind which the curtains are usually hung?
2 What is 'fringe' theatre?
3 What was the name of the first British film to be made from a number of scenes being joined together?
4 What three new genres became popular once 'the talkies' had arrived?
5 Name two directors who produced 'art movies' during the 1970s.

5 Robert Altman and Woody Allen.
4 Musicals, and films about gangsters and newspaper men.
3 'Come Along Do' – made by the Robert Paul Company.
2 Non-commercial theatre, often created with a specific goal – political, literary, artistic, or avant-garde for example.
1 A proscenium arch

Sample question and model answer

1

Show how religion, defence, travel and civic pride have influenced styles of buildings over our history.

Step 1
Introduction.

- Briefly set out the types of buildings that you are going to use to answer the question, e.g.
  - the vast medieval cathedrals, or striking modern churches
  - the castles built to subdue hostile local populations
  - a range of possibilities from coaching inns, to the large railway stations mainly built in Queen Victoria's reign
  - the great Town Halls of our industrial cities.
- Do not go into any detail in your introduction, or you will be repeating yourself.

Step 2
Development.

It is vital that you provide a range of examples to illustrate your answer.

- It is important that you illustrate your answer with lots of actual examples, as well as being able to discuss the specific functions of the differing types of building, e.g.

When standing before one of the great Medieval cathedrals, such as Lincoln or Salisbury, it is impossible not to be impressed by the craftsmanship and building skill of the builders. Even if one does not have Christian views, it is still possible to feel the spirits soar as your eyes are drawn heavenwards by the immense architecture, the pillars supporting ornate ceilings and the stained glass throwing a coloured light that we are sharing with countless others who have been into these buildings hoping for eternal life, over the past centuries.

- You should seek to highlight the differences between the differing types of buildings in the question. You could also comment on the way in which the great railway stations have been described as 'the cathedrals of the steam age' in the enormity of their design.

Step 3
Conclusion.

- Your conclusion should focus on the way in which architects have always produced buildings to match specific needs.
  - The buildings you have set out to describe did not happen by accident, but rather came into being because those who wanted them gave a specific brief. The role of the architect has therefore been important throughout recent history.

Practice examination questions

Short answer questions

1 What was the earliest building technique that enabled buildings to support a roof?

2 Analyse the work of a chosen school of artists.

3 Outline the lost-wax method for sculpting metal figures.

Essay question

4 Discuss the history of the cinema over the 20th century.

Chapter 6

Art, culture and society

The following topics are covered in this chapter:

- *Aesthetics in art*
- *The arts in different communities*
- *Factors shaping the arts*

6.1 Aesthetics in art

After studying this section you should be able to:

- *discuss ideas of beauty, reality and the 'spiritual' experience*
- *outline arguments around the validity that there should be 'art for art's sake'*
- *explain arguments put forward in philosophy, politics and psychology around the role of art*

LEARNING SUMMARY

What is aesthetics?

AQA A	M4
AQA B	M4, M6
EDEXCEL	M4
OCR	M4, M6

Key points from AS

- **Aesthetics**
  Revise AS pages 63–64

Try to think of examples of these that you could use as illustration in your exam.

The term 'aesthetics' was first used in 1753 and was coined by the German philosopher Alexander Baumgarten, although the actual study and pursuit of beauty can be traced back to the Ancient Greeks. The traditional view of aestheticism in art during the 18th and first two-thirds of the 19th centuries was dominated by the idea that art is the imitator of nature. If this imitation was accurate, then it was *per se* beautiful since God's creation was beautiful. In terms of artistic style, this created the need for careful attention to life-like detail.

If part of what is encompassed by that branch of philosophy that is called 'aesthetics' is to seek to understand concepts of beauty and ugliness, then art has always provided plenty of scope and example for detailed consideration in this way. Whether it comes from the deeply religious images of the Mediaeval (for example, angels or saints in rapturous devotion, or evil spirits and devils tormenting souls in everlasting domination), or from the modern (in which the image itself, not any message it is trying to communicate, is of primary importance) people have long argued about the aesthetic qualities of art.

Traditional aesthetics assumed that things in art should be useful as well as beautiful. For example, a painting could commemorate a historic event, or encourage a belief in morality. Music could inspire piety (like some of the great requiem masses, for example) or patriotism. Drama might criticise society and in so doing seek to bring about improvements.

However, towards the latter years of the 19th century these traditional views were increasingly challenged. As discussed in Chapter 5, the artists known as the Impressionists (and perhaps Monet in particular) were critical of 'academic' painters for painting what they **thought** they saw, not what they **actually** saw – for example, surfaces constantly changing as a result of light and shade. As the century ended men like Paul Gaugin and Vincent van Gogh were more concerned with the actual structure of paintings, and with expressing their own psyche, rather than with representing objects in the world of nature. Tastes in painting were certainly changing, but it should also be remembered that van Gogh only sold one of his paintings during his own lifetime. The 20th century saw painting, at least in some quarters, moving even further away from the re-creation of 'reality'. The works of the Spanish Cubist Pablo Picasso or the Expressionists Henri Matisse (French) or the German Ernst Kirchner are good examples of this process.

Remember that the AQA-A specification says you should be able to discuss spiritual experience of Art. The other specs are not so precise.

If we accept the modern view that a painting does not have to be a life-like replica of an original scene in order to be considered 'good', what about the role of painting and the arts in promoting the 'spiritual experience'? In Mediaeval times such representations were often considered to be just as much a reality as anything in the physical world – in fact the majority of works of art had devotional themes and were regarded as assisting the beholder to develop their knowledge and understanding of God. The whole question of the importance of art to the spiritual life of people is discussed in Chapter 4. It is not just in painting, but also in stained glass, in the soaring pillars of our great churches and in the music that accompanies acts of worship, that artists in the broadest sense have sought to bring people to God.

Art for art's sake

AQA A	M4
AQA B	M4, M6
EDEXCEL	M4
OCR	M4, M6

This well-known phrase was first used by the French philosopher Victor Cousin in 1818. It expresses the basic idea that beauty can exist for its own sake – and from here it is a small step to say that to seek out beauty just because it is there is a valid artistic exercise. This doctrine (which had its origins in the earlier philosophical concept of aesthetics and which was not dissimilar to the ideas of 'hedonism' – the pursuit of pleasure for its own sake) was sometimes nicknamed 'aestheticism' by the Victorians – who certainly created an ideal environment in which it could thrive. On the one hand was the immense wealth and prestige of Victorian England, but on the other was squalor, disease and deprivation existing almost side by side in the country known by 1851 as 'the workshop of the world'. The aesthetic movement covered a variety of the arts and membership belonged to anyone with long flowing hair, a large ego, and a love of things Mediaeval (i.e. it was a severe reaction against advancing industry and technology).

Its peak came in the 1870s and 1880s and in 1881 Gilbert and Sullivan produced their satirical operetta 'Patience', in which two aesthetic poets and a group of traditional British soldiers vie for the affection of the local women! This was first produced five years after the painter James Whistler, the 'high priest' of aesthetic art, had famously sued the critic John Ruskin who had described one of Whistler's paintings as 'flinging a pot of paint in the public's face'. Whistler famously won – only for the judge to award him damages of one penny. Then in 1878 Oscar Wilde arrived in London from Oxford clutching his sacred lily (one of the poets in 'Patience' carries a lily by total coincidence!), enthusing about blue and white china, the paintings of the Pre-Raphaelite Brotherhood and describing in his aesthetically affected manner the legs of the actor Henry Irvine as being 'distinctly precious'.

Philosophical support of art for art's sake

Just as Gilbert and Sullivan were able to lampoon the aesthetic movement there were others who maintained a powerful philosophical justification for it.

- **Henri Bergson** (1859–1941) (French) defined science as the use of intelligence to create a system of symbols that supposedly describes reality, but actually falsifies it. Art, on the other hand, being intuitive, is a direct apprehension of reality, cutting through conventional symbols and beliefs about people, life and society, and leaving reality itself.
- **Benedetto Croce** (1866–1952) (Italian) also praised intuition – he said it was the immediate awareness of an object that gave that object form, before you have the chance to think about it. Works of art are the physical expressions of such intuitions. He said that beauty and ugliness were not qualities of the work of art itself, but qualities of the spirit expressed intuitively in these works of art.

- George Santayana (1863–1952) (American) believed that when you took pleasure in something, the pleasure may be seen as a quality of the thing itself, not just as a human response to it. Just as you can claim that some acts by humans are good in themselves (and not just because you might personally approve of them), so you can also say that some objects are beautiful, not just because of a delight in their form and colour.
- John Dewey (1859–1952) (American) saw life as being fragmented, full of beginnings but with few ends. It was those exceptional things that went right through from start to conclusion that are aesthetic. Aesthetic experience is enjoyment for its own sake, it is complete and self-contained – an end in itself, not merely a part of other purposes.

Political and psychological objection to art for art's sake

Opposition to aestheticism was not just based on the idea that:

- all aesthetes are long-haired, mamby-pamby dreamers after a lost world; or
- that Art should reflect the world in which people live, and both reflect and help shape the reality of what people see around them.

Two very different men, both of whom were having deep and profound effects on society in the latter part of the nineteenth century, rejected aestheticism. They were Karl Marx, the writer and revolutionary thinker and Sigmund Freud, a doctor and the founder of psychoanalysis.

- Karl Marx believed that all art was an expression of the underlying economic relations in its society. Art could only be described as 'great' when it was 'progressive' – that is, it is helping to drive forward the inevitable eventual victory of the working class (the proletariat). In a country that has already become Communist the role of art is to further the values of the society in which it is created. Far from existing for its own sake, the role of art is to act as one of the supports for the power of the proletariat.
- Sigmund Freud believed that the value of art lay in its therapeutic use – both the artist and the audience can reveal hidden conflicts and get rid of tensions. As fantasies and daydreams become art they are transformed from being an escape from life into ways of meeting it.

> It is not the purpose of this book to tell you what sort of art you should like, or what is 'best'. You should try to build up a 'portfolio' of your favourite pieces of art, music, literature, etc. In the exam you may get the chance to write about them, but going further. You will also need to offer some analysis and some thoughts on whether 'art for art's sake' is justifiable – is art a vehicle for other things (such as the expression of hidden conflict) or is a painting a creation that exists in its own right? Whatever your conclusion never simply say that you 'don't like' art without aiming to explain why.

KEY POINT

Progress check

1 What term was first used by German philosopher Alexander Baumgarten in 1753?
2 What two useful functions was it thought that music could help a person achieve?
3 Name the 20th-century Spanish painter who lead the Cubist movement away from the idea that a painting has to a 'photographic' view of reality.
4 What phrase was first used by Victor Cousin in 1818?
5 Who believed that art helped to reveal hidden conflicts?

1 Aesthetics. 2 Piety and patriotism. 3 Pablo Picasso. 4 'Art for art's sake'. 5 Sigmund Freud.

6.2 The arts in different communities

After studying this section you should be able to:

- briefly describe the Arts in different ages and in different social settings
- discuss the vibrant tradition of 'folk art' that exists in communities around the world

LEARNING SUMMARY

Art and society

AQA A	M4
AQA B	M4
EDEXCEL	M4
OCR	M4, M6

Key points from AS

- **Creativity and innovation**
  Revise AS pages 81–88

Do not be so simplistic as to write-off a type of Art that you do not understand.

While successful artists can be viewed as creative geniuses, it also has to be recognised that they are the products of their own society. It is perhaps easier to appreciate the particular genius when looking at the works of an artist from a similar cultural background – from Europe, North America, Australia or New Zealand, for example. (Never forget, however, that European culture was imposed over existing, and still surviving, art forms in all communities subjected to colonialism.) However, because something is culturally very different – and as a result we may not understand it fully – it may well have a tradition as long, if not longer, than our own in Europe.

In order to promote the arts, a society has to have sufficient wealth to enable both those producing the artistic works to be 'non-productive' in economic terms and those appreciating it to have sufficient leisure time to do so. In simple terms, primitive hunter-gatherer communities needed every single person to be involved in the struggle of looking constantly for new food sources – the idea of some people being full-time artists would not even have been dreamt of. Society has to be sufficiently wealthy to produce 'patrons of the arts' – that is, people who provide the resources to allow artists to create their works. The earliest known examples of patrons are the priests of ancient Sumaria – as we can see from evidence in the stone tablets from that time. However, perhaps the best known patrons of the arts were the great Renaissance popes and princes coming from the great Italian families such as the de Medicis. They had acquired fabulous wealth through the opening of the trade routes with the East and used some of it to fund artists and sculptors like Leonardo de Vinci and Michaelangelo. The role of the sponsor and the artist in creating religious works in a European world that was totally dominated by the church is discussed in Chapter 4. We look in more detail at the idea of the patron later in this chapter.

In some societies even the opportunity to become an artist in the first place can be culturally influenced. In traditional societies like Japan until recently, it was the norm for a boy to follow into his father's profession and this included actors and painters. Those who became monks in the Middle Ages not only dedicated themselves to a life of prayer and abstinence, but in purely historical terms became guardians of the traditions of art, music, book making, writing, and so on. In Europe much early art and music comes from this monastic tradition, although that is certainly not to deny that there was also a vibrant 'folk tradition' of the arts – the occasional remnants of which survive, sometimes as tourist attractions, right through to the 21st century.

Until the world of mass production and cheap transportation in which we live started to develop, the forms taken by the arts in different communities were influenced by the materials available to the artists. Nomadic Asian herders created beautiful rugs from the wool of their sheep. Painters in Mediaeval Europe used wooden panels, plaster walls, parchment and stained glass in the days before paper was known in the West.

The subjects of artistic works have also been strongly influenced by the society in which they were created. In Ancient Egypt, for example, art was totally dominated by the state and the priests, and the desire to glorify the pharaoh and life after death. In Mediaeval Europe virtually all of the formal arts, in all their forms, were based on the prevalent Christian view of the time – that life was a time of trial and the Earth a vale of tears, with the prospect of either eternal bliss or eternal damnation depending on the individual's response to God.

Twentieth-century totalitarian regimes have used art in the service of the state. As mentioned, Marx wrote about the importance of 'progressive' art in furthering the revolution and the Nazi regime was a master at staging huge exhibitions, concerts and so on to create a feeling of awe and wonder in those who saw them. Music and artistic symbolism (the swastika came from Hindu art) were used to carefully choreograph rallies which glorified the regime. It cannot therefore be claimed that the arts are inherently 'innocent' and 'uplifting' to the soul. In the wrong hands the arts can be used to manipulate and control – although it should be stressed that this is a mis-use of the arts. Most artists working in the Western world today have virtually total freedom to express themselves how they like. This is a reflection of the affluence of contemporary society and the ability of at least a proportion of those who see themselves as creative artists to earn enough without having to rely on producing commissioned works.

> Many great devotional works can still be seen in our art galleries. Get out and see them!

Folk Art

AQA A   M4
AQA B   M4
EDEXCEL   M4
OCR   M4, M6

This can be seen as almost the opposite to the formal, grand art that is the subject of academic study and analysis. It is work produced anonymously by local artists and craftsmen following often deeply rooted traditional forms and styles associated with that area. Although it rejects innovation, it is nevertheless marked by a freshness and vitality. Skills in the 'domestic arts' – embroidery, weaving and textiles – have traditionally been the realm of women.

Such work is far from the preserve of those living in undeveloped economies. For example, there is still a living tradition of weaving and quilting in Wales. Welsh patchwork quilts follow traditional patterns and are still made for public display and sale by quilters, who collect pieces of patterned cloth to enable them to acquire their raw materials.

Another good example of folk art that can be seen over the length and breadth of Britain is the painted pub sign – not the mass-produced metal signs beloved of the big brewers, but the hand-painted signs that maintain a tradition going back for centuries. Some are quite memorable in their own way, such as the sign hanging outside 'The Quiet Woman' in the Derbyshire village of Earl Sterndale which shows a woman with no head. 'The Great George' in Abergavenny, south Wales, is unique in having a different portrait on each of its faces – both great Georges: one side is George Washington, and the other is George Bernard Shaw. In Britain if something is described as 'folk' art it suggests it belongs to pre-industrial communities, but this is not always the case. Some vibrant folk art can be seen in the 'castles and roses' art style associated with the canals – both on the sides of the boats and the 'furniture' on them, down to buckets and cooking utensils.

> Take care not to equate 'folk art' with a lack of talent or skill – it is simply a different tradition.

Nowhere is the idea of folk art stronger than in the United States. Not only is there the whole body of Native American art – of which perhaps the best known examples to us in Britain are the tall, ornately carved and painted totem poles – but there is also a wide collection of styles of folk art from around the world brought to the States by the original immigrant families.

Interesting fusions of traditional and formal art forms can be found in South America where traditional peasant art and culture and the Spanish importation of Christianity have become joined. Christianity has always taken over and adapted indigenous customs and festivals. This can also be seen in Mexico in the striking, brightly coloured figures made for display during the festival of the Day of the Dead. The formal religious art of Catholic Europe is adapted in the form of statues or paintings of saints by transforming them into figures of folk art and traditional pre-Christian religion.

> The arts in their broadest sense have to operate within the contexts of the societies in which they are created. Some forms are formal and 'academic', others are popular and traditional, but all help to shape the societies in which they exist.
>
> **KEY POINT**

Progress check

1 Who were the earliest known patrons of artists?
2 Name one of the great Medieval Italian families who sponsored artists.
3 Which political writer believed that the best art existed to serve the state?
4 Give an example of a still surviving form of a Welsh folk art.
5 Which country maintains the strongest concept of folk art?

1 Ancient Sumarian priests. 2 The Medici family. 3 Karl Marx. 4 Patchwork quilting. 5 The United States.

6.3 Factors shaping the arts

After studying this section you should be able to:

- *discuss the role of the critics*
- *appreciate the advantages and drawbacks of patronage and sponsorship*
- *understand the roles of art galleries and museums*

LEARNING SUMMARY

The critics

AQA A	M4
AQA B	M5
EDEXCEL	M4
OCR	M4, M6

Key points from AS

- **Creativity and innovation**
  Revise AS pages 83–88

The critics have a major role in informing the public about the arts, which they do through writing articles and books and appearing on the arts programmes in the media and so on. A good illustration of the power of critics to shape opinion and fashion in the arts is the annual award in the UK of the Turner Prize. A panel is appointed to choose the recipient of the £20 000 prize and it is in their gift to determine who 'has made the greatest contribution to art in Great Britain over the previous 12 months'. This competition has been instrumental in bringing innovative new art to a wider audience, although it has not been without controversy such as that surrounding Damien Hirst's work using parts of animals preserved in formaldehyde, or Tracy Emin's unmade bed (which seemed so full of detritus that it must have been occupied virtually full time!).

See the section on the Impressionists in Chapter 5.

Critics are often conservative in their tastes. One example of this was noted in the section on the Impressionists in Chapter 5, where we mentioned that it was a critic who invented the title 'Impressionist', intending it as a slur, not a compliment. Similarly in 1863, when Manet displayed his 'Dejeuner sur L'Herbe' which showed a naked woman sitting next to two fully clothed men at a woodland picnic, he was bitterly attacked by the critics. It seemed that nudity was acceptable in religious themes, or others similarly removed from real life, but Manet's picture was hailed as immoral.

Worse condemnation still came two years later in 1865 when Manet's 'Olympia' was displayed at the Paris salon. This painting was of a nude, based on the famous 'Venus of Urbino' by the classical Italian, Titian. However, the model was clearly a modern Frenchwoman, with an overt sexuality and direct gaze that the critics said was an affront to morality.

On the other hand, artists who won (and today manage to win) critical acclaim were (and are) much sought after. To be liked by the critics can certainly give an artist fame and influence within the artistic community, although few could claim to earn a lot of money from their profession. At the same time some modern artists set out to shock or cause offence. Damien Hirst would be far from upset if the critics condemned his efforts, he would be pleased to have upset the establishment!

Funding for the arts

AQA A	M4
AQA B	M5
EDEXCEL	M4
OCR	M4, M6

Patrons

As mentioned earlier, over the whole of the history of the European arts the role of the patron has been of the highest importance. As far back as Ancient Greece rich individuals would provide employment for a variety of types of artists, who created wall paintings, mosaics, jewellery and highly decorated furniture. In Roman times patronage saw the design and creation of monuments that were designed to reflect the needs of the patron, not the creative personality of the artist. The Mediaeval popes and princes were also great patrons, the best-known being the families who ruled northern Italy in the 15th century. They were wealthy enough from commerce to patronise the arts and this was vital for the success of the flourishing Renaissance art movements.

Patrons have often insisted that they are included in some way in the works that they funded. They might want to be a figure in a painting or even to be the 'star' (particularly in Protestant northern Europe where commissioning a religious work was no longer seen as a way of buying a place in eternity) – not unlike modern-day sponsors wanting to see their logos associated with their product. However, this desire by the early patrons was not because they were advertising themselves for sales purposes – it was purely for self-aggrandisement. Certainly the major difficulty with being employed directly by somebody to create works of art is that they have the ability to specify what must be done – with the threat of withdrawal of funding if it isn't.

After the Reformation, in the Protestant countries of northern Europe, the rising merchant class became important patrons of the arts. This was important since the Protestant churches tended not to go in for the display of pictures, sculptures and the other artistic forms that wealthy Catholic patrons had previously requested. The effect of this was primarily to make the arts much more domestic, with paintings of individuals or family scenes, for example.

In the days when Britain had an empire and sent governors to the colonies around the world, their wives would often be seen as supporters and patrons of the arts. This did much to encourage local styles and schools of art – which can be seen to good effect in Australia, for example. Similarly, many of the wealthy Britons who embarked on the Grand Tour of the major sites of Europe commissioned the local Venetian artist Canaletto to paint them a Venice scene to bring back memories – which explains why there are so many of his Venetian scenes in the UK!

Sponsors

This is a modern development of patronage. Sponsorship tends to provide funding from commercial sources in return for which the name of the sponsor is acknowledged – a form of advertising that in the age of TV can be quite lucrative.

However, sponsorship can be much more low key than this. It might be a group of local shops providing support and accommodation to stage a local exhibition, for example. The earliest sponsorship was in Ancient Greece, where the elaborate costumes and masks of the actors in the tragic dramas would be provided by wealthy supporters.

Early Christian architecture benefited greatly from sponsorship by Imperial Rome, after Christianity became the established religion of the Empire. Some sponsored buildings were on a monumental scale.

The Turner Prize, mentioned above, is a good example of contemporary sponsorship of the arts. It has had several major sponsors – at present it is Channel 4. Other examples are the Booker prize for literature and the Sainsbury Arts Centre at the University of East Anglia.

Public subsidy

In the UK, public subsidies to the arts amounts to millions of pounds a year. The main channels for direct government support are the separate Arts Councils in each of the countries of the UK. They provide direct subsidy to sustain major opera, dance and drama companies; touring companies and experimental groups; orchestras and festivals. The National Lottery is also a major source of funding, not always without controversy – for example, the grant of millions of pounds to the Opera House, Covent Garden. It was said by some that this represented the subsidy of the entertainment of the rich by those who are often amongst the poorest in society.

Galleries and Museums

AQA A	M4
AQA B	M5
EDEXCEL	M4
OCR	M4, M6

Art galleries

At their most simple these can be a room in a building for the public exhibition of works of art. There are also private galleries, where dealers organise the display of works for sale. Their origins were in Ancient Greece and Rome. In Greece, there was a space at the entrance to a temple where depictions of the gods were displayed. In Rome there was a room in many private homes where statues and other works of art were kept.

Art has been commissioned and collected by the wealthy and powerful – or acquired through looting during military campaigns – for many centuries. The idea that art can collectively belong to the nation emerged in the 19th century. During this period previously private collections were also opened to the public – notably The Louvre (1793), a French royal residence until the Revolution, and the Hermitage (1852) which housed the collections of the Tsars in St Petersburg.

Purpose-built national galleries included one in London (1837), the Rijksmuseum in Amsterdam in 1817 and the Prado in Madrid in 1818. Some national galleries were based on a core of donated works, with government funding to support subsequent acquisitions.

The government announced in 2001 that it has plans to abolish all admission charges to major galleries and museums so you will have no excuse for not visiting! Some are already free to visit – for example, the National Gallery and the National Portrait Gallery, both in London.

Traditional national galleries are housed in imposing neo-classical buildings, reflecting the earnest spirit in which they were created. However, more recent galleries have tended to be more flamboyant – such as the Guggenheim in New York (1959), the Hayward Gallery in London (1968) and, perhaps most notably, the Georges Pompidou Centre in Paris (1977).

In the UK the Arts Councils provide support to a range of galleries, as do local councils. Sponsorship is also important – sometimes on quite a grand scale, such as the Sainsbury wing of the National Gallery, opened in 1991.

Museums

These are institutes for the housing of collections of artistic, historic or scientific interest, conserved and displayed for the education and enjoyment of the public.

The first museum to be opened in the world was at the university in Basel, Switzerland, in 1671. The first one to use the name 'museum' was the Ashmolean Museum in Oxford University, opened in 1683.

There are three main types of museum.

- **Historical museums** devoted to national, regional or local history. Some are housed in traditional buildings, others faithfully re-create old buildings, artefacts and so on in outdoor settings – for example, the Museum of Welsh life at St Fagans, part of the Welsh National Museum.
- **Science museums** – notable museums dedicated to science and technology were opened in the 19th century in cities such as London, Birmingham, Manchester and Newcastle. They celebrated the triumph of the machine age and of scientific progress. London, for example, has over 600 working exhibits.
- **Specialist museums** – devoted to single subjects, such as the Museum of Childhood in Bethnal Green, the National Maritime Museum in Greenwich, the National Railway Museum in York and the National Museum of Photography, Film and Television in Bradford.

Education has always been a major focus of museums – with the use of:

- permanent displays
- school visits
- travelling exhibitions
- libraries of books and journals
- lectures
- support to the media
- loans
- original documents.

Collections held in museums are acquired in various ways:

- through purchase – although this can be expensive
- through donations, gifts and bequests
- through field expeditions.

(This could cover a wide variety of 'practical' things – archaeological digs, seed collection, etc. Within the UK there are clear regulations covering finds, even by amateurs finding buried artefacts (treasure trove), which have been amended by the current government to strengthen the powers of museums to acquire them. There are fewer overseas expeditions now, but sometimes – where specific expertise is being used, for example – clear contractual arrangements are made in advance on rights to display any finds, etc.)

Most controversially, in colonial days things were plundered. This begs the question whether we still have the moral or legal right to retain these things when most countries now have their own national museums. A good example of an ongoing controversy in this area is that concerning the Elgin Marbles. These are parts of the frieze from the walls of the Parthenon in Athens which were purchased by Lord Elgin. They are still in the British Museum in London, although Greece has been fighting for their return for years. Arguments that are made in favour of keeping artefacts include the following.

- In the case of the Elgin Marbles, lots of things got destroyed and the British protected them by removing them. The Parthenon, from which they came, is now suffering badly from acid rain because of bad pollution in Athens.
- The major world galleries and museums have an acknowledged expertise in the conservation of artefacts.
- 'Centres of excellence' can be built up, showing examples of specific types of artefact from different places under one roof, rather than just showing some purely local examples.

- Allows scholars access to major collections of artefacts and associated academic materials (libraries, etc. associated with the museum/gallery are often built up over time).
- The major world galleries, museums/galleries attract visitors from around the world – they are therefore truly international centres.

KEY POINT

The arts would not have evolved in the way they have if there had been no patrons or sponsors. Similarly, critics inform us of new works, and galleries and museums allow us to see existing collections. The arts are sustained in an interwoven and connected way, with each part needing the other.

KEY POINT

Note for candidates following the AQA A specification

When you take the exam paper covering Module 4 of the specification ('Culture, Morality, Arts and Humanities') you will have to attempt a compulsory question in a modern European language. This gives you a choice of reading a passage in French, German or Spanish and then answering a series of multiple-choice questions. The questions are in English, and there will be a glossary to explain any unusual words.

The aim of this test is to seek to discover whether you have retained a GCSE (grade C) understanding of your chosen European language during your post-16 studies. However, the reality is that few candidates for General Studies other than those studying languages will have spent very much, if any, time reading anything that is not in English. If you fall into this category – don't panic! There are a couple of tips that are worth following up:

- Look at some past papers so you know what to expect.
- In the comprehension passage try to identify words that look similar to English words – they will often have virtually identical meanings, and could give you a reasonable idea of meaning.
- Look carefully at the four possible answers to the question (questions and possible answers are printed in English) – a couple could hopefully be discounted at once, leaving you with a choice of one from two. Do you know any of the words in the passage – do they relate to either of these alternatives?
- In the period before you take the exam you could try reading passages in your chosen European language. Your school or college's languages department will probably have something suitable, or you could look out for European newspapers at bigger newsagents. *The Guardian*'s education supplement on Tuesdays also often has an article in a European language – it might be a good idea to make a collection of these during the duration of your course (which is always better than leaving things until the last minute!).

Progress check

1 Where was the first building to be opened as a specifically named museum?
2 Which former French royal residence was opened as an art gallery in 1793, following the Revolution?
3 What famous gallery was opened in New York in 1959?
4 Where is the National Railway Museum?
5 What are the three usual ways in which museums acquire new pieces today?

1 The Ashmolean Museum in Oxford University. 2 The Louvre in Paris. 3 The Guggenheim. 4 York. 5 Through purchase; through donation; through field expeditions.

Sample question and model answer

1

The Arts are an expensive luxury that at the end of the day do nothing to make the world a better place.' Discuss this view with particular reference to the idea of 'art for art's sake'.

Step 1
Introduction.

- Briefly acknowledge the basic premise contained in the question – that the arts are an expensive luxury.
- Without going into any detail, make the point that since virtually all societies throughout history have had some kind of artistic tradition there must be an alternative, frequently held view.

Try to spend a few minutes noting the arguments that supporters of the assertion could put forward.

Step 2
Arguments to support the assertion.

- Art as an end in itself achieves nothing beyond earning a fee for the artist.
- Art is 'style not substance' – it is a closed world of self satisfaction in which sometimes ludicrous parodies are hailed as 'masterpieces' – a dirty bed, parts of the bodies of real animals, piles of bricks could be cited as actual recent examples.

Take care – this can be a dangerous line of argument. Do not push it too hard if in reality you are actually saying you don't know much about painting!

- The millions of pounds paid out for these affectations would be better spent on helping people who are homeless or sick.
- Styles come into and out of fashion so quickly that there can be nothing inherently 'good' and worthy of the high praise heaped onto 'trendy' styles of any one time.
- Society is better judged by its physical creativity and inventiveness than by paintings.

Step 3 Arguments to counter the assertion.

Again, do not rush straight into concocting a mere list. Spend a few minutes trying to line up arguments so that they flow into each other in a complementary way:

- Paintings encourage us and challenge us about our world.
- Works of art enhance and beautify our surroundings.
- They can help us to express and find outlets for our emotions, for our political or religious views, and so on.
- They help to establish the values and traditions of a society when they are well known and seen by many people.
- Paintings help to stimulate social and political debate – they can challenge us to think more carefully about our world.
- They can provide entertainment and pleasure during our leisure time, helping us to escape some of the pressures of our modern way of life.

NB The question refers to 'art for art's sake' – so the best examples you can give will not be those that set out to achieve some specific purpose (such as the Medieval images of the divine that were intended to help the viewer in the quest for heaven). The concept really belongs to the period since the latter part of the 19th century – so try to illustrate your answers with references to the works of the Impressionists or to the better known artists of the 20th century.

Step 4
Conclusion.

- Try to pull the arguments together, without merely repeating yourself.
- Try to come to a personal conclusion, which would be strengthened if you could support it with reference to a couple of examples of paintings and painters known to you. For example:

It is easy to say that the money spent on paintings would be better spent on other things like healthcare. However, the reality is that every society in the history of humanity has expressed itself through the arts and if we were to try to change this we would lose part of our soul. Great paintings inspire us, they give us insights both into ourselves and into our society, whether it is

Sample question and model answer (continued)

the sheer happiness of the early Impressionists, such as Monet and Renoir with their pictures of the bathers on the river Seine, or the more disturbing and challenging works of painters such as Picasso, with works such as Guernica which portrayed the destruction of a Spanish fishing village by German aircraft during the Civil War. Without art we would lose so much — each picture tells a thousand stories. To claim that the arts are an expensive luxury is the thinking of a philistine — it should be given no credence in our contemporary world.

Practice examination questions

Short answer questions

1 Briefly explain why Karl Marx was opposed to the concept of 'art for art's sake'.

2 Illustrate some of the materials used to create forms of art by people in their localities before the era of mass production and cheap transport.

3 Outline the two major areas of public subsidy that provide funding to the arts in the UK.

Essay question

4 What are the main roles and responsibilities for art galleries and museums?

Chapter 7

Scientific and technological progress

The following topics are covered in this chapter:

- *Medicine and health*
- *Food supply and distribution*
- *Herbicides and pesticides*
- *Telecommunications*
- *The impact of computers*

7.1 Medicine and health

After studying this section you should be able to:

- *explain different kinds of illness*
- *describe important developments in medical science relating to surgery*

LEARNING SUMMARY

Different kinds of illness

AQA A	M5
AQA B	M4, M6
EDEXCEL	M6
OCR	M4, M6

Illness can be looked at in terms of **physical** illness and **mental** illness – in simple terms, illness of the body and illness of the mind. However, it should be appreciated that some medical conditions have aspects of both.

Key points from AS

- **Medical ethics**
  Revise AS page 125

Physical illness

There are two main types of disease: – infectious and non-infectious.

Infectious illness

This has four main causes:

- viruses
- bacteria
- fungi
- parasites.

These are transmitted from person to person. Infection can be defined as 'the invasion of the body by disease creating organisms which become established, multiply and produce symptoms'.

> Infection is transmitted in a variety of ways:
> - through the air
> - by direct contact (contagion)
> - through blood
> - through contamination
> - by sexual transmission
> - from animals.
>
> **KEY POINT**

Be aware of the main ways in which infection is passed on.

- **Airborne infection** – caught from infected droplets from the nose, throat/lungs or saliva. (The infection is based in these areas and is then spread through coughing, sneezing, kissing.)
- **Contamination** – often from food or water supplies. There have, for example, been several headline stories concerning serious outbreaks of food poisoning, sometimes fatal. Infected faeces and urine are other causes – hence the importance of personal hygiene.
- **Contagion** – illness is picked up from close contact with an infected person.
- **Sexual transmission** – comes directly from vaginal or anal intercourse, or oral sex.
- **Blood infection** – often comes from infection of contaminated blood or blood products. It is common among intravenous drug users and made headlines during the 1990s when the consequences of treating haemophiliacs with blood products that were infected with the HIV virus became known.
- **Animal carriers** (or vectors) – include for example, the injection into humans

of contaminated saliva by the insect that carries malaria. In history (but also showing signs of revival) there was the spreading of bubonic plague (Black Death) by rats.

The causes of infection

You might want to look in more detail at HIV/AIDS, which also has wide economic and social consequences.

- **Viruses** These are the most basic forms of life – a protein coat protecting a strand of DNA. They can only reproduce within the cells of other organisms where they multiply, and then destroy the cell. In this way they cause many diseases, from the common cold to AIDS.
  The only natural defence in the body is the production of antibodies. Only two or three drugs are of any use, and these only against a limited number of viruses. Hence the importance of immunisation – most children are injected against a range of previously fatal illnesses, such as measles and rubella. There is increasing medical concern at what seems to be a growing reluctance by parents to have their children immunised – an outbreak of measles in Dublin in 2000 resulted in two child deaths.

- **Bacteria** These are much bigger than viruses and can be seen under an ordinary microscope. They become parasitic on more complex organisms. Certain bacteria cause specific diseases, examples being acne and salmonella (serious food poisoning). Two groups of drugs are used to treat bacterial infections:
  - **antibiotics**, which act as direct poisons on bacteria. However, in recent years bacteria have been developing resistance to them, with potentially serious consequences for the effectiveness of treatments
  - **bacteriostats**, which work to prevent the multiplication of bacteria.

Bacteriophages attack E.coli bacterium

- **Fungi** These are probably the most widespread of organisms, being found in virtually all animal and plant species and their habitats. Few fungi infect humans – those that do mainly colonise the skin, nails and hair, e.g. Athlete's Foot. The spores of fungi may be responsible for asthma and a range of allergies, but technically these are not infectious illnesses.

- **Parasites** divide into three groups:
  - **protozoans**, which can be seen as large bacteria. They include the amoeba that cause amoebic dysentery and malaria
  - **worms**, which affect human intestines in various ways, and in some cases migrate to other organs. They include tapeworms and threadworms. In the tropics the disease bilharzia is a major killer
  - **anthropoids**, such as lice, fleas and mites. They not only infect humans, but also act as carriers (vectors) of micro-organisms, such as those carrying typhus and plague.

Non-infectious diseases

In developed countries the ability to protect against many infectious diseases means that non-infectious diseases are now the main health problem. Cancer, heart disease and strokes are now the major killers in our contemporary society.

Table 7.1 Some infectious diseases

Disease	Cause	Transmission	Characteristics
AIDS	HIV virus	Sexual; blood	Destruction of the immune system
Common cold	Virus	Airborne	Inflammation of nose and upper respiratory tract
Food poisoning	Bacteria	Contaminated food	Vomiting and diarrhoea
Malaria	Parasite	Mosquito bites	Destruction of red blood cells
Chicken pox	Virus	Airborne	Itchy, blistering rash
Whooping cough	Bacteria	Airborne, direct contact	Infection of trachea and bronchi, producing severe coughs

Cancers

These can attack many parts of the human body. Cancer (malignant) cells are usually degenerate, capable only of reproducing themselves. Normally, the cells in our body divide and multiply in a controlled way determined by our genes to replace those that naturally die off. Our genes therefore switch cell growth and division 'on and off', and also the direction and extent of cell development. When these growth-controlling genes malfunction there is unrestrained growth. Sometimes this leads to relatively harmless growth (a 'benign' tumour), but if several of the genes within a cell mutate it can form a growth (a 'malignant' tumour) that sets about re-creating itself and invading/destroying other tissue in an uncontrolled way. Malignant cells spread from their original site through the bloodstream or lymphatic system.

We are still developing our understanding of cancers and this is a major area of medical research, much of it involving experiments on animals. There are some agents – called carcinogens – known to trigger cancer, such as cigarette smoke, asbestos dust and exhaust fumes. Some viruses also trigger the cancerous growth of cells, as can radioactivity (including X-rays). Diet also seems to have some effect in some cancers, for example, a lack of fibre can contribute to bowel cancer. Environmental factors also play a part – for example, excessive exposure to sunlight can lead to skin cancer. Almost 33% of cancers could be avoided if people stopped smoking tobacco. This leads most commonly to lung cancer, but also causes cancers of the pancreas, oesophagus and larynx. Smokers are also more likely to suffer heart attacks, chronic bronchitis and emphysema.

> Animal experiments are a major source of controversy – in this context, think of the medical issues.

> There are broader issues to consider in General Studies – e.g. should the NHS treat self-inflicted lung cancer, etc?

Hereditary diseases

There are a range of diseases passed on by inheritance. Some are apparent from birth, others can take decades to develop. There are more than 4000 genetic diseases, but recent medical breakthroughs in the area of genetic modification could herald the ability to provide cures for the first time. Huntington's disease and sickle-cell disease (which affects people of African origins in the main) are two serious diseases that might be cured by such developments.

> Genetic modification is not without ethical problems – see Chapter 8.

Physical and chemical causes of non-infectious diseases

- **Environmental** – Some non-infectious diseases are the result of the environment in which we live. People who have a high exposure to radiation are a well-known group of sufferers from these, as are workers who have been exposed to coal or asbestos dusts.
- **Diet (including alcohol consumption)** – The diet of many people in our society is too low in fibre and too high in sugar and other refined carbohydrates, and fat. The growing popularity of fast foods is tending to make this worse. Heart disease, diabetes, cancer of the colon and of the large bowel, obesity, constipation and haemorrhoids are some of the major diseases that result from this diet. Obesity is also more likely to result in heart disease, diabetes and strokes. A diet too high in saturated fat can increase the cholesterol level, leading to the build up of fatty deposits on artery walls. This can lead to angina (severe chest pains) and heart attacks.

> Society has been guilty of putting people at risk – this could be an issue for an exam question.

Many people drink alcohol on a regular basis, and there is evidence that in moderation this can have some beneficial results, most likely through helping people to relax. However, alcohol is in fact a drug that acts as a powerful depressant. Excessive intake takes a huge toll on physical health, with associated costs to the Health Service. Long-term effects include cirrhosis of the liver (liver cells replaced by scar tissue), alcoholic hepatitis (inflamed liver) and liver cancer. Alcohol can also damage the heart, brain and nervous system. Cancers of the larynx, oesophagus and pancreas are also associated with the consumption of alcohol.

> Alcohol also has huge social costs that could also be covered in a General Studies exam.

Mental illness

The ways in which people have traditionally viewed mental illness has reflected the prevailing culture of their society. Until the later 19th century Christian society tended to regard the mentally ill as being possessed by spirits, or the Devil, while other societies have seen divine inspiration in madness. It is often said that there is a thin line between genius and insanity and people point to people like Van Gogh as an example.

There are four broad categories of mental illness:
- psychotic
- neurotic
- organic
- other disorders.

There are links with social attitudes – e.g. 'care in the community' policies, which might provide the focus of a question in the exam.

Psychoses

People suffering from psychoses are out of touch with reality, show bizarre behaviour in normal settings and experience delusions and hallucinations. Sufferers are not always aware of their illness. Schizophrenia is perhaps the best known example and manic depression is another.

Neuroses

These are a form of psychological illness – for example, anxiety can become such a dominant emotion that normal life is impossible. A compulsive disorder can lead to long complicated rituals, such as repeated hand-washing. Phobias, such as fear of confined spaces or certain animals, result from things which many people have a capacity to fear, but which get grossly exaggerated.

Organic mental illnesses

These are caused by physical disease, for example, delirium (an acute short-term clouding of the consciousness) often caused by high fever. Dementia is a long-term brain dysfunction often associated with old age, but also caused by syphilis or some forms of drug abuse.

Other disorders

Many factors can also contribute to forms of mental illness. These include hereditary factors (especially from in-breeding amongst people having the same genetic make up), upbringing, and neglect.

Treatment of mental illnesses

Anti-psychotic drugs have been developed over the last half-century. This has helped a large number of people to lead normal lives and not have to be admitted to psychiatric hospital.

Anti-depressants and tranquillisers have also been useful – although in the latter there is some risk of addiction if taken for an extended period.

Psychotherapy covers a range of activities aimed at helping patients to understand themselves. Psychoanalysis, counselling, drama therapy and art therapy are examples of forms of psychotherapy. Family therapy can also be useful in conditions brought on by patterns of behaviour within families.

Surgical treatments for illness

AQA A	M5
AQA B	M4, M6
EDEXCEL	M6
OCR	M4, M6

There are two basic categories of surgery:

- **Elective** (where the patient elects to undergo the treatment or the parents of the patient request it on the child's behalf), e.g.
  - hip replacement
  - pacemaker fitment

– cochlea implant

Such treatment is aimed at improving the quality of life.

- **Non-elective** (often emergency operations needed to preserve life), e.g.
  – removal of an inflamed appendix
  – amputation
  – organ transplants.

Transplants

The removal of organs is not without controversy – see Chapter 8.

These have been one of the most well-known and best-publicised developments in medicine over the last half-century.

Pioneering work on the transplantation of kidneys took place in the 1950s on identical twins, removing the risk of rejection which is otherwise a major problem. Rejection is a problem because the body knows the transplant is alien and will try to reject it. This problem was addressed through the drug cyclosporin, developed in 1978, which suppresses the immune system, so preventing rejection.

The four main transplant procedures involve the liver, kidney, heart and heart–lung.

When heart transplants (the best known) were first attempted – starting in 1967 when Christian Barnard operated in South Africa – no recipients survived for long. However, techniques have now been refined and 80% of recipients today enjoy a one-year survival at least. Many recipients in recent years have been children, including newborn babies, who had inoperable heart diseases.

In the longer term the procedure may no longer be needed. Research being undertaken into the growth of replacement organs from stem-cells, and other work in genetic medicine, could mean that organs will no longer be taken from dead donors to help save the life of another.

> **KEY POINT**
>
> The treatment of illness costs billions of pounds a year in the UK. Many diseases are unavoidable, but others can be seen as self inflicted – such as disease resulting from smoking, alcohol abuse or obesity. In a society with limited resources, on what basis do we prioritise treatments if it is necessary? Or, should we treat *all* people regardless?

Progress check

1 What are the four causes of infectious disease?
2 What are six ways in which infection is transmitted?
3 What is a carcinogen?
4 Name the four broad causes of mental illness.
5 What is the importance of the drug cyclosporin in transplants?

5 Helps prevent rejection of the organ.
4 Psychosis; neurosis; organic; other disorders.
3 An agent that triggers cancers.
2 Through air; contamination; contagion; sexual transmission; blood; animals.
1 Viruses; bacteria; fungi; parasites.

7.2 Food supply and distribution

After studying this section you should be able to:

- describe some of the problems of world food supply
- outline a model to set up self-sufficiency

LEARNING SUMMARY

The rise of the supermarket

AQA A	M5
AQA B	M4
EDEXCEL	M6
OCR	M4, M6

Key points from AS

- **Environmental concerns**
  Revise AS pages 112–115

To the general reader of this revision guide the most common manifestation of food distribution will be the giant supermarket lorries that travel the length and breadth of the country to ensure that the shelves are stocked. The supermarkets have contracts with producers which enable them to buy in huge amounts. However, many livestock farmers are complaining that unless they are big enough to have a contract with a supermarket the price of meat had been driven down so far that they could no longer make a profit. UK farming, particularly amongst smaller producers, has certainly been going through a crisis.

It was also claimed that the high cost of fuel was causing a rise in food-distribution costs. However, while this may or may not be true, it is certainly true that the greater use of science and technology in farming – in developing new crop strains, for example – has seen production per acre reaching new highs.

The global problem

AQA A	M5
AQA B	M4
EDEXCEL	M6
OCR	M4, M6

A General Studies exam question is just as likely to take a global perspective.

While the going might be tough for some British farmers, and while the diets of some people in the UK may be far from perfect, the problems of food supply and distribution are far more critical on a global scale.

In many countries in the developing world, food production is hampered by the following factors:
- climate
- poor soil
- lack of water
- poor quality seed and livestock
- lack of a supporting infrastructure – funding, – transport, – research, etc.
- war
- virulent plant and animal diseases.

There is also the need – resulting from increasing population, particularly in the developing economies – to increase food production merely to maintain the status quo. At the same time the world's richest countries often exploit the poorest.

- They hold the poorest countries to ransom over their interest-repayment debts (there is pressure on governments, including that of the UK, to address this).
- Land-owning by European and north American companies exploits much productive land, e.g. tea production in India provides drinks – and employment – for the British.
- Cash-crop purchases – luxury vegetables and fruit grown to be sold at high prices and high profit in the shops of the developed world. Local labourers help to produce them in order to help earn foreign capital – which is often necessary to repay part of the interest on international capitalist's loans.

Try looking at 'country of origin' labels on most fresh fruit and vegetables in supermarkets.

Table 7.2 illustrates the problems facing the developing economies in keeping up with food requirements.

Table 7.2 Global birth, death and growth rates 1998 (UN figures)

	World	Developing nations	Developed nations
Live births (for every 1 000 population)	30	38	17
Deaths (for every 1 000 population)	12	14	9
Growth rate (%)	1.8	2.4	0.8
Doubling time (years)	39	29	88

Source: United Nations (Food and Agriculture Organisation)

Defining world food supply

The world food supply is the ratio of food produced to the population of the world.

However, other factors complicate this seemingly simple formula:
- the extent of hunger and malnutrition (food demand)
- distribution
- loss and wastage
- availability.

By the year 2000, 75% of the world's population lived in developing regions. About 20% of the populations of developing regions have inadequate supplies, despite an average increase of 3% a year in food production in such regions. Sadly, in many places this is virtually entirely taken up in feeding the increasing population at the same inadequate levels.

There are increasing numbers of live stock – much of it for 'fast food'. Cattle are grazed in former rainforest areas. The value of maintaining such high numbers of livestock can be questioned – particularly when the meat produced will be exported to provide food for fast-food outlets. Millions of tonnes of grain a year go to feed livestock. Only around 10% of the available energy is transferred from one nutritional link in the food chain to the next. It is therefore far more energy-efficient to consume plants and grain, rather than to consume herbivores that have eaten plants and grain as their diet. However, this is more of a problem for the richest countries, who eat a disproportionately large amount of meat.

There is probably enough food in the world at the moment to provide adequate levels for its entire population. However:

This creates large problems, which are considered in Chapter 8.

- distribution is uneven and inequitable
- many human practices, particularly in the advanced world, fail to take account of the need for sustainability
- there is an urgent need to reduce the birth rate. However, the steepest increases tend to be in Catholic countries, where it is taught that artificial contraception is sinful.

The need to spread knowledge and understanding

AQA A	M5
AQA B	M4
EDEXCEL	M6
OCR	M4, M6

The United Nations, as a global organisation, is well placed to have a global impact, and it does this through two main channels:
- the UN Food and Agriculture Organisation (FAO)
- the World Food Programme (WFP).

The Food and Agriculture Organisation

The FAO is based in Rome and has 161 member nations. A 49-member Council monitors the world food situation and suggests any necessary actions. Its activities include:

- distributing data and information
- fostering conservation
- promoting agricultural credit
- development of soil and water resources
- international exchange of new types of plants
- control of animal and plant diseases
- providing technical assistance in nutrition, irrigation and soil conservation.

Its constitution states its objectives as 'revising levels of nutrition and standards of living and securing improvements in the efficiency of the production and distribution of all food and agricultural products'.

The World Food Programme

The WFP seeks to provide food and to assist in the implementation of programmes to support development in food-deficient countries. It also provides support after disasters and emergencies.

There is a clear need to balance food supplies with demand, but also in a global context to improve equity, reduce poverty and ensure supplies for all.

This issue is considered in Chapter 8.

There are also other major issues, such as the development of genetically modified foods. While this could have huge beneficial effects in, for example, opening up new areas for crop-growing in areas that are currently marginal, there may also be the potential for environmental catastrophe.

The transfer of knowledge

One model by which the skills and progress of the richest economies could be passed on to those still at subsistence level has been proposed by the US agronomist Norman Borlang, who some see as the founder of the green revolution movement.

He proposes a four-step process:

A General Studies exam question might well be seeking a positive way forward.

1 a shift from local, traditional strains of plants and livestock, and production techniques to a new, imported package of new strains and techniques reflecting progress in plant and animal husbandry.

2 using local adaptive studies to ensure that this is adjusted to local constraints, such as the local environment and to social forces within the country.

3 the provision of long-term support from the government of the country involved for the development of applied knowledge, and the transfer of this to local producers and distributors.

4 the introduction of supportive changes to the local social infrastructure – possibly amending local systems of property ownership, communications, education, transport and laws, for example. A major reason for this would be population stabilisation.

> China has shown that it is possible to feed a country with a huge population. Its concentration on equitable resource distribution, agricultural development and programmes of birth control lies at the heart of their success. The challenge is there for other developing countries to do likewise, but rich countries like the UK have an important part to play in enabling this to happen.
>
> **KEY POINT**

1 What are the main physical problems facing some developing countries in trying to produce food?

2 Give three ways in which the governments of some undeveloped economies are hindered from developing their agricultural production by the world's rich countries.

3 What was the percentage growth rate of the population of the developing countries in the late-20th century?

4 In 2000 what percentage of the world's population lived in non-industrialised countries?

5 Which UN agency is concerned with food supplies?

1 Climate; soils; lack of water. 2 Debt repayments; loss of local land to foreign owners; production of cash crops to be sold abroad. 3 2.4% per year. 4 75%. 5 UN Food and Agricultural Organisation (FAO).

7.3 Herbicides and pesticides

After studying this section you should be able to:

- *explain why these chemicals were developed*
- *describe the serious environmental damage that some of them caused*

LEARNING SUMMARY

Why were herbicides and pesticides developed?

AQA A	M5
AQA B	M4
EDEXCEL	M6
OCR	M4, M6

Key points from AS

- Water pollution
  Revise AS page 114

Herbicides and pesticides are chemicals produced to control weeds and insects that would otherwise seriously reduce the amount of crops produced per acre.

Nobody would argue that some early chemicals that were developed to control pests had very serious and damaging long-term effects on the food chain. However, the chemical industry claims that it is now producing selective pesticides that quickly break down into harmless by-products that do not enter the food chain.

Another modern development is in the area of biotechnology. This entails the development of man-made viruses that attack only certain larvae or insects when they are sprayed, and quickly self-destruct when their work has been done. However, many environmentalists have serious concerns about the unknown possibilities that could result from such dramatic interventions.

The argument for chemical controls

Arguments put forward in favour of these chemical controls are as follows.

- Ninety per cent of the world's people are dependent on 15 major crops and 7 animal species, and it is vital to maximise production if the ever-growing population is to be fed.
- Pests destroy around 35% of the world's crops (add to this losses caused after harvesting by insects, micro-organisms, rodents and birds and the total loss could reach 50%). Pest control dramatically increases yield without needing additional land area.
- The estimated cost of the cereals that are lost to pests every year is £300 million. In Japan and South-East Asia herbicides used to control rice blast and rice blight prevent a £340 million crop loss.
- In the mid-1990s the estimated cost of insecticides used in the world was £4.5 billion a year, but the savings were several times that amount.
- Modern chemicals have a short persistence and break down into harmless elements.

In a General Studies exam you might well be asked for both the plus and minus aspects of the use of chemicals.

The arguments against chemical controls

Many would argue that it is wrong to say that *all* chemicals should be rejected, but, without doubt, there have been some very serious environmental side effects arising from the use of agro-chemicals.

* The most serious concern is that the regular and frequent use of chemicals leaves residues of the most persistent in the soil.
* Birds of prey, especially the Peregrine falcon and the Golden Eagle declined sharply in numbers in the early 1960s, and there is considerable evidence that this was due to being poisoned by chemical residues. Many other birds have also been found dead, while others have been severely reduced in numbers because of a declining ability to produce offspring. This was caused by the shells of their eggs becoming very thin and smashing under the weight of the parent birds on the nest.
* Indiscriminate use of chemicals kills useful insects such as honeybees, and the natural predators on insects and other pests. Some insects were developing resistance to sprays and, since their natural predators were being wiped out, these pests were multiplying rather than reducing in number. A good example would be the plague of red-spider mites in orchards in the 1960s.
* The group of chemicals known as the 'chlorinated hydrocarbons' are now notorious for their persistence. During the late 1950s and in the 1960s they tended to be replaced by organic phosphates and carbamates. These tended to be less persistent, but they also included some that were the most toxic, such as Parathion. The use of this, and another phosphate called Malathion, caused 600 deaths in Japan between 1958 and 1963.
* The rich countries of the developed world can now be very selective in the use of chemicals. However, there is still a need to enable farmers in the developing nations to move away from the traditional, powerful chemicals – which are available to use. The problem of pests in warmer climates is undeniably large.

The case of DDT is a classic example of the need to move away from traditional agro-chemicals.

* The best-documented example of the bad side-effects of chlorinated hydrocarbons is that of DDT. Isolated in Germany in 1874, it was not until 1939 that it became recognised as a potent nerve poison on insects. It was used heavily as a crop spray in Europe during World War II, and was later used around the world to combat yellow fever, typhus and other insect-borne diseases.

In India the use of DDT reduced malaria from 75 million identified cases to fewer than 5 million within a decade. Crops and livestock sprayed with the chemical as much as doubled their yield. The chemical was hailed as a major scientific success story. However, by the 1960s there were clear indications that DDT had entered the food chain and was becoming concentrated in the bodies of the higher animals. Traces of the chemical were found in the Arctic and Antarctic regions, where it had obviously not been sprayed directly. It was simply not breaking down in the environment. As a result, steps were taken to ban it in many countries, but it has still not totally disappeared from the world.

Is genetic modification (GM) of crops the way forward?

AQA A   M5
AQA B   M4
EDEXCEL   M6
OCR   M4, M6

Work is now being undertaken, both in laboratories and in field trials, of genetically modified crops. There could be major advantages to these, e.g. crops could be grown in areas where they are not economically viable at the moment. They might also be developed so that they were resistant to weed or insect infestation. This would certainly reduce the need for chemicals if such crops could be developed.

Many people have serious concerns about GM research, because of unknown environmental consequences and the wider effects on wildlife. If the natural weeds and insects of a crop are wiped out, then so are those other creatures that feed on them. There is thus a risk of upsetting the balance of nature in using GM crops.

There is no easy right and wrong answer in relation to the use of chemicals. Without them we would lose millions of tons of food a year, with them we have seen the damage that can be done to the environment. Since farmers do use chemicals perhaps the chemical industry needs to seek to develop ever more eco-friendly or more organic ways of dealing with pests so that food production is not damaged.

Progress check

1 90% of the world's population rely on what number of major crops and animal species for food?
2 What percentage of the world's crops is lost to pests?
3 Which birds of prey reduced in numbers in the early 1960s, probably due to agricultural chemicals?
4 DDT belongs to what group of chemicals?
5 What tropical diseases, carried by insects, were dealt with by spraying with DDT in the 1950s?

1 15 crops and 7 animal species.
2 35%.
3 Peregrine falcons and Golden eagles.
4 Chlorinated hydrocarbons.
5 Yellow fever and typhus, amongst others.

7.4 Telecommunications

After studying this section you should be able to:

• *discuss the development of telecommunications*
• *describe some important principles of telecommunication*

What is telecommunications?

AQA A	M5
AQA B	M5, M6
EDEXCEL	M4, M6
OCR	M6

Key points from AS

• **Our changing lifestyle**
  Revise AS page 107

A basic definition of telecommunication is the ability to communicate over a distance using equipment to overcome that distance. The term usually refers to the transmission of either words, sounds, pictures or data in the form of electronic signals or impulses. Behind this simple definition is a revolution that has had a powerful and dramatic effect on life, particularly over the last quarter of a century.

Until the latter part of the 20th century the telephone was the most familiar form, but today there is a range of computer-based telecommunications. In particular, the Internet has provided millions of people with the means of exchanging information through a vast computer network stretching around the world.

Key dates in the development of telecommunications

AQA A	M5
AQA B	M5, M6
EDEXCEL	M4, M6
OCR	M6

Even if you have trouble remembering dates, try to remember developments for the exam.

1876 Alexander Graham Bell makes the first ever telephone call.
1901 Guglielmo Marconi transmitted radio waves to carry a message across the Atlantic Ocean. Radio remains an important form of communication.
1910 Almon Strowger developed an automatic switching system, enabling telephone calls to be automated.
1947 William Shockley, John Bardee and Walter Brattain invented the transistor – this was a vital breakthrough in the electronics revolution, enabling miniaturisation. It provided the basis for a computerised, rather than a mechanical, telecommunications network.
1965 Charles Kao first developed the theory that information could be carried using optical fibres, which subsequently became the basis of the global transmission service.

Key concepts at the heart of telecommunications

AQA A	M5
AQA B	M5, M6
EDEXCEL	M4, M6
OCR	M6

Networks

At the heart of the telecommunications global systems are three basic network components that enable the whole thing to happen:

- user equipment, a telephone or computer at each end of the communication
- transmission equipment, which provides the ability to send millions of telephone messages every second
- switches, creating a hierarchy of local, national and international rates for messages, allowing any user to connect to any other user.

Equipment

- **Hardware** – telephones, transmitters, cables, interface devices, switches and computers.
- **Software** – the packages that provide the codes that instruct the computer or other hardware. The development of digital systems and data networks has led to a range of network services.

Analogue and digital networks

The earliest systems used analogue technology – continuously variable signals which conveyed information. This frequently involved transmitting the human voice and the quality of speech achievable was determined by the amount of the speech spectrum that could be carried.

Since the 1990s computer capacity has grown enormously through the use of digital networks, which can carry a mix of voice, data pictures and text.

> This very practical detail creates a context in which you should be able to discuss developments in telecoms.

Circuit-switching and packet-switching

The traditional telephone system is a good example of a circuit-switching system that uses end-to-end connection between the communicating people which is maintained until the communication is complete.

However, communication between computers, or between terminals and computers, involves transferring blocks of data, rather than continuous data streams. Packet switching is the system that exploits the ability to send data blocks between terminals without setting up end-to-end communications through the network. Instead, it is possible to transmit on a link-by-link basis, with each data block being temporarily stored at each switch along the route, where they queue for transmission along an appropriate outgoing link. Decisions on the automatic routing are taken by analysis of the information contained in the 'header' appended to the front of each data block. The term 'packet' refers to the collection of the headers of the attached block of data, i.e. groups of messages are collected as 'packets' for transmission.

Congestion and blocking

In a packet-switched network each packet is competing for its own part of the resources of the network. When the system accepts a packet the switch does not know if the entire network has the resources to handle it. This means it is possible for more traffic to be accepted than can be carried, so affecting the quality of service unless something is done. Controls are therefore needed to stop such congestion happening frequently.

In simple circuit-switched networks the user's call stops others from getting access for the duration of the call (on a telephone call you get the engaged tone). Circuit-switched networks are designed to balance the amount of equipment used, set against a reasonable level of access for users of that network. Economic decisions of costs and results have to be balanced in this equation.

Performance

Circuit-switched networks like public telephones provide end-to-end connections on demand so long as the resources are available. Other uses cannot interfere with the quality of communication and end-to-end delays are small.

However, in packet-switched systems each packet is queuing for onward transmission at each switch. The volume of traffic along a transmission route will therefore affect the amount of delay across the network. If you try to use a computer that is networked to other computers you will notice that sometimes the machine is slower than at other times.

The information superhighway

AQA A	M5
AQA B	M5, M6
EDEXCEL	M4, M6
OCR	M6

The internet has a wider social use – try to consider the social aspects of use.

The internet has become an important part of our lives in a very short space of time. Students can use it for a variety of key functions – providing information; enabling purchases or banking transactions to be made; acting as a source of recreation, etc. Many people use the internet at home, but the provision of terminals in a wide variety of places like cafés or even bars give it a more social aspect, including 'surfing the net'.

A history of the internet

The internet is an expanded group of computer networks that share a common set of protocols and address-space that links tens of millions of people worldwide – and is growing rapidly. It was originally conceived by the US military who wanted to end a reliance on central computers. It is now a global community of users who send and receive mail, exchange files and gain access to shared data. The internet provides a means by which any computer can communicate with any other.

The worldwide web (WWW) is an internet-based application that exploits this ability to provide a global information service. It can support multi-media, such as giving access to papers containing pictures, video clips and sound, as well as text. It provides links that allow users to trawl between information held on different computers by clicking on the screen in front of the user. Many companies, organisations, interest groups, schools and colleges, etc. now have well established and often detailed websites, many containing a wide range of individual pages.

> It is the development of telecommunications over the past century, but especially during the latter years of the 20th century, that has transformed global communication and allows us to have almost instant access to people and organisations around the world.
>
> **KEY POINT**

Progress check

1 Who was the first person to transmit radio waves across the Atlantic?
2 What is the purpose of switches within a telecommunications system?
3 What are the two basic types of systems used in telecommunications?
4 What was the origin of the internet?

1 Guglielmo Marconi. 2 They create routes for the transmission of messages at local, national and international levels. 3 Circuit-switching and packet switching systems. 4 The desire of the US military to escape reliance on central computers.

7.5 The impact of computers

After studying the section you should be able to:

- describe the development of the computer and its uses
- discuss the role of Information and Communication Technology in education

LEARNING SUMMARY

The history of the computer

AQA A	M5
AQA B	M4, M6
EDEXCEL	M6
OCR	M4, M6

We might all know what a computer is and does, but make sure you can offer a definition if your exam calls for one.

The first counting machine was made in the 16th century by Pascal, the French mathematician and philosopher. Increasingly complex mechanical machines able to carry out a range of mathematical functions were then developed during the 19th century by people such as the Cambridge University mathematician and inventor Sir Charles Babbage. However, it was during World War II that the first all-electronic digital computer was built.

A computer can be defined as an electronic device that receives instructions (programs) and carries them out through the performance of calculations based on numerical data, or the manipulation of other forms of information.

Over the last half a century computers have revolutionised manufacturing through automation, and have transformed communications systems. They have become essential tools in every field of research and applied technology. The computer industry is global. Its main economic base is in the United States, in Seattle (the HQ of Microsoft – the company established and controlled by Bill Gates) and the so-called 'Silicon Valley' in California, where so many computer firms and research facilities are based. However, taking as an example an Intel Pentium processor which was designed in the US, the assembly might be undertaken in Ireland, using a Japanese semi-conductor wafer inserted into a circuit board made in Taiwan.

Many parts of a personal computer (PC) are now made in Asia, where there is a large pool of computer-science graduates and where general wage levels are comparatively low. At the same time, all the top operating systems and applications programs have been developed and written in the United States. This is certainly a factor in the emergence of the USA as the world's leading super-power in the latter years of the 20th century. Early computers were seen as a way of performing mathematical calculations. Today almost any kind of information can be represented in a form that a computer can handle – letters, dots, telecommunication signals and graphical information, for example. Between 1950 and 1990 computer performance increased about a *million* times. The speed of the basic circuitry improved about 10 000 times, and the remainder of the improvement came from changes in the internal organisation of computers. In practical terms, the maximum power of a computer is limited by the heat it generates internally and by the time taken for a signal to travel within it. Researchers are looking to develop a machine that uses laser lights rather than electronic signals, which could lead to the production of even more powerful machines.

Some landmarks in computing

1945 'Colossus' was developed at Bletchley Park by British scientists working on cracking the codes used by the Nazis for passing military information. This was the first all-electronic digital computer.

ENIAC was developed in the United States. A general-purpose machine, used to calculate the trajectory of bombs and shells, it contained 18 000 valves, weighed 30 tonnes, used 140 kilowatts of electricity and took up 85 cubic metres!

1946 The leading US scientists who developed ENIAC set up the world's first computer firm, making the Universal Automatic computer – UNIVAC. Machines such as the Ferranti Mark I were also developed in the UK.

1952 First use of germanium semiconducter diodes in a machine called Gamma 3

1957 Computer languages such as FORTRAN (Formula Translation), ALGOL
–59 (Algorithmic Language) and COBOL (Commercial Business Orientated Language) were introduced.

1958 First computers to use transistors, e.g. Elliott 802

1964 The first integrated circuits, e.g. IBM System 360

1974 First micro-processor based computer systems developed commercially by Intel, using an 8-bit micro-processor

1978 First 32-bit mini-computer, the VAX-11/780

1979 The IBM Personal Computer launched

1989 First optical computer demonstrated

1990 Microsoft launch Windows 3 for PCs.

Types of computer

AQA A	M5
AQA B	M4, M6
EDEXCEL	M6
OCR	M4, M6

Exam questions might ask about the different uses of computers.

- The **personal computer** (PC), used by individuals in industry and commerce for their own personal work, or by people at home for a wide range of activities, including leisure. There is a huge software market making games, or information disks that can be loaded into PCs. These machines are usually desk-top size, but as the computer industry has developed in sophistication they can also be 'lap-top', which enables a business person to carry one in a briefcase to meetings and so on. Current developments are seeing further miniaturisation to palm-top machines that are hand-held.
- The **workstation** is a machine with enhanced graphics and communications, which is useful in offices and other commercial settings.
- The **mini-computer** is often too expensive for personal use. Its capabilities make it ideal for business or research.
- **Mainframe** machines can contain huge capability and act as the centre of a network of other machines. They are found in industry, local government, universities – in fact in any large organisation where a lot of people need access to the same type of central information.

Some uses for computers

AQA A	M5
AQA B	M4, M6
EDEXCEL	M6
OCR	M4, M6

It is their practical uses that could form the basis of an exam question.

Automation

In industry and commerce many processes are now undertaken by automated techniques, including the use of robots. Processes that at one time used a lot of manpower now only need someone to control the machines. Not only can the basic process be speeded up and performed to absolutely identical specifications every time, production can also be increased because machines do not need regular rest breaks and could operate 24-hours a day if necessary.

Computer-art and design

Industry can now create and modify designs for new products using computers. In the art world, in its broadest sense, the use of computers is important in architecture, film animation and music.

Computer-assisted learning

This has transformed many aspects of traditional teaching and learning. Information and communication technology (ICT) is now at the heart of the

Think how IT has affected your own learning.

National Curriculum in schools in the UK. The government have introduced the National Grid for Learning, which aims to create a national system linking up all schools by computer, going on to link up with libraries, homes, etc. so that learning can become far more interactive. Schools' expenditure on IT was around £20 million in 1984 – ten years later (1994) it had risen to £250 million. Computers today are used across the whole of the curriculum. By linking up with satellites it is also possible to develop schemes for distance learning, for example, in India it is being used to provide adult education in remote areas where there have been high levels of illiteracy in the past.

Computer games

The production of software to enable people to use their PCs for playing games has developed into a multi-million pound industry around the world. This became possible with the development of the microprocessor in the mid-1970s. However, there is controversy around the wider social effects of computer games as many games involve war and violence, for example. There is also a concern expressed by some that we are creating a generation of 'computer nerds' who do not get any physical exercise, or develop normal social contact with other people.

Computer graphics

These can be as simple as a pie chart or as complex as a 3D engineering blueprint. Increasingly, these are being used to generate models and simulations in engineering, meteorology, medicine and the sciences.

Computerised axial tomography

The CAT scan used in medicine – a sophisticated form of X-ray imaging. It can aid diagnosis and pinpoint problem areas without the need for exploratory surgery. A 3D picture of an organ or tissue can be built up and any irregularities analysed.

Computer simulations

These are the representation of real-life situations in a computer program. This has many uses, and is particularly helpful in situations when it is too dangerous, time consuming, or simply impossible to carry out a real experiment.

> **KEY POINT**
>
> The 20th century has seen the emergence of science and technology as key elements transforming life for every person living in the world's advanced economy. Within a century life has changed on a scale previously unknown. Try to grasp some of the consequences of this, as well as noting the concrete examples that have been outlined in this chapter. Consider how different your life, from birth to death, would have been had you been born 100 years ago.

Progress check

1 Name two important centres for the US computer industry.
2 What was Colossus?
3 When did Microsoft launch Windows 3 for PCs?
4 How has industrial output been increased by the use of computers?
5 What is the value of a computer-based CAT scan?

1 Seattle (Microsoft's HQ) and Silicon Valley in California. 2 The first all-electric digital computer, built in 1945. 3 1990. 4 Through the introduction of automated production controlled by computers. 5 Allows doctors to undertake medical investigations of internal organs and tissue without the need for surgery.

Sample question and model answer

1

How have developments in science and technology increased the production of food from British farms?

Step 1
Introduction.

- Be brief and succinct – just set out an outline of what you aim to establish in your answer, without going into detail or analysis.
- The key point is that science and technology play a vital part in modern agriculture, ranging from the machinery that is used to the chemicals that are utilised in maximising production.

The question refers to both science *and* technology – look at each aspect separately.

Step 2
Development.

- Scientific developments could include:
  - the use of fertilisers to increase yield and to increase, or at least to sustain, the fertility of the soil. Sometimes soil has been used so heavily that its natural fertility has become so depleted that crops can *only* be sustained through the heavy use of chemical fertilisers.
  - the use of pesticides and herbicides to reduce the enormous loss of food crops to pests

N B The question is not about the pros and cons of these points – only about the amount of production. This is where marks will be allocated.

  - the development of new strains of seeds and the developments in genetically modified crops (although not yet as advanced as in the United States), will allow the use of more marginal land, or the production of pest-resistant crops.
- Discussing technological developments will involve describing how general technological development has affected the farming industry in particular. This ability to put wider learning into a specific context is one of the skills of General Studies.
  - machinery is faster and often more effective than human labour, so more can be undertaken
  - the existence of tractors and other vehicles mean bigger fields can be created and utilised for production
  - the creation of controlled environments for livestock in battery farming inside buildings maximises output by creating 'ideal' amounts of light, heat and food for the animals, with minimal human intervention.

Step 3
Conclusion.

- It would certainly be in order to mention that many of the methods used to increase agricultural production of both crops and animals are highly controversial. However, this is not a question that asks you to look at this in detail, so the mark scheme will not allocate many marks to this area.
- The importance of increased production in the context of the ever-reducing availability of land and the increasing population should be stressed.
- The role of scientists and technologists in supporting farmers in increasing their production should provide an effective close to your answer, for example:

For centuries it was the agricultural wisdom passed down through the generations that sustained the methods and techniques of farming. It is true that there have been improvements to livestock and to seeds over the past 200 years or so, but over the last half-century the scientist and technologist have produced the capabilities for farmers to produce outputs per acre that their predecessors would never have thought possible. Whatever the controversies that have accompanied much of this development, it cannot be denied that the partnership of science, technology and farming has transformed the production of food from British farms.

Practice examination questions

Short answer questions

1 Outline the main ways in which infectious diseases are transmitted.

2 How does the Food and Agriculture Organisation (FAO) seek to improve food supplies in the world?

3 Name three computer languages developed in the second-half of the 1950s.

Essay question

4 What are the arguments both for and against the use of herbicides in farming?

A note for candidates taking the AQA A specification exam

The question paper covering Unit 5 (M5) of the AQA A specification contains a unique feature, found in no other General Studies A2 papers – the **Spatial and Mechanical Relations** section.

The aim of this is for you to show that you understand the principles that govern the way that simple tools, machines and devices work. You will be given a diagram, often in 3D, and asked questions that test your ability to visualise the whole thing. In the past, diagrams have included Newcomen's atmospheric engine, a taxi meter, a hand loom, house plans and bicycle gears.

The best way to prepare for this is simply to look at, and practise using, past papers. You could also look at machines in a local museum, or on a CD-Rom. However, this skill cannot be taught in a traditional way – so don't expect lessons from your teachers on this during the course!

KEY POINT

Chapter 8

Controversies in science and technology

The following topics are covered in this chapter:

- *Medical procedures*
- *Pollution*
- *Environmental destruction*
- *Cloning*
- *Genetically modified foods*

8.1 Medical procedures

After studying this section you should be able to:

- *discuss some of the controversial advances in medical procedures*
- *explain why some people have serious concerns about the morality of these procedures*

LEARNING SUMMARY

A 'right to die' or a 'right to live?'

AQA A	M5
AQA B	M4, M6
EDEXCEL	M4, M6
OCR	M4, M6

Key points from AS

- **Some contemporary controversies**
  Revise AS pages 121–125

During the year 2000 the parliament of The Netherlands became the first in a modern democracy to legalise the right of people, in certain circumstances to choose to die – euthanasia.

In the UK there may be a shift in public opinion towards this 'right' becoming acceptable. but it is still far from the statute book. However, as the new millennium gets underway there have been some interesting cases in which the courts have had to rule on medical intervention. We will look at five such cases in this section.

In October 2000, following the introduction of the Human Rights Act (which seeks to guarantee the right to life) the President of the High Court Family Division, Dame Elizabeth Butler-Sloss, had to rule on whether this right to life can be over-ruled.

The facts of the case were:

- two women, both suffering from permanent vegetative state (PVS), described in court as 'a state of living death'.
- both were completely oblivious to their surroundings with no hope of recovery, BUT doctors could keep them alive.
- they survived because they were fed with liquids through a tube, if this was stopped both women would die.
- between 1993 and 2000 around 20 people with PVS had been allowed to die, following a ruling by the House of Lords that Tony Bland, a victim of the Hillsborough Stadium disaster, could be allowed to die.

The judge ruled that doctors did have the right to stop feeding both patients in this case and in so doing set an important precedent for the future.

So far as a student of General Studies is concerned there are some important questions that need to be considered, such as:

- How far is the right to life that is enshrined in the Human Rights Convention an absolute right?
- If doctors know that by turning off life-support equipment they will directly cause the death of a patient, are they committing murder?
- How far should members of the patient's family be allowed to sway a doctor's medical decision?
- Should judges, doctors or family members take the decision to end life-support?

CASE STUDY 1

The second 'new millennium' controversy we consider hinges around our definition of death and the removal of organs for transplant. In 1999 there were over 5400 people waiting for solid organ transplants (heart, lung, liver and kidney), but only 2500 operations took place. Hearts, lungs and livers need to be removed in 'beating heart operations', and are mostly from younger drivers and car passengers. However, in recent years, largely due to increased seat-belt use, the numbers of younger people dying and donating organs has dropped.

Consider the balance of 'rights' – the right to a 'new' life for a patient receiving a new organ as opposed to the rights, if appropriate, of the donor to be finally proved dead, or to be treated as if they were still alive.

The Information in this case study originated in the editorial in the August 2000 edition of *Anaesthesia*, the journal of the Royal College of Anaesthetists, which called for routine anaesthesia when organs are removed from clinically dead bodies.

This controversy raises the question of how we define 'death'. Society's definition of death has changed over time:

- In the Middle Ages many Christians in Europe considered that death came when the soul left the body and went to heaven or hell.
- By the 20th century death was considered to have occurred when the heart stopped beating.
- Today in the UK the definition is of 'brainstem death,' which is when no activity can be detected in the brainstem – the 'motorway' for messages between the brain and the nervous system, which initiates breathing and is responsible for consciousness.
- This definition is not acceptable in the United States and much of Europe, where the definition is the 'irreversible cessation of all functions of the entire brain, including the brainstem'.

The current controversy hinges around whether the clinically dead person should be given an anaesthetic before organs are removed – and whether the UK definition is enough to guarantee death. (The issue around whether an anaesthetic is necessary centres on the belief that some anaesthetists have that because the body moves when organs are removed this could indicate that the patient might well feel pain even if there is no activity in the brainstem. Those who believe anaesthetics are unnecessary believe such movement to be a simple reflex and not the result of pain.) One leading anaesthetist sees no problem, even if the person having an organ removed cannot be finally and totally proved to be dead. He was quoted as saying 'I'm very much in favour of transplants. I see no problem at all in squaring it with the family, saying your relative can't survive and it is absolutely pointless to go on like this – why not let me anaesthetise them and we will take the organs out.'

- In August 2000 the Royal College of Anaesthetists called for anaesthetics to be given routinely during operations to remove hearts, lungs, livers and pancreas – all of which occur while a patient is on a ventilator that keeps their heart beating.
- Another consultant anaesthetist wrote, 'If you don't give anything at all the patient will start moving and wriggling around and it's impossible to do the operation. The surgeon has always asked us to paralyse the patient.'
- On the other hand the President of the Intensive Care Society, which represents 85% of UK anaesthetists, said, 'Brainstem dead patients do not require analgesia or sedation during surgery to remove their organs. In simple terms, if you are dead, you are dead and so dead people don't require anaesthesia… If you aren't dead, you shouldn't be having your organs taken away.'

CASE STUDY 2

Our next 'millennium case study' concerns a case which went to court in October 2000 and deals with the 'right' of parents to choose the sex of their next child.

- Alan and Louise Masterson have four sons, and wanted to have a clinical genetic diagnosis and implantation of a female embryo to ensure their next child was a girl.
- Their daughter had died the previous summer in a bonfire accident which had led to 90% burns. The father said, 'We are

looking for the opportunity to try for another daughter, not another Nicola, but to bring a female dimension to our family.'
- The law as it stands makes embryo screening available only for prospective parents who are carriers of medical conditions related to a particular gender.
- The case was brought against the Human Fertilisation and Embryology Authority (HFEA), which regulates 'test-tube baby' clinics and their work in the UK.

CASE STUDY 3

The Mastersons based their case upon the European Convention on Human Rights which guarantee a fair hearing from public authorities.

The following quotes from people with differing perspectives sum up the two sides in this argument:

- The Bishop of Edinburgh, a former HFEA member, said that the Authority was being cautious because of a public fear over sex selection. 'I think, in this case, it ought to look hard at it because, while you could probably make a case for a general regulation that sex selection is a bad thing, there must be exceptional circumstances. I would think this one probably was, and I hope they (the Mastersons) can get a centre to send in an application to the HFEA.'

- Ken Mason, lecturer in medical law and ethics and Edinburgh University, said, however, that the case crossed the boundaries of ethically acceptable medical practice. 'You could take this to the point of absurdity – for example, you could say you had five children with red hair and wanted one with black hair.'

When the case came to court, the judgement rejected the Mastersons case and said that the law did not permit couples to choose the sex of their children other than for the medical reason outlined above. Do you think that the court came to the right decision?

When medical science advances rapidly, existing laws often fail to give clear guidance on new situations. When this happens it is often judge, not doctors, who can determine a medical outcome.

As the new millennium gets underway, another controversial test-tube baby hit the headlines – the family, called Nash, came from the United States. In this case a baby boy, Adam, was born after genetic screening showed him to have precisely the right cells for him to act as a donor to his seriously ill older sister. In essence, he was 'created' as a way of saving another person's life.

- The older sister, Molly, has a rare inherited disorder called Fanconi Anaemia, which stops cell production of bone marrow. At his birth doctors collected cells from Adam's umbilical cord which were then infused into his sister. Without a successful transplant her disease is 100% fatal, but she now has a 85–90% chance of full recovery.

- Prior to Mrs Nash being made pregnant doctors created 12 embryos by standard *in vitro* fertilisation (IVF) and single cells were taken from each to test for the Fanconi gene and for measures of compatibility with Molly. One embryo was considered fully suitable and transferred to Lisa Nash's uterus – from this embryo came baby Adam – born so that his sister can live.

This case was the first of its kind to come to light, and opened a fierce debate on the ethics of designing babies with specific genetic traits.

Just as in the previous case study there are conflicting medical opinions:

- Dr Paul Veys, a bone-marrow transplant specialist at Great Ormond Street Children's Hospital said he believed the Illinois case was a rare instance in which designing a baby to be a donor was ethically justified – 'In this case, hopefully, you're going to end up with two children who are healthy. How can you argue against that?' he said.

- On the other hand some bio-ethicists regard Adam's birth as a mixed blessing – a step along the road to a society in which parents can choose 'boutique babies.' Jeffrey Kahn, Director of the University of Minnesota's Centre for Bioethics said, 'I suspect that it's only because we don't yet have the tests that we're not having parents asking for embryos without a predisposition to homosexuality or for kids who will grow to more than six feet tall.'

Dr Veys makes an important point – if 'designer babies' can be justified in a few cases, who draws the line on what is acceptable and what is unacceptable? Who sways public opinion – should philosophers, judges or parents be the key deciders? There is no clear answer – this is why the courts can become involved in cases of medical ethics.

Our final example of a new dilemma for the new millennium is the case of Mary and Jodie which became a cause célèbre as many people, including doctors, theologians and philosophers, agonised over the right course of action in the case of two conjoined twins (what were formerly described as 'Siamese twins'). Medical technology made one course possible, but did that make it right? Professor McCall Smith, specialist in medical law at the University of Edinburgh, summarised the basis of this case, writing in *The Guardian* in September 2000:

'Two parents come to Britain to have their babies. Conjoined twins were delivered and it was discovered that surgery to separate them would result in the death of one, although possibly saving the life of the other. The parents declared that they did not want this, for religious reasons, and they were supported in their opposition by the Catholic church. But the twins were born into a society in which there is sufficient attachment to the principle that the welfare of children is generally more important than the wishes of the parents.'

The background to the case

Conjoined twins were born on 8 August 2000 at St Mary's Hospital in Manchester, their parents having come from Gozo, a small and strongly Catholic island in the Mediterranean near Malta. The twins were joined at the lower abdomen and were, for legal purposes, given the English names of Mary and Jodie so that their family could not be identified. Doctors believed that without an operation to separate them they would both be dead within six months. However, if separated it was felt that Jodie could go on to live a relatively normal life, but the inevitable consequence of the operation would be the death of Mary, since she had no functioning heart or lungs and only a primitive brain. She was, in effect, being kept alive by Jodie, but the increasing strain of this as both grew would mean that Jodie's heart would at some point become unable to cope and she would die from a heart attack, leaving Mary to die also.

The Central Manchester Healthcare Trust obtained the consent of the High Court to carry out the separation, leading the parents to appeal to a bench of three judges in the Court of Appeal. It was at this second court that many of the medical and ethical issues were fully aired – the fact that the judges allowed representations from the Catholic Archbishop of Westminster and from the Pro-Life Alliance suggested they were unsure of many ethical issues. Two of the three Appeal judges later admitted the case had caused them sleepless nights as they struggled with the issues:

- Would separation constitute murder, or at least manslaughter, by the doctors who would end Mary's life?
- Should Mary's life be ended by a surgeon's knife, or by 'God's will?'
- Should Mary be allowed to kill Jodie?
- Should the parents' express wishes be ignored?
- Would the case become 'the thin end of the wedge', leading later to people born less than perfect being put to death?

One of the Appeal judges, Lord Justice Ward, put a central concern bluntly, 'The moment the knife goes into that united body, it touches the body of unhappy little Mary. It is in that second an assault. You fiddle about, re-arrange the plumbing. An hour later you put a clamp on the aorta [cutting the blood supply to Mary]. You cannot pretend that this is not actively engaged in assaulting her integrity. For what justification? None of hers.'

The central moral argument is whether it can ever be right for a doctor to save one life at the expense of another. The Catholic view is that nobody may commit a wrong action that good may come from it. On the other hand, a utilitarian argument would be that saving one life, rather than losing two might be justified.

One thing that it would not have been legal for the court to do would have been to authorise a step that would 'actively terminate a life' – even if it relieved misery, and the patient or a parent consented. However, if Mary's death was caused by the interruption or withdrawal of Jodie's blood supply it could be compared with the withholding of nourishment for those in a persistent vegetative state (see Case Study 1).

An individual's view of the best outcome in a case such as this may well be influenced by whether they have a belief in an after life. In a secular society, physical existence assumes a greater importance, but if there is a view that after death the individual goes on, either to some kind of eternal bliss, or to return through incarnation, then 'God's will' does not seem so terrifying and final.

The arguments presented to the Court of Appeal

The arguments against separating the twins

- The twins' parents quoted Article 2 of the European convention on Human Rights – 'Everyone's right to life shall be protected by law.'

- The parents' initial case to the High Court said, 'We cannot begin to accept or contemplate that one of our children should die to allow the other one to survive. That is not God's will. Everyone has the right to life, so why should we kill one of our daughters to enable the other one to survive?… We have faith in God and we are quite happy for God's will to decide what happens to our daughters.'

- The Catholic Archbishop of Westminster submitted to the Court of Appeal, 'God has given to humankind the gift of life, and as such it is to be revered and cherished… In this case, if what is envisaged is the killing of, or a deliberate lethal assault on, one of the twins, Mary, in order to save the other, Jodie, there is a grave injustice involved.'

- David Harris QC, the barrister representing Mary for the Official Solicitor (appointed under the Children Act regulations) insisted it would be unlawful to operate – there was no evidence that she was in any kind of pain and although her life would be short it would not be 'so intolerable as to render it in the child's best interests that it should end'.

- The family's parish priest at home in Gozo said, 'It is the same principle as organ donation. Transplants are valid and moral when the donor is dead, but Mary is not dead. She is alive, she is a human being. It is wrong to kill her, no matter how good the intention.'

- Speaking about a similar medical case in the United States in 1993 the Professor of Medical Ethics at Chicago University medical centre said, 'I remember during the debate how quickly people who wanted to intervene could move into the idea that one twin was like a parasite, or an appendage – language that makes one morally able to divide them.'

- Richard Nicolson, Editor of the *Bulletin of Medical Ethics* wrote, 'In a situation like this when there isn't an obvious right answer, do we need to put the onus for the decision back on those who are going to have to live with the consequences of the decision? Surely we have to give great power and credence to the parents?'

- There was also a more general concern expressed that if Mary was not thought of as a human being – and therefore having the right to life – then a precedent would be set that might in future be used against others born with severe disabilities.

Arguments in favour *of separating the twins*

- Lord Justice Ward, one of the Appeal Judges, said during the appeal, 'It was not God's will that this baby (Mary) should live, because she was not born with the capacity to live… nobody in their right mind would hook this child onto a life support system, given the utter deformity of her heart and lungs.'

- The same judge said to Mary's counsel, 'You invite us to treat her as an independent life, when everyone knows that if she had been born a single person she would have been left to die.'

- The team of independent doctors appointed by the Court of Appeal to consider the medical perspective were unanimous in concluding that the twins should be separated, despite the wishes of the parents.

- In English law 'great weight' has to be given to parental views, but courts have a clear duty to ignore these when that would be in the best interests of the child or children concerned.

- It was not disputed that Mary was dying of her own condition, so in effect the withdrawal of Jodie's 'life support' would not be the substantial cause of death. 'It would follow that there was no criminal intent in the present case', concluded her barrister.

- He argued that doctors had two choices – to operate, or to do nothing. The latter would, he argued, be a derogation of their duty of care and protection to Jodie.

- With regard to the European Convention on Human Rights declaration on the right to life, and whether this can be seen as an absolute right at all costs, it was argued that if this was indeed the case there would be wider implications. For example, doctors might not be able to carry out an abortion to save a mother's life. If the right was absolute, in the case of the twins it would mean that Jodie could not be saved, because the only way of doing this would be to end Mary's life. Hence, in time both twins would die.

The legal conclusion to the case

For the student of General Studies there will be few, if any, cases where advances in medical science has brought such major ethical questions into such sharp focus. Whatever specification you are following there will be areas in which such debate could provide the basis for a question, or for an argument.

What was the legal outcome? All three judges

came to the same conclusion in their detailed statements. To quote key phrases from the ruling by Lord Justice Ward, 'The only solution is to balance the welfare of each child against the other to find the least detrimental alternative. Into each scale goes their right to life... Jodie is entitled to protest that Mary is killing her. Nobody but the doctors can help Jodie. Mary sadly is beyond any help. She is designated for death... The law must allow an escape by permitting the doctors to choose the lesser of two evils... I conclude, therefore, that this operation can be lawfully carried out.'

Postscript

Following the judgement, the twins' parents said they would take the case no further – all four judges (the original High Court judge and the three Appeal judges) had all come to the same conclusion. A last minute attempt to re-open the case by the Pro-Life Alliance was rejected by the court and the operation went ahead.

Following her separation, Mary was tended and kept warm by theatre staff until her inevitable death. A subsequent post-mortem came to the unique judgement that Mary had her life terminated as a result of a legally carried out surgical operation.

Jodie returned to her family home in Gozo early in 2001.

Progress check

1 Which was the first European country to legalise euthanasia in some circumstances?

2 What was the court ruling on the ending of artificial feeding in two cases of people suffering from permanent vegetative state in October 2000?

3 What European Convention gives the right to life and the protection of life?

4 What organs are removed for transplantation in 'beating heart' operations?

5 In UK law what part of the brain is looked to in order to determine death?

6 Why did Alan and Louise Masterson bring a case against the Human Fertilisation and Embryology Authority?

7 How did one child get over Fanconi anaemia?

8 What were the names of the conjoined twins born in Manchester in August 2000?

1 The Netherlands.

2 That doctors could stop feeding the two patients.

3 The European Convention on Human Rights.

4 Hearts, lungs, livers and pancreas.

5 The brainstem.

6 They wanted to ensure, through genetic screening, that their next child would be a girl – a process which is currently not legal in UK.

7 By her parents selecting an embryo for implantation which had the right cells to act as donor cells. Cells from the child's umbilical cord at birth were transplanted so the child with Fanconi anaemia could develop her own bone marrow.

8 'Mary' and 'Jodie' – not their real names, so the family could not be identified.

8.2 Pollution

After studying this section you should be able to:

- identify some of the key causes of pollution
- discuss why the advanced economies of the world seem reluctant to address the issue in a serious way
- link pollution with environmental destruction (next section)

What causes pollution?

AQA A	M5
AQA B	M4, M5, M6
EDEXCEL	M6
OCR	M4, M6

Key points from AS

- Industrial and technological issues
  Revise AS page 111
- Environmental concerns
  Revise AS pages 112–114

Pollution is brought about by human activity, its effects can be extremely serious and sometimes deadly, yet the advanced economies of the world seem unwilling, or unable to address a problem of our own making. The world conference looking at pollution and climate change held in The Hague at the end of 2000 (which was intended to turn some of the fine words of the earlier UN conference held at Kyoto in Japan into practical action) broke up without any agreement being reached.

- Pollution is the largely unintended and unwanted result of human activities in the areas of manufacturing, transport, agriculture and waste disposal.
- It is classified by the part of the environment that is primarily affected – air, water or land. The substances that cause pollution are usually in the form of gases, finely divided solids or finely dispersed aerosols.

Types of pollution

AQA A	M5
AQA B	M4, M5, M6
EDEXCEL	M6
OCR	M4, M6

Air pollution

There are five major classes of pollutants that are discharged into the air:

- carbon oxides
- sulphur oxides
- hydrocarbons
- nitrogen oxides
- particulates (dust and ash, for example).

The main cause of air pollution is the burning of fossil fuels – coal and oil. The biggest single cause is the exhaust from cars and lorries, which contains carbon and nitrogen oxides and hydrocarbons. There are also problems from the sulphur oxides emitted primarily by industries that burn coal and oil.

> Make sure you do not confuse global warming and the greenhouse effect (see the AS Revise Guide).

Levels of pollution have risen consistently through the 20th century. This is in large part because the consumption of fossil fuels has led the levels of carbon dioxide in the atmosphere to increase. Many believe we are now seeing tangible signs of a potentially catastrophic consequence – global warming (of which more later in this section).

Ways of reducing air pollution

There are various ways in which air pollution can be reduced or controlled. However, the most obvious – the severe limitation of cars and lorries powered by internal combustion engines – is a political non-starter. Can you imagine a political party being elected to government on a policy of banning or severely reducing private car use? Yet the reality is that this would lead to a dramatic reduction in air pollution and the illnesses often associated with this.

> A General Studies exam question might ask you why you think this is the case.

There are steps which are now taken with new vehicles in an attempt to control exhaust emissions – re-designed engines and catalytic converters, for example.

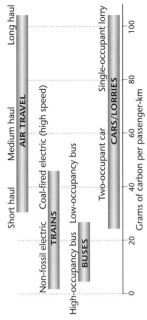

Carbon dioxide emissions by type of transport

There is also a move to 'cleaner' fuels and fuel additives.

Over the last two decades there has also been a marked movement away from coal-burning power stations – often in favour of electricity generation using natural gas. The British press dubbed this rapid move in the UK 'the dash for gas'.

Factories have been compelled by legislation to remove or reduce the pollutants entering the atmosphere from their chimneys, which is often done by introducing electrostatic precipitation.

Water pollution

Any body of water has a capability to break down or absorb materials put into it using micro-organisms. However, if the input of added material is greater than the water's ability to cope with it, the additional materials become pollutants.

The principal sources of water pollution are:

- sewage
- industrial waste
- rubbish/refuse
- agricultural fertilisers
- pesticides and herbicides.

Domestic waste water used in sewage systems can be artificially treated and purified before being discharged back into the environment, although some untreated raw sewage continues to be pumped directly into the sea below the low-tide level in the UK.

Agricultural wastes are generally less concentrated, taking longer to produce aggravating effects. However, many streams and rivers that look clean and have large amounts of bright green plant life are in fact being 'choked to death' by this vigorous plant growth – which is stimulated by the run-off of nitrates and other fertilisers from surrounding fields.

Land pollution

Pollution of the surface of the land has historically been primarily the result of the dumping of waste from industrial and mineral activities – slag run-off from blast furnaces, or the spoil heaps of collieries, for example. To this can be added the more recent burial of nuclear material.

There has always been household waste to dispose of, but the amount has escalated dramatically as a result of:

- the population reaching an all-time high
- the huge increase in pre-packaged food
- the decline of the deposit system on glass bottles
- the use of 'fancy packaging' to make a product more enticing.

Land pollution today consists mainly of solid wastes:

- cans
- glass and plastic bottles
- plastic containers
- papers.

Far more could be done to recycle much of this waste and local councils (who are responsible for organising refuse collection) have challenging targets for the amount of recycling they will be expected by the government to achieve.

In the meantime the principal means of disposal remain:

- landfill – although the number of suitable sites not yet full is ever-declining
- incineration – some schemes use the heat generated by burning rubbish to

provide for central heating systems. However, the act of burning itself creates air pollution

- ocean dumping – no longer seen as a 'green' solution, with its potential to pollute the seas. (It was believed that micro-organisms in the sea quickly broke down the pollutants; this might have been the case with small amounts.)

> **KEY POINT**
>
> Pollution can be defined as 'the addition to the environment of any substance, or energy form (e.g. heat) at a rate faster than the environment can accommodate it by dispersion, breakdown, recycling or storage in some harmless form.'

Why do we put up with pollution?

The first point to make is that not everybody does! There are increasing numbers of people who campaign for a better environment, and provide education to make people more aware – even if they are not sure what to do about it. In Britain there are many environmental groups, both local and national – if you have debated environmental issues during your General Studies course you might well have been in touch with some of them. Perhaps the best known is Friends of the Earth, a national group with local branches.

The Friends of the Earth website contains some excellent material for General Studies students.

Does democracy itself make it difficult to oppose pollution? Much pollution is generated as a result of our desire to acquire more and more possessions, to travel freely and cheaply in our own individual cars and so on. Under our political system the Opposition can always claim that government action is an infringement of freedom and liberty if it suggests legislation to reduce pollution. This was vividly seen in the widespread campaign to reduce fuel tax in Autumn 2000. The leader of the Conservative opposition, William Hague, publicly praised the actions of those who had brought the country to a virtual standstill. What this failed to acknowledge was that it was the Conservative Chancellor of the Exchequer, Kenneth Clarke, who introduced in the first place the financial mechanism that increased duties on fuel at above rates of inflation as a direct way of trying to reduce individual car use.

Consider the following quote by Polly Toynbee in an article in *The Guardian* in September 2000:

In your General Studies exam you should be able to put pollution into a global context.

> 'Can Western democracies ever deliver the politics necessary to save the world? To stop global warming as it is now – just to halt it – world emissions of carbon dioxide have to be cut by between 60% and 80% according to the intergovernmental panel on climate change: targets set at Kyoto which some countries won't reach were a pathetically modest first step. But outside wartime, no democracy has ever asked its voters for such savage belt tightening or such a radical lifestyle change as would be required to get anywhere near that goal.
>
> Will it have to wait until citizens can see for themselves that climate change threatens them now, not in the future? Dying polar bears, water at the North Pole, fires blazing across great tracts of land, or even tropical diseases like West Nile Fever breaking out in Boston make interesting newspaper stories, but they don't scare the people into a wartime frame of mind: presumably that will take water flooding over the spire of the Empire State Building.'

Until the latter part of the 20th century most people considered pollution to be a local problem. Smog (thick fog mixed with smoke from domestic and industrial chimneys) was one such issue – notoriously, 4000 Londoners were killed by smog in three weeks during December 1952 and this was instrumental in bringing about the Clean Air Act in 1953. Sometimes pollution was seen in even more local terms

– but its consequences could still be devastating. For example, in 1967 the huge spoil heap from the local colliery that was on the hillside above the south Wales valley community of Aberfan collapsed onto the village school, killing nearly all the children and their teachers.

Disappearing sea caused by irrigation; Aral Sea, Usbekistan

Pollution has always been a deadly risk, but today the problem is becoming global. The advanced economies of the world could be said to be threatening the future of life on earth as we know it. Why, therefore, do people not take direct action to reduce pollution – particularly those emissions leading to global warming and the greenhouse effect? Possible reasons are:

- ignorance of the process that is going on
- the benefits of an increasingly comfortable and affluent lifestyle encouraging us to turn a blind eye
- the feeling that the future consequences of present-day actions have been exaggerated
- putting oneself and one's immediate lifestyle before others and the longer term.

Our planet is warming by an average of half a degree every decade – and even with intergovernmental action to reduce CO_2 emissions this looks set to continue until at least 2030. In the UK the immediate effects of this might mean that it will be easier to grow grain crops and winter heating bills will reduce. However,

> Computer models and scientific opinion vary – so some predictions appear to be contradictory.

- habitats and wildlife will find it hard to keep pace with the northward migration of the earth's climate, which is moving approximately 10 km a year (habitats can only move at around 10 km a decade).
- the price of vegetables may rise by up to 25% as pests thrive and more water is required to produce traditional British vegetables
- the south-east will become warmer and dryer (the UN now classifies East Anglia as a 'semi-arid zone')
- there will be increasing levels of 'freak' weather
- the risk of significant destabilisation of our planetary ecosystem is possible. Changes in ocean currents could push the warm waters of the Gulf Stream Drift (which gives the UK temperate seas and moderate extremes in our temperatures) further north – making the temperatures in Britain around 10° colder.

> **KEY POINT**
>
> The richest 20% of the human population own and control 82% of the world's wealth and resources. This 20% includes most of us in this country. If we want to stop climate change, habitat destruction, species extinction and the increase in respiratory disease we must take action on pollution – or risk global consequences.

Progress check

1 Where was the world conference looking at issues around pollution and global warming held in 2000?
2 Which three oxides are among the major pollutants discharged into the air?
3 What are the main agricultural contributors to water pollution?
4 Name three means for the disposal of rubbish?
5 What level of reduction of CO_2 emission has been called for by the intergovernmental panel on climate change?

5 60–80%.
4 Landfill, incineration, ocean dumping.
3 Fertilisers, pesticides and herbicides.
2 Carbon, sulphur and nitrogen.
1 The Hague.

8.3 Environmental destruction

After studying this section you should be able to:

- *discuss some of the major concerns around the destruction of environments*
- *describe one model advanced to help industry and commerce address these*

LEARNING SUMMARY

Use of resources

AQA A	M5
AQA B	M4, M5, M6
EDEXCEL	M6
OCR	M4

> In the exam you might be asked to think about issues such as our own purchasing of goods that cause pollution – does that imply any personal responsibility?

Key points from AS

- **Environmental concerns**
  Revise AS pages 112–117

Industry uses materials – animal, vegetable and mineral – that Nature has provided, and has traditionally paid little attention to the waste thereby produced. However, goods are only manufactured for those who consume them. In other words, we provide industry with the market it needs. To what extent do we therefore have a moral responsibility – or even a duty – to protect our environment; to be a 'friend of the Earth'?

Industry has been progressively destroying Nature and its ability to create new resources in three ways.

- By the extraction of millions of tons of materials from the Earth's crust every year. It is a basic scientific law that matter cannot disappear – so petrol used to drive a car does not simply vanish, it breaks down into a mixture of gases such as carbon monoxide and sulphur dioxide. The burning of fossil fuels, in particular, produces large volumes of waste such as carbon dioxide, to the extent that Nature cannot re-absorb this. It is in large part the accumulation of CO_2 in the atmosphere which is leading to global warming
- By creating volumes of waste that are far beyond the ability of Nature to cope with, leading to a gradual accumulation of waste and destruction of habitats and ecosystems. Some of this waste is virtually un-degradable, is harmful to life and will be with us for many years to come. Pollutants such as dioxins, for example, cause a range of serious effects from cancers to abnormalities of the human reproductive system.
- By removing from Nature far more of its living resources than it is capable of renewing – so that natural resources are sometimes at risk of disappearing altogether. The over-fishing of areas like the North Sea provides a good example, and the species cod is now on the brink of extinction.

> The major problem:
> - Industry is ecologically destructive and is creating waste that nature cannot destroy.
> - Nature cannot create new resources at a fast enough rate.
>
> **KEY POINT**

'Unnatural disasters'

AQA A	M5
AQA B	M4, M5, M6
EDEXCEL	M6
OCR	M4

The above is the title of a Christian Aid report published in May 2000. It makes painful reading for those of us living in advanced economies. It claims that rich countries, like Britain, are condemning poor countries to an 'ever increasing number of overwhelming humanitarian catastrophes... 9 of the past 11 disasters to which we have responded have been caused by extreme weather conditions... The terrible irony is that the poorest countries are suffering and we believe that this is because of pollution by the wealthiest.'

Some of the appalling conclusions of the report are as follows.

- By 2020 75% of the world's population, mostly in poor countries, could be at risk from drought or flood, as a result of the 'creeping menace' of global warming due to the continued burning of fossil fuel.

- In 1998 alone environmental catastrophes created 25 million refugees – more than wars. 300 million were affected by storms, rain, landslips, mudslides and tidal waves.
- 45 countries were afflicted by serious drought.
- Mosquitoes have appeared in new areas – malaria cases could increase.
- Lack of water could affect 3 billion people in India, Africa and the Middle East – nearly half the world's population.
- 94 million people are at risk from rising sea levels in Bangladesh, India and South-East Asia.
- Environmental problems will lead to continuing mass migration into cities, creating ever larger shanty towns that are vulnerable to disease and crime.
- The UK emitted 9.5 tonnes of carbon dioxide per person, compared to 0.7 tonnes per person in Honduras in 1998.

> How are statistics like these balanced against our 'freedom' to use our cars freely?

Should we all become vegetarians?

AQA A	M5
AQA B	M4, M5, M6
EDEXCEL	M6
OCR	M4

A large majority of people in Britain eat meat, but the number of vegetarians is growing. In terms of the destruction of habitats and our environment perhaps those of us who enjoy meat should consider the following.

- Methane gas emitted by livestock and their decomposing manure accounts for 44% of Europe's annual emission – contributing to global warming.
- Millions of trees have been destroyed around the world to create grazing land for animals – up to 40% of the Amazon rainforest clearance has been to provide more land for cattle.
- Intensive cattle and pig farming is the single biggest cause of river pollution, with slurry being washed into waterways. Cattle slurry is 20–40 times stronger than human effluent in removing oxygen from water, killing fish and plant life.
- It takes 100 times more water to produce one kilo of beef than one kilo of vegetable protein, while demand for water is doubling every 21 years.
- In around 40 years the world's population might have doubled – too many are already suffering from malnutrition or starvation. One acre of land devoted to grain produces five times more protein than when used for meat production.
- One-third of the world's fish catch and more than one-third of the world's total grain output are fed to livestock, while some estimates put the numbers of people dying, either directly or indirectly, from malnutrition at 20 million a year.

> The rich have the resources to buy meat often produced in poor countries.

Broader consequences of global warming

AQA A	M5
AQA B	M4, M5, M6
EDEXCEL	M6
OCR	M4

In May 2000 the UK government was the first to try to quantify the cost of maintaining our environment in the face of global warming. Among costs that will have to be met:

- £95 million a year for the next 50 years merely to prevent existing defences from being overwhelmed by sea and rivers
- predicted 20% shortfall in water supplies in 30 years time will cost £5 billion to address
- a similar sum will have to be spent on strengthening buildings, in order to withstand the predicted increase in storm winds
- even with such spending some sparsely inhabited low-lying areas, mainly in eastern England, will be lost to water inundation as sea levels rise.

The then Minister for the Environment, Michael Meacher, said, 'Even if the international community succeeded in cutting its carbon dioxide emissions by 60–70% we would still face these costs because of the greenhouse gases we have already put into the atmosphere.'

127

- The UK Round Table on Sustainable Development reported in May 2000 that setting targets for reducing the pace of climate change and cutting traffic pollution had to be priorities. It concluded, 'we believe the signal is showing red and that the world is still proceeding at a reckless pace towards disaster.'
- The World Wildlife Fund reported in August 2000 that global warming is likely to destroy more than half the earth's colder habitats within the next 100 years, leading to the extinction of many species. The bleak predictions are based on the conservative estimate that concentrations of carbon dioxide will only be double those of pre-industrial days, but unless drastic steps are taken to reduce the amount of fossil fuel being used for energy production the level of CO_2 could easily be treble that of pre-industrial days.

A possible model for ecologically sound industry and commerce

AQA A	M5
AQA B	M4, M5, M6
EDEXCEL	M6
OCR	M4

In 1998 the Co-operative Bank plc published its four rules for ecologically sound businesses:

1 Substances derived from the Earth's crust should not be allowed to build up in Nature – we should not exceed Nature's capacity to transport a given substance back into the Earth's crust. In practical terms this will lead to a radical decrease in mining activity and the use of fossil fuels, and an increase in the use of recycling methods and sustainable energy sources, such as solar and hydro electricity.

2 Products we create, and the waste they leave behind, should not be allowed to build up in Nature. We should not manufacture products, or generate waste at levels that exceeds Nature's ability to break down a given substance and render it harmless. This means phasing out the production of long-lived substances that Nature has little capacity to break down, such as CFCs or the insecticide DDT.

To what extent do these rules fly in the face of the pressures to acquire more and more possessions?

3 Nature should not be allowed to deteriorate in terms of quality (its diversity), or quantity (its volume). This means not harvesting resources at rates that exceed the ability to replace them. Fishing is a good example. This will lead to sweeping changes in our systems of forestry, agriculture, fishing and in our urban-planning policies.

4 Resources should be used by society and business in a fair and efficient manner. If people don't see the system as being fair to all they could think that others are profiting, and so would not support any of the other ideas above. This includes the urgent need for living more resource-efficient lifestyles in the wealthy world.

> Is such a plan unrealistic? Today such diverse organisations as the Co-op Bank, the manufacturer Electrolux and the furnishing retailer IKEA are using these four rules to guide their investment. One thing is clear – if nothing is done our environment is under a very serious threat.

KEY POINT

Progress check

1 In which three ways has industry been progressively destroying Nature?
2 Which is the main gas being emitted into the atmosphere responsible for global warming?
3 Name the Christian Aid report published in 2000 that set out some consequences of man-made environmental disasters.
4 How much carbon dioxide did the UK emit per person in 1998?
5 Without drastic action, what proportion of the world's colder habitats might be lost in the next 100 years?

1 The extraction of materials from the earth's crust; the creation of large amounts of waste; the removal of the ability to renew living resources through over-exploitation. 2 Carbon dioxide (methane is also mentioned in the section). 3 *Unnatural Disasters.* 4 9.5 tonnes per person. 5 More than 50% of existing cold habitats.

8.4 Cloning

After studying this section you should be able to:

- describe current research into cloning
- discuss ethical and religious aspects of developments in cloning

What is the purpose of cloning?

AQA A	M5
AQA B	M5
EDEXCEL	M6
OCR	M4, M6

Developments in cloning, especially in what the Press sometimes calls 'spare-part surgery', is a major area of research, both in medicine and more widely as the 21st century gets underway. Some people see huge opportunities to treat a range of so far lethal diseases, others see the whole process as meddling with God's creation and usurping the act of creation itself. There are also broader possibilities that could benefit nature in general such as developing the ability to breed animals that are currently endangered species, or have indeed become extinct, through the manipulation of DNA.

Research using human embryos

AQA A	M5
AQA B	M5
EDEXCEL	M6
OCR	M4, M6

If you do not accept this, you need to consider the question 'On what specific day in a pregnancy does a bundle of cells become a human?'

Key points from AS

- Ethical dilemmas in science and technology; genetic engineering
Revise AS pages 110–111, 122–123.

At present researchers are permitted to work on human embryos that are the unwanted result of IVF treatment, when an embryo has been implanted but other fertilised embryos remain in the laboratory. This can only be done until the 14th day of development and is restricted to work on fertility, miscarriage and congenital disease. The donor's full consent is required in order to carry out any work. The ethical/religious question here is, when does life begin? Some, particularly the Catholic church, believe that life begins with the act of conception – the fusing of sperm and egg. They argue that life is a gift from God and that an embryo is an individual from the start, not merely a collection of cells.

The Head of the government's Human Fertility and Embryology Authority has indicated at least qualified support for some research: 'Nobody anywhere wants reproductive cloning, the cloning of babies, but right round the world there is a growing consensus that there would not be any harm, indeed there would be much good, in therapeutic cloning of embryos.'

The particular concentration of research would be to focus on inherited diseases, like Parkinson's disease and Huntington's disease, and on Alzheimer's disease, breast cancer and the repair of burns and fractures. Such work opens up the possibility of medical cures without the use of sometimes costly medicines.

At present, medical research is being hindered by having to use embryos that are frequently of poor quality – those from people who are needing fertility treatment in order to fertilise the eggs. The head of the Centre for Genome Research – a world centre – at Edinburgh University has called for a change in the law to allow women undergoing a range of gynaecological treatments to offer embryos.

The basis of medical research

If you personally oppose such development do you have the right to stop others from benefiting?

The essence of the process involves taking 'stem cells' – a tiny clump of general cells with no specific purpose in the earliest days of the embryo's development – and coaxing them into growing into becoming a single, large mass of specialised human tissue – hearts, lungs, livers, nerves and skin for example.

The embryos used would be clumps of cells, ranging from a single fertilised egg, to a ball of a few scores of cells. They have no nervous system, discernible feeling,

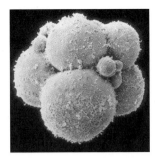

A human embryo at the 8-cell stage

thoughts or consciousness. The stem cells have the ability to develop into any of the specialist cells that make up the human body. Scientists hope that they will be able to 'instruct' these to develop into the required specialist cells and organs, that could then be used to treat someone.

So far scientists have been able to isolate stem cells in mice and make them specialise, but have not been able to create specific organs. Research is also being undertaken in 'growing' tissues in animals that can be transplanted into humans. Pigs in particular have been used in recent experiments, but there is a very serious concern that new diseases might also be passed on together with the new organ. The Roslin Institute in Scotland (the creators of Dolly the sheep) stopped its research with pigs in 2000 for this very reason. The professor in charge was quoted as saying, 'I think the concern is mainly unknown viruses. That's the frightening thing.'

Screening of women for some inherited diseases is already going on. Genetic counselling has so far consisted largely of warning couples of possible illnesses of an inherited nature so that they can decide whether to risk a pregnancy, or in the case of detecting a disease in a foetus of offering a termination of the pregnancy. However, if such genetic illness are curable in the future then the prospect opens up of screening for a much wider range of illness in the future. Is this a step towards 'perfect babies' by design, rather than letting nature take its course?

> These moral questions are likely to feature in exam questions.

What if a baby, when it is born, can provide the cells needed to cure another family member? Does this mean it is right to create a baby as a 'cure' for someone else (see the story of the Nash family in 8.1 above)? Also, if the disease for which the cells are needed to provide the cure is in one of the parents could this lead to babies being planned specifically to provide cells for their parent's treatment and thus become 'spare parts' for the parent?

As medical developments continue to come along our ethical viewpoint on these issues as a society is likely to change and perhaps become more liberal. However, some will always have objections, often of a religious nature. Tim Hedgley, who chairs the fertility charity 'Issue' said, 'If I had said to you 20 years ago that I knew a consultant who wanted to rip the heart out of a dead body and put it in a living person, and attach electrodes to restart it, you'd think I was mad, but now heart transplants are normal' (quoted in the *Observer*, September 2000).

The preservation of endangered species

AQA A	M5
AQA B	M5
EDEXCEL	M6
OCR	M4, M6

One advantage of cloning is that it gives humans the potential to repair the damage it has inflicted on the world's wildlife. In November 2000, Bessie, an ordinary American cow, gave birth to a gaur (an Indian bison), a giant ox-like creature from southern Asia, which is at present under threat. This was done using the same medical technique as used to create Dolly the sheep. 692 cells from the skin of a bull gaur were taken after the beast had died a natural death. The DNA from the eggs of a group of cows was then removed and the gaur cells implanted in its place before the eggs were returned to the cows – meaning they would give birth to a gaur if they became fertilised and pregnancy went to full term. The gaur DNA and the eggs were fused together by a small jolt of electricity. It is a reflection of how primitive our current work is that of the 692 eggs implanted with the alien DNA only 81 grew sufficiently to be implanted, only eight cows became pregnant, five of these miscarried. Bessie became the first large animal in the world to have conceived another species of animal. If the technique can be refined some scientists talk of being able to produce large numbers of animals at present under threat of extinction – such as giant pandas, who could have bears as surrogate mothers, for example.

> Even if humanity is responsible for the decline of some species – is this a case of two wrongs don't make a right?

The possibility of recreating extinct species also raises its head. This has so far only been attempted with the bucardo – a Pyrenean mountain goat, the very last one of which died when it was killed by a falling tree in 2000. Scientists were able to take tissue samples for freezing very quickly after the death, so the DNA would not be damaged. It could now be possible to use the egg of an ordinary goat, with its own DNA replaced by that of the last bucardo, to re-create the species that is now extinct. However, a major problem of an entire species created from a single animal is that they would all be genetically identical, and therefore likely to fall prey to the same diseases, which could then threaten them all.

The possibility of obtaining DNA from animals long dead, but found preserved in perma-frost has also been discussed – for example, the creation of a living woolly mammoth, which died out in the last Ice Age. However, it is most likely that the DNA will have been damaged over time and so this possibility belongs, for the time being at least, in the realms of science fiction.

Is there anything actually wrong with re-creating extinct species?

> **KEY POINT**
>
> Scientists will need to be joined by ethicists and philosophers for the wider debate about the extent to which cloning is acceptable. There are times when society places limits on what science would be able to achieve in theory. For the moment human cloning and 'designer babies', for example, remain socially unacceptable.

Progress check

1 What are the only human embryos currently available for research?
2 What areas of research are permitted on embryos by current law?
3 What diseases are currently those being talked of as the most likely to be cured by genetic means?
4 What are the immature cells serving no specific purpose in a newly developing embryo called?
5 Why is Bessy the cow important in the development of cloning?

5 She was the first large animal to give birth to an offspring of another species implanted in her egg.
4 Stem cells.
3 Parkinson's disease; Huntington's disease; Alzheimer's disease.
2 Treatment for fertility, miscarriage and congenital disease.
1 Embryos that are left over following the completion of fertility treatment.

8.5 Genetically modified foods

After studying this section you should be able to:

- *identify issues of scientific controversy surrounding GM food development*
- *state arguments for and against GM foods*

LEARNING SUMMARY

Why do we need GM foods?

AQA A	M5
AQA B	M4, M5
EDEXCEL	M6
OCR	M4, M6

Key points from AS

- **Genetically modified foods**
  Revise AS pages 114–115

Genetically modified foods are foods whose original genetic composition has been modified by scientists – e.g. made disease resistant, able to produce increased yield, able to withstand harsher temperatures, etc.

Prince Charles, who farms organically on his estate in Gloucestershire, raised the following ten questions that hit at the heart of the GM food controversy.

1 *Do we need GM food in this country?*
   - He feels the technology is for those who farm on an industrial scale.
   - The government says biotechnology offers enormous opportunities.

2 *Is GM food safe for us to eat?*
   - The Prince says independent research, not work by GM firms themselves, is needed.
   - The government says scientists, not politicians have to answer.

3 *Why are the rules for approving GM foods so much less stringent than those for new medicines that use the same technology?*
   - The Prince says drugs have to undergo rigorous testing.
   - The government says seeds are subject to testing before approval is given to grow a crop from them.

4 *How much do we know about environmental consequences of GM crops?*
   - The Prince is concerned that pollen from GM maize in the USA has caused damage to the caterpillars of the Monarch butterfly.
   - The government says that it is the chance of unforeseen long-term effects that makes large-scale independent monitoring and testing so important.

5 *Is it sensible to plant test crops without strict regulations?*
   - The Prince worries that there is only a voluntary code of practice.
   - The Government is looking for an agreement with the GM industry to form the basics for future statutory regulations.

6 *How will consumers be able to exercise genuine choice?*
   - The Prince is concerned that GM crops will contaminate non-GM crops, whatever food labels might say.
   - The government says that testing will establish the dangers, if any, of contamination of non-GM crops.

7 *If something goes wrong with a GM crop, who will be held responsible?*
   - The Prince has concerns about both human health and the environment.
   - The government says liability is being discussed, but there are no regulations.

8 *Are GM crops really the only way to feed the world's growing population?*
   - The Prince feels that argument is like emotional blackmail.
   - The government says it is a question for scientists.

9 *What effect will GM crops have on the people of the world's poorest countries?*
   - The Prince believes the creation of sustainable livelihoods is key, and is not sure how GM crops will help.
   - The government says that individual states should in future be able to have power over multinationals to move GM crops and food between countries.

10 *What sort of world do we want to live in?*
   - The Prince talks about the industrialisation of life itself – redesigning the natural world for the sake of convenience.
   - The government says it wants a safe world – so it is proceeding with caution.

Arguments put forward in favour of GM foods

- Over the next 25 years and more, the world will find it increasingly difficult to feed itself. The supply of arable land will continue to shrink, while the population increases. The only alternative to GM foods is to dramatically increase the use of powerful chemical herbicides and pesticides.
- People in Britain have been eating and drinking products from chicken, pork and beef fed on GM-rich diets for more than a decade with no ill effects.
- Half the soya bean crop in the USA is GM – yields have increased by 25% because they are no longer susceptible to pests like the corn borer.
- Current research to genetically modify tomatoes and bananas so they contain the hepatitis-B vaccine could provide an extremely cheap and effective way of ridding the world of this potentially lethal illness. Similar vaccines could be given in the same way in future.
- It would be possible to produce seed strains that would allow 10–20% of a crop to be weeds before their resistance to the weeds kicks in, so that food sources would still be available for natural wildlife, such as farmland birds.
- If plants could be modified so that a fixed proportion of their nitrogen came from the air, rather than all coming from the soil, there would be less need to spray fertilisers – which have bad side-effects, on water courses in particular.

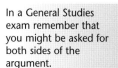

In a General Studies exam remember that you might be asked for both sides of the argument.

Arguments put forward by opponents of GM foods

Greenpeace activists destroying a GM crop

- Broader ecosystems and biodiversity, including wildlife, would be wiped out by the creation of what are in effect sterile monocultures.
- There is a threat that genes could leap species barriers. A German study found the genes used in modifying a crop of oilseed rape was found in bees that gathered its pollen. With the consequences of BSE still prominent in our minds, can we risk such a step into the unknown?
- Over 2 million tonnes of GM crops are imported to make animal feed. The government had said that the heating process used in the process of manufacturing animal feed containing GM material would destroy it, but there is now evidence that some survives. There is a fear that this could introduce alien genes to animals and potentially to humans. Farmworkers inhaling dust could also be affected.
- Greenpeace is concerned that GM crops risk inflicting irreparable damage to the environment.

> **KEY POINT**
>
> Many who oppose the growing of GM crops on UK farms are not necessarily totally opposed to the concept. They are worried about the current lack of laboratory research and the possible danger to environments and wildlife, including humans. Many are seeking a five-year ban until laboratory research has been able to provide answers, followed by a detailed review of the evidence.

Progress check

1. Who do both Prince Charles and the government think should be responsible for ensuring the safety of GM food?
2. Why will arable land be required to produce greater amounts of food over the coming years?
3. The use of GM maize in the USA has increased crop yields by how much?
4. Evidence from what insects has suggested that GM food enables genes to jump species?

1 Independent scientists. 2 Because of increasing world population and diminishing land availability. 3 25%.
4 Bees in a German study.

Sample question and model answer

1

Discuss the view that 'cloning is a promise, not a threat'.

Step 1
Introduction.

- Define 'cloning' – e.g. 'Cloning is the process by which single cells of an animal or plant are used to create another part or whole of the same species with exactly the same form of the parent.'

Take care not to undertake analysis in the introduction.

- Establish in one or two sentences that there are scientific, religious and ethical questions that need to be examined.
- Explain that it holds out hope of cure for many people who will currently die from genetic illnesses like Huntington's disease.

Step 2
Arguments to support the view that cloning is a promise.

- For some illnesses it could herald the idea of treatment without medicines.
- Will allow for effective treatment of physical damage to the body – burns and fractures, for example.

Support these with some of the examples from the chapter.

- Cells taken from a healthy member of a family could be used to treat some forms of illness in other family members – e.g. to enable the development of bone marrow where a person's body could not do this without treatment.
- In Nature – surrogate parents could be used to increase numbers where a species is threatened, by placing the DNA of a threatened animal inside the prepared egg of the host mother.
- Even extinct species could be re-created with good DNA to help repair the damage humanity has done to the Earth.

Step 3
Arguments that cloning is a threat.

- The act of creation belongs to God and not to human beings.
- There are examples of terrible consequences where man has attempted to manipulate nature – we simply do not know what we might unleash.
- The possibility that children will be conceived and born so that some of their cells could be used to treat brothers, sisters, or parents suggests that they have been born as 'spare parts'.

Again – seek to qualify by giving examples and illustration from the chapter.

- There is the distinct possibility that we would quickly move into a world of 'designer babies' in which doctors would be able to become very wealthy by charging parents to create the exact baby they want.
- Nature will always have its way in the end – the re-creation of a species from single cells of a dead example will give the whole population an identical genetic make up, making them highly susceptible to disease, in-breeding, etc.

Conclusion.

- Pull both sides of the argument together in a couple of succinct sentences.
- Come to a reasoned conclusion that acknowledges there are conflicting perspectives, but nevertheless setting out whether you believe that cloning is indeed a 'promise', or a 'threat'.

For example:

Medical and scientific progress involving the manipulation of cells in both humans and animals is an area for much research at the moment. While many take the view, often based on their personal religious views, that God is the sole creator of life and that we 'mock' Him by trying to copy His creation, it seems probable that within a generation we will be regarding 'cloning' as a normal part of medicine. Hopefully we will not be talking about the cloning of entire human beings, but rather about the new lives gained by millions of people who in the past would have been condemned to die from genetic diseases. This will indeed be a promise worth striving to attain: 'cloning' is indeed a promise for the future.

Practice examination questions

Short answer questions

1 Briefly summarise the issues that need to be considered in determining whether life support should be withdrawn from a patient who will never recover and is in a permanent vegetative state.

2 Outline the main steps that have been taken to limit air pollution.

3 What three areas of research are currently permitted using human embryos?

Essay question

4 Discuss the view that there will be times when it will be morally acceptable for a doctor to terminate the life of another human being.

Chapter 9

Science and culture

The following topics are covered in this chapter:

- The nature of scientific and religious beliefs
- How technology has supported cultural development
- The social and cultural acceptance of scientific advances

9.1 The nature of scientific and religious beliefs

After studying this section you should be able to:

- describe differences between the nature of beliefs in science and religion
- discuss whether science invalidates religion
- examine critically arguments for the existence of a deity

The nature of beliefs in science and religion

AQA A	M4, M5
AQA B	M4, M6
EDEXCEL	M6
OCR	M4, M6

Key points from AS

- **Science and culture**
  Revise AS pages 119–121

> The idea of objective research is at the heart of scientific study.

It is in the nature of science that its 'beliefs' are based on systematic verification. This goes back to the time of Galileo and Descartes who lived in the 17th century. They took the idea of induction and deduction, (discussed in Revise AS General Studies) and added the requirement that scientific work be based on a research model underpinned by a mathematical basis. It was this that led to the development of the laws of science, starting with Newton's Law on Gravity published in 1687. Newton and others were also working on the invention of calculus, and it was this that provided the foundation for today's sophisticated level of science and maths.

The 18th century saw the rise of the materialistic sciences, such as chemistry. This led to the systematic development of the understanding of the physical world in which we live – including the discovery of the gasses that make up the air that we breathe to sustain our lives. Life could begin to be explained on a 'physio-chemical' basis, rather than simply in theological terms in which all of creation was part of the work of a deity. The 19th century saw the rise to prominence of work in the biological sciences, most prominent being the mighty work *On The Origin of Species* in 1859 – the published research work of Charles Darwin. This caused a huge and sustained clash between scientists and theologians over the theory that human beings developed as a result of evolution rather than creation by God.

From a scientific perspective (a perspective that seeks to eliminate the unknown) the history and development of the universe can be thought of as follows.

- At some point, up to 18 billion years ago, the universe began with a 'Big Bang' – a huge explosion of gaseous material that resulted in the creation of the universe, which has been expanding ever since.
- Matter emerged from the Big Bang which began to undergo a process whereby stars and galaxies were formed, which developed in predictable ways.
- Our solar system was formed 4–5 billion years ago, although the mechanism for this remains unclear.
- Life on our planet began with micro-organisms around 3.5–4 billion years ago, leading to the appearance of multi-cellular creatures around 700 million years ago, developing into humans who colonised land around 4.25 million years ago. The point at which primitive micro-organisms changed into multi-cellular creatures was a profound development.
- A variety of creatures evolved with the process of natural selection leading to changes and divergence of life forms that became increasingly specialised to fit particular niches in the natural environment.

> Many people who believe in God have no problem with this rational view of creation.

- Human beings evolved in their modern form around 100 000 years ago, and continue to evolve (in terms of growing taller, for example).

How does scientific and religious thinking differ?

- Science is objective and its ideas are constructed through thought and observation that is tested through experiment. Definitive answers are sought and there is no room for mystery.
- Religion is a world of personal experience and trust. It is believed that the development of the world since its creation could not have happened as an accident, that there has to be some guiding force. For example, Dr John Polkinghorne, a theoretical physicist and mathematician at Queens' College Cambridge who is also a Christian priest, argues that the equilibrium that governs the relative strengths of the forces of nature is very fine. If there was just one small change in the balance, such as an increase in gravity, it would become impossible for complex molecules, such as carbon, to form. Without carbon, life on Earth would not be possible. This suggests that this planet is unique in the universe. Its existence could be either coincidence or the result of divine creation. Dr Polkinghorne argues that since science follows mathematical models there is an order to everything, so creation was no accident. If humans developed simply as a result of natural selection – the survival of the fittest – our brains would not have progressed beyond the stage of solving the Stone Age problems of survival. The fact that the human brain has such extraordinary powers points, he believes, to divine creation.
- Science is limited in its areas of study. Professor Stephen Hawking, another believer in a deity, wrote that, 'Although science may solve the problem of how the universe began, it cannot answer the question, "Why does the universe bother to exist?" I don't know the answer to that' (*Black Holes and Baby Universes*, 1993).

> Science does not *rule out* the idea of a deity, nor does it seek to prove it.

Science can tell us about:
- atoms and molecules (physics and chemistry)
- the mechanisms of living things (biology)
- the structure of the Earth (geology).

However, it cannot tell us about:
- right and wrong
- purpose and meaning
- the importance of personal opinion.

The idea of faith

Faith is a belief, not a knowledge. St Paul, writing in the New Testament of the Bible, says it is, 'the assurance of things hoped for, the conviction of things not seen.' It often consists of two elements:
- the belief in the existence of a deity
- the 'objective' element of the acceptance of a 'body of truth' that tells us about this God. For example, Christians believe in the birth, death and coming back to life of Jesus who they believe was not only a historical human figure, but also one part of the God they worship. Similarly, Muslims believe the teachings of the prophet Mohammed about their God, Allah.

Some religious thinkers have written about a 'leap of faith', with the believer making the jump from the world of the known and the verifiable to the world of faith and personal knowledge of God that leads to the promise of an eternal after life. To those with religious faith death is very much a beginning, not an end.

Although all philosophers who believe in a deity believe that while He is a mystery beyond human understanding, we can nevertheless begin to have a limited knowledge of God. However, as far back as the 17th century the French mathematician Pascal contrasted the 'God of philosophers', with complex 'proofs' for His existence, with the 'God of faith', who millions experienced as a caring and loving reality. While many theologians may feel it is wrong to try to give God a gender, or a personality, many believers create human analogies – in fact Christianity talks about 'God the Father'.

Many in our modern society would argue that belief in a God was necessary at one time to provide a rationale for the unknown and unexplained. Such a belief also held out a hope, in a world in which disease and starvation were an everyday occurrence, of a better life that would come after death. In Medieval times the world was referred to as a 'vale of tears'. With our ability to cure illness, feed people and live contented lives lasting, on average, over 70 years have we now lost the need to have some kind of belief in the supernatural? For those who believe that there is a God, there are four basic areas that underpin their faith:

- **Purpose** – that God planned and created the universe, that it has purpose and was not some kind of fantastic accident that led to the amazingly complex and intelligent creatures known as humans.
- **Personhood** – that God created us as a personal act. We are not an accidental by-product of the random movement of atoms, but beings, people.
- **Morality** – if we are merely accidents in space and time how can words like 'right' and 'wrong' have any meaning, and how can they apply to human beings any more than they could to any other randomly created creatures on the Earth?
- **Future** – if we humans are accidental by-products of a physical universe then we have no future – our experience ends at death, and all life will end when the sun expands (if we have not managed to kill each other by that stage!).

Arguments for the existence of God

There have been many attempts to 'prove' the existence of God, particularly in Christianity following the development of the ideas in the 'Age of Reason'. The 17th-century theologian St Thomas Aquinas put forward his five proofs forming the basis of the doctrine of the Catholic Church.

The 'proof' of God is not based on scientific law or thinking, i.e. 'experiment and verification'.

1 Any change that comes about needs something to cause it to happen – an agent of change. There therefore needed to be something to bring about the first change – God.
2 If everything in the world has a cause and effect then the 'chain of causation' that triggered this off has to exist.
3 The 'contingent' facts of the world – the facts that might not have been as they actually are – presupposes a 'necessary being' who guided their paths.
4 If we can grade things, and put them into an order of 'higher' and 'lower' (with humans being the highest form of life) there is a hierarchy that is like a triangle and that at some point there has to be the pinnacle of that hierarchy – the ultimate perfection.
5 The order and design in nature demands as its source a Being possessing the highest wisdom who has created everything according to a Divine plan.

It is thought by many that the existence of a God cannot be proved, or disproved, by humans. Believers think that there is a cumulative force to their beliefs that amounts to a strong probability, especially when these are set beside the personal religious experience felt by believers. Ultimately, belief is an act of faith.

Will we eventually live in a world without religion?

In the advanced economies of the world the percentage of people proclaiming a religious belief and attending acts of worship is in decline. In the UK this decline seems to be accelerating, although there are many examples of places of worship that can still attract large numbers, particularly in the evangelical tradition. The steepest decline has been in attendance at the Church of England, maybe because at one time it was merely part of 'polite society' to go to church.

People have always sought explanations for the world around them. Over the centuries we have been able to explain more and more about the world, and create more and more things. At the start of the new millennium this process seems to be speeding up – developments such as genetic modification and cloning helping us discover new aspects to the creation of life. In such circumstances do we still need a God – or are we, in fact, in danger of trying to become God-like ourselves?

There are many scientists still committed and practising members of religious groups. However, studies have shown that declining numbers of scientists believe in God. Even in the United States, where a high percentage of the general population still profess a belief in God, a study undertaken by Larson and Witham in 1998 showed that among scientists who were members of the National Academy of Sciences only 7% had a personal belief in God, compared with 20.8% who declared themselves agnostic and 72.2% who disbelieved (published in the *Scientific American*, 1998).

> **KEY POINT**
>
> Science is based on laws, hypotheses, experiment and verification. It seeks to be rational and objective. Religion is based on faith and personal experience. They are therefore not directly comparable – science does not even attempt to prove or disprove religion. However, as science makes ever greater strides it would seem to many that there is no longer a need to seek to explain the world in terms of its creation by a God.

Progress check

1 The development of modern scientific methodology owes much to which two 17th-century scientists?
2 Which academic work stirred up a huge controversy between science and religion in the 19th century?
3 Who wrote the five 'proofs' for the existence of God?
4 A recent study showed what percentage of scientists in the US National Academy of Sciences had a personal belief in God?

1 Galileo and Descartes. 2 The Origin of Species. 3 St Thomas Aquinas. 4 7%.

9.2 How technology has supported cultural development

After studying this section you should be able to:

- *describe how popular culture is dependent on technology for its transmission*
- *explain the basis on which this transmission takes place*

LEARNING SUMMARY

Radio, TV and video

AQA A	M4
AQA B	M4, M6
EDEXCEL	M4, M6
OCR	M4, M6

Over the last century popular culture has changed dramatically. In Victorian times domestic entertainment was based around the piano, reading or story-telling. Trips out might include visits to the theatre or concert hall. Since that era, popular culture has been transformed by technological developments in many fields – for example, radio, TV and video, hi-fi, photography and cinema.

Key points from AS

• **Creativity and innovation**
Revise AS pages 81–84

Since radio and TV are so important in today's world it's important for you to understand the basic principles of how they work.

Radio and television has had a bigger impact on our lives than any other single thing, allowing access to entertainment and sport, news and education, and the ability to get access to a wide range of culture, both popular and classical.

How radio and TV work

The use of electromagnetic waves to carry sounds and pictures has revolutionised communications. Radio waves are at the low frequency end of the electromagnetic spectrum, carrying information at the speed of light (186 000 miles per second). Long, medium and short radio waves, with wavelengths between 2 kilometres and 10 metres long, can 'bend' round obstacles like hills and therefore these waves are suitable for local radio broadcasts. The waves are reflected both by the Earth and by the ionosphere (a layer in the atmosphere) – they bounce between the two and can be transmitted over very long distances. Short waves are the best reflected, hence their use in international broadcasts. VHF (very high frequency) and UHF (ultra high frequency) have shorter wavelengths. They can only travel in a straight line and pass straight through the ionosphere, and these waves are therefore chiefly used for TV and local radio.

The transmission of music and voice by radio needs a 'carrier wave' to supplement the basic fixed-frequency wave, this second signal being imposed in a process called 'modulation'. One form is 'amplitude modulation' (AM) where the amplitude (volume) of the wave is varied, the second is 'frequency modulation' (FM) which determines pitch, where the frequency is varied. A microphone produces a small electrical current representing the sounds made into it. The wave profile that equates to this current is then superimposed on the carrier wave, broadcast and finally separated out again at the other end by the radio receiver. An amplifier increases the power of the signal so it can operate a speaker, re-creating the original sounds made into the microphone.

The use of radio waves to carry pictures, only became practical in 1926. The basic principle in the creation of a television picture is the breaking down of the image into a series of dots which are transmitted and displayed on the screen so quickly that the eye sees them as a complete picture. John Logie Baird was the first to demonstrate a TV picture, based on a mechanical method of scanning an image into lines of dots of light. This was quickly superseded by an all-electric system developed by Zurorykin, a Russian-born engineer working in the USA, whose first practical camera was produced in 1931. A modern TV camera measures the light intensity at each point of an image and this is encoded on the radio wave and transmitted. In the television set the signal then has to be decoded. The set is basically a cathode tube in which a 'gun' fires a beam of electrons at a luminescent screen – as they strike it, the screen lights up. To make up the complete picture the beam is scanned to and fro in a series of 625 horizontal lines covering the whole screen in 1/25th of a second.

Because the VHF and UHF wavebands that carry TV signals are not reflected by the ionosphere many transmitters are needed to achieve complete national coverage. For TV transmissions between longer distances satellites are used to pick up signals and beam them back to Earth. The satellite signals are too weak to be picked up by an ordinary aerial, so they have to be re-broadcast by ground transmitters. In recent years special satellite-dish-aerials have been developed so that direct broadcasting from satellites is now possible (satellite channels). TV signals can also be fed through cable, so networks featuring films, sport, news and so on can be offered exclusively to those paying a subscription.

Videotext can also be displayed on a TV screen. It is transmitted as part of the signal and decoded by the receiver. Each page takes about a quarter of a second to transmit and the system runs through a 'magazine' of around 150 pages, taking

30 seconds to complete the whole cycle. The viewer can stop the cycle at any page by keying in its number.

Video recorders allow TV programmes to be recorded onto magnetic tape. Signals are recorded as magnetic patterns on the tape. In order to get the mass of details needed, the recording head in the video machine rotates as the tape runs past it, so that, in effect, the information is laid out diagonally across the tape, reducing the length needed to make a recording.

Hi-fi

AQA A	M4
AQA B	M4, M6
EDEXCEL	M4, M6
OCR	M4, M6

Hi-fi is short for 'high fidelity' and refers to the high quality of the sound reproduction that is now possible. Sound has been recorded and transmitted for over 100 years, but there has been a revolution in quality since the 1980s.

There are three forms of recorded sound:

• vinyl discs, where a stylus travels along a groove picking up the sound
• tapes, onto which sound is recorded as magnetic patterns
• digital (compact) discs, or CDs in which a laser light beam reads patterns of binary digits.

The first recording was by Thomas Edison's phonograph in 1877. Sound vibrations were converted into a groove on the surface of a cylinder. These could not, however, be easily mass produced, so they were superseded by flat discs which became called gramophone records. Once a master copy of a recording had been produced as many copies as needed could be produced. Electrical systems of recording using microphones was introduced in 1920 – a big step forward.

Long playing records (LPs) were first introduced in 1946. They had a very fine groove, needing a much lighter stylus pressure and a finer point, so that diamonds or sapphires were used as the 'needles'. These discs could play for more than 20 minutes on each side (as opposed to the previous four minutes) and had high-quality sound reproduction. They marked the arrival of the hi-fi age.

Recording onto tape originated in the early 1930s using tapes made of steel. However, in 1935 the introduction of strong plastic tape covered by iron (ferrous) oxide came from Germany. Domestic tape recorders became popular from the 1950s. Sound is recorded by passing the tape in front of a recording head that is an electromagnet fed by the electrical signals originating from a microphone. A magnetic pattern corresponding to the sounds is created on the tape as the iron oxide aligns itself to the magnetic field. The commonest format for listening to tapes is the compact cassette, introduced by the Dutch electrical firm Philips in 1963. Their effectiveness as a hi-fi medium was enormously enhanced by the invention of a noise reduction system which eliminated hiss by Roy Dolby, an American engineer.

Popular culture on discs can be both pop and classical music – both can have their place in a General Studies exam.

Compact disc players have been made possible by modern electronics. The discs contain sounds recorded digitally as a series of binary numbers, or 'bits'. The sound is sampled 40 000 times a second as its amplitude and frequency (sound and pitch) are recorded as a binary number. The bits are recorded as a series of pits or blank spaces in the surface of the disc – each pit measuring less than a 100th of a millimetre across. Made of clear PVC coated with shiny aluminium and covered with a plastic laminate, CDs have the major advantage of low distortion and a good signal-to-noise ratio – and they don't get scratched like vinyl discs. They were first launched commercially in 1982.

As the CD spins in its player the laser light beam is either reflected or scattered depending on whether it hits a blank space or a pit. As it scans, the laser picks up a series of binary signals, either 1s or 0s, the original binary digits of the recording. These are converted into analogue currents, amplified and fed to speakers.

Photography

Remember that photography is not only a leisure pursuit – it is also a recognised art medium.

The first photographic image was produced onto a sheet of pewter by Frenchman Nicéphore Niepce in 1826. Today, digital cameras produce images that are produced through computers.

A traditional camera is basically a box that is lightproof except for the lens which can be opened to project an image onto a film inside the camera. The film is coated with an emulsion whose chemical properties are changed by exposure to light and which, after processing, can reproduce the image. The emulsion is made of silver halide grains suspended in gelatine. After exposure to light and chemical processing (developing) the grains become black metallic silver. When unexposed silver halide in parts wholly or partially untouched by light is dissolved away, the picture becomes permanent (fixed). However, it is a negative that is created – dark areas show up as light and vice versa. This was overcome by the invention of the negative/positive technique by Englishman William Fox Talbot in 1841. The paper negative was placed against another, unexposed, piece of sensitised paper and light passed through the back of the negative. The sensitised paper, when developed, became a positive print. With this step forward multiple copies of positive photographs could be produced from the original negative.

Later developments occurred with the wet-plate process, followed later by the dry-plate process. The former originated in 1851 – a jelly-like coating called collodion was poured onto a glass plate which was then dipped into silver-nitrate solution. The plate was then exposed in the camera and developed before the plate dried. This enabled portrait and landscape photography to develop, and photographers started to go on expeditions taking their tripods (since the process needed a long exposure during which the camera had to be perfectly still to avoid blur), glass plates and darkroom tent.

The dry-plate method started in 1870, and led to the commercial manufacture of glass plates. The dry emulsion was far more sensitive and, using a spring-operated shutter for the first time, exposure time was cut to 1/25th of a second, so a tripod was no longer essential.

In 1888 the American George Eastman made the first Kodak camera, advertised with the slogan, 'You press the button, we do the rest'. The major advance in this was the introduction of roll film that was wound on between shots. In the 1920s the first 'miniature' camera (all things are relative) that could use 35mm film was marketed by Leica. This led to the popularisation of the single lens reflex (SLR) camera, which allowed the user to see the exact picture being taken through the view finder.

Colour photography became practical after the appearance of Kodachrome and Agfacolor film in the 1930s, using three separate emulsions to record blue, green and red parts of the image. The film was processed by dyeing each layer with the corresponding complementary colour (yellow, magenta and cyan), which produced three positive images, one above the other, which together reproduced the original colours of the image. In the mid-20th century the Polaroid camera was developed by American Edwin Land. This creates instant pictures by processing the picture inside the camera.

The very latest technology has now created the digital camera, which has done away with the need to use film. Images are seen instantly on a small screen on the back of the camera, and if you want to keep it you can store it, before later downloading it onto a computer. It can then be printed off, but it could also be enhanced, or directly e-mailed to somebody. This represents a very major advance in the development of photography.

Cinema

AQA A	M4
AQA B	M4, M6
EDEXCEL	M4, M6
OCR	M4, M6

The first photographer to record movement was English-born Eadweard Muybridge, who photographed animals and people at a zoo, and in 1880 projected them through his 200Praxiscope. More practical was Frenchman Etienne Marey's invention of 1882 which was a 'gun' that took a sequence of pictures on a revolving photographic plate. However, it was the invention of plastic film by George Eastman (see 'Photography' above) that enabled Thomas Edison to invent a practical method of photographing movement. His assistant W.K.L. Dickson went on to develop a camera and a viewer that enabled an observer to watch a continuous loop of film, launched commercially in 1894 as a slot machine for solo viewing. To prove that Thomas Edison, although a practical genius, did not get everything right – he did not try to develop projected films because he thought they would be seen by too many people at once to make any money! However, there were also others who could lay claim to having invented motion pictures – in particular the brothers August and Louis Lumière, who gave their first public show in December 1895.

Edison's first film was called 'Fred Ott's Sneeze' and showed a lab assistant sneezing – it was less than a minute long. All his film was shot in a studio using very cumbersome equipment, while the Lumières had a portable camera and filmed real life, including famous footage of a train arriving at a Paris terminus.

The early films were made in black and white, although some were tinted into an appropriate colour for the scene. The films had no sound track, and the cinemas often employed pianists to play appropriate mood music. In 1926 Warner Brothers produced a synchronised music track on a disc to be played alongside the film. The following year, 1927, saw Al Jolson starring in 'The Jazz Singer', which was the first 'talkie' that contained songs and a snatch of dialogue. The method by which the sound was recorded onto the film itself as a varying strip of light came into use in 1928 using a system developed in Germany. The first experiments in colour were as early as 1915. In 1941 Technicolor introduced a three-colour system onto a single film. This was superseded by the Eastman Color system in 1952.

Animation became popular in the 1930s and remains so to the present day. Walt Disney's studio first introduced Mickey Mouse in the film 'Steamboat Willy' in the late 1920s and went on to make many classic animated films. There are two types of animation – the first consists of a series of individually drawn pictures filmed in sequence (like the classic Disney films), the second uses models filmed using stop-action photography, (the Wallace and Grommit films are successful recent examples of this).

> **KEY POINT**
> Radio, television, recorded music, photography and film constitute important aspects of the arts – the first two as channels for 'onward transmission' of the arts and popular culture. All of these aspects have blossomed as a result of technological developments. As well as appreciating these various media, you should also appreciate their relevant technology.

Progress check

1 What do AM and FM stand for in radio transmission?
2 How are live TV transmissions between continents sent?
3 What are the three forms of recorded sound?
4 In which field was William Fox Talbot a pioneer?
5 Which two firms pioneered the production of colour film?

1 Amplitude modulation and frequency modulation. 2 Via satellite, because the radio waves used don't 'bend'. 3 Vinyl discs; tapes; digital (compact) discs. 4 Photography. 5 Kodachrome and Agfacolor, produced by the Eastman and Agfa companies.

9.3 The social and cultural acceptance of scientific advances

After studying this section you should be able to:

- *explain how technology is introducing positive change to our lives*
- *describe one area where religious belief has been transformed through our scientific knowledge*
- *discuss the morality of a medical procedure*
- *outline a controversial area in which science has sought to support agriculture*

LEARNING SUMMARY

Key points from AS

- **Genetically modified foods**
  Revise AS pages 114–115
- **Science and God**
  Revise AS pages 120–121
- **Medical ethics**
  Revise AS page 125

We often take advances in science and technology for granted and rarely reflect on what a dramatic effect they have on changing our society and culture. The aim of this section is therefore to take four areas and look at how changes in them have altered the thinking and way of life of millions of people – and brought with them associated problems.

These four issues are representative of ones that might crop up in your exam.

Home computing

AQA A	M5
AQA B	M4, M5, M6
EDEXCEL	M6
OCR	M4, M6

Try to think of positive ways in which you personally use ICT for study.

Many young people use computers at home to supplement the work they do in ICT as part of their school work. Computers are used to teach subjects across the whole curriculum and learning can be added to at home through working on projects. As part of your post-16 studies you may be following a Key Skills course containing a range of ICT elements. You might use your computer to store information, tabulate research or look for details on the internet or on CD-Roms.

All of this is obviously very important in supporting your studies, but for the wider population the computer at home has far wider uses and for increasing numbers it enables them to abandon having to work in an office. A home computer allows you to communicate immediately with colleagues, often supported by e-mail (electronic-mail). This is perhaps the principal way in which our society and culture (and our view of the work ethic, for example) has been affected by the computer.

Teleworking

By the turn of the new millennium the global number of 'teleworkers', as they are known, had reached 10 million and by 2005 it will be over 16 million. Alan Denbigh, who is the Chair of the Telework and Telecentre Association said, 'The conventional 9–5 workplace is actually unsuitable for work. The buildings are often unhealthy and there are constant interruptions.'

What are the best and worst features of teleworking?

Best features
- It saves time and money on travelling.
- There is more control over your work and other parts of your life.
- There are no interruptions, gossip or office politics.
- It gives an improved quality of life.
- It allows greater opportunity for community involvement.
- It is better for the environment.

Worst features
- It requires high personal motivation.
- It requires space at home to work in.

- It makes people more dependent on technology.
- There is a potential lack of human contact.
- People can be 'frozen out' of office politics.
- It is harder to escape from the 'office'.
- There is less distinction between work and home.

e-mail and the internet

The instant global communication provided by e-mail and the internet is a staggering concept. However, it can be abused and there have been several high-profile stories of the system being abused by office workers circulating obscene material to work colleagues – which led in some cases to people being dismissed from their jobs. What we often forget is that our messages can be read by people other than the intended recipients. In 2000 the Home Office confirmed it was spending £25 million on building an e-mail surveillance centre at MI5 because of concern at its use by criminals. Service providers like Freeserve have tracking mechanisms, so that the government will be able to read everything that passes over the internet.

There are now some examples of government interference from around the world:

Any debate on freedom of speech should now include electronic communication.

- 'cyber dissidents' have been imprisoned in China after circumventing the government-run internet provider.
- In Burma, the government's 'cyberspace warfare centre' hacks into computers that receive or send 'forbidden messages' and penalties include up to 15 years in prison.
- 45 countries restrict internet access in some way according to a study by Censor Dot Gov – including Australia which is trying to prevent access to websites peddling pornography.
- Saudia Arabia has delayed providing access to the internet until technology is available to bar access to information contrary to Islamic values and dangerous to society.

The internet has certainly affected the way in which pupils learn at school or college. A survey reported in *The Guardian* in May 2000 found that:

- 10% of children no longer used reference books and relied on electronic sources, mainly the internet, for their information.
- By the age of five 15% of children have started looking things up on the Net or CD-Rom.
- By the age of 15 this has gone up to 58% – only 2% less than those using non-fiction books.

(The survey was undertaken by the Library and Information Commission.)

What about making purchases electronically? By 2000 one in 10 Britons shop on-line, and it is in the wealthy suburbs of our more prosperous towns and cities that it is most common. In fact in 'boom towns' like Chester, Southampton and Brighton internet shopping is beginning to pose real threats to traditional shops who do not trade on-line. However, other parts of the country remain largely untouched by this revolution. In the north of England, Scotland and Wales in 2000 only 16% of adults were on-line and less than 6% were frequent on-line buyers. Rural counties, and village dwellers, especially those in remote counties like Cornwall, show the greatest reluctance to shop on the net.

Problems associated with home computing

Concerns in this area relate to the fact that not everyone will have equal access to this kind of technology and people may therefore be excluded and marginalised in future society. Another concern is that some people overuse the technology and lose contact with other humans.

'Big Bang' theory

AQA A	M5
AQA B	M4, M5, M6
EDEXCEL	M6
OCR	M4, M6

As ever-fewer people attend acts of Christian worship in Britain it is hard for young people today to understand why during the reign of Queen Victoria one of the main intellectual debates was between the believers in the newly published theory of evolution and those who maintained that the creation of the world had happened exactly as set out in the Bible.

Those who continued to believe that the account contained in the Book of Genesis was literal truth took the view that the whole of creation, from the formation of the world through to its habitation by the first humans, took place in six days. Those who believed this found the new theory put forward by Charles Darwin to be totally unacceptable that all life on Earth had evolved over millions of years according to the principle of natural selection.

Today, there are still some who believe in the Genesis account and this is still taught as Creation Science in some American states, where it is illegal to teach evolution. However, most people, including modern followers in all religions, accept that evolution is a fact. This does not disprove God, but this is another area where science has transformed our lives by challenging our belief in the Divine and in creation.

The creation and destruction of the world

It is probably helpful at this point to re-read the section on science and religion earlier in this chapter. We will now contrast the pre-Darwin Christian view that on the first day of creation God created the heavens and the Earth with what modern science says about the Earth's creation and its future.

- The Earth and the universe originated in a huge, incomparably large explosion of gasses in space – the 'big bang' – that took place probably between 12–20 billion years ago.
- The universe has always been, and still is, expanding. Its ultimate fate will depend on how much matter it contains, which we do not know.
- If there is enough matter (the 'critical density') the expansion will eventually slow and stop as a result of the gravitational pull that every object will exert on each other. The expansion will then go into reverse, and with increasing speed head for the 'big crunch'.
- If the universe does not contain enough matter to reach this critical mass, gravity will not stop its expansion. About a million-million years from now all the star-making material will have been used up. The galaxies will then start to fade as stars die and are not re-cycled. Some will end up as black holes, others as cold balls of matter in which, over enormous periods of time, even the protons will decay into radiation and positrons (the positive counterparts to electrons). Neutrons will also decay into electrons and protons, so that ultimately all that currently exists in the universe will have been converted to radiation, and electrons and protons which will annihilate each other to leave yet more radiation. Black holes will 'evaporate', emitting radiation as they do so until nothing exists except radiation.
- If the amount of critical balance is precisely balanced in the universe, it would continue to expand but at an ever-decreasing speed, coming to be on the point of collapse for eternity. The two alternatives – reaching the critical density or failing to reach critical density will lead to the destruction of the universe – but if there is a critical balance the universe can survive so long as the balance exists. Some theories suggest that the 'big bang' produced this exact ratio.

The termination of pregnancy (abortion)

AQA A	M5
AQA B	M4, M5, M6
EDEXCEL	M6
OCR	M4, M6

This is an interesting area of study for students of A Level General Studies, since it is a live debate and there are people on both sides of the moral arguments who believe passionately that they are correct. The degree of passion involved has even led to the murder of people who work in abortion clinics by people seeking to defend the 'unborn child'. To the millions of followers of Roman Catholicism abortion is a serious sin against God, yet abortions have always been performed for women who, for a variety of reasons, did not want to be pregnant.

The history of abortion legislation

- Abortion was widespread in ancient times, but later became restricted or forbidden by most world religions.
- It did not become illegal in the UK until the 19th century. Parliament did this in part to protect women from the perils of unsafe surgery. The only legal grounds for an abortion was a serious risk to the life of the mother.
- The 20th century saw legislation to permit the operation in many countries – the first of which was Soviet Russia in 1920, following the Communist revolution and creation of the world's first officially atheist state. This was followed in the years after World War II by Japan and several East European states that became Communist.

> This is a good example of a 'classic' moral argument. As such it is the sort of thing often found in General Studies exams.

In the 1960s liberalised legislation became widespread, including the 1967 Act to legalise abortion in England, Scotland and Wales (it was not then, and still has not been, legalised in Northern Ireland or Eire).

There were three basic reasons for this legalisation:

- the unacceptable level of infanticide (child murder), and the death rate of women after illegal abortions
- the rapidly growing world population
- the rise of the feminist movement for the first time asserting it was 'a woman's right to choose'.

Abortion is still illegal in many Catholic and Islamic countries, although the operation can sometimes be carried out if there is a risk to the woman's life.

The reality is that in the advanced economies of the world opinion polls show clear support for abortion. This, though, brings the doctors and nurses who carry out this operation into conflict with traditional moral objections. Medicine has created a very safe technique and procedure, but does that make it right to use it?

What are the moral arguments?

Both sides would agree that it is morally wrong to kill another person, but the disagreement is over the status of the foetus – is it a living person, an 'unborn child' having the same rights to life as the child who has been born?

Arguments of those who oppose abortion

- Those who believe the foetus is a living person argue that there is no single moment between the original fertilisation of the egg to the moment of birth when the cells that make up the child are not multiplying. They believe that you cannot therefore say that on one day the foetus is a bundle of cells, but the next it is a person. Therefore it should always be regarded as human and to end the existence of a foetus is therefore to kill a person.
- Opponents of abortion show X-ray photographs of a foetus when barely the size of an adult's thumb. It clearly has elements of human appearance. They say a foetus can feel pain and distress, so it cannot merely be seen as an 'appendage' of the mother.

- The Catholic church, and Islam, claims that all life comes from God. It is His creation, and a woman becomes pregnant because it is His will. If this is accepted, then artificial contraception and abortion are attempts to thwart the will of God and therefore a sin.

Arguments of those in favour of abortion

- Supporters of abortion say that a foetus is totally a part of its mother – that without her it could not survive for an instant. To think of it as a person is therefore incorrect. They say it has the potential for life, but does not in itself have any ability to sustain its life – it is not an independent being.
- They further argue that it is possible to draw a line at which the foetus, if it were to be born, even prematurely, could be sustained and kept alive, even if this meant a major medical input. It is at this point when a foetus can start to be thought of as a person, not before.

The global development of genetically modified crops

AQA A	M5
AQA B	M4, M5, M6
EDEXCEL	M6
OCR	M4, M6

In Chapter 8 we looked at the scientific controversy surrounding the development of genetically modified food. As the 20th century ended Britain saw a 'consumer's revolt' against it, leading many of the main supermarket chains to either label clearly all the foods they sell that contain genetically modified material, or in the case of their 'own label' goods, to stop using GM ingredients at all. It is argued that the reaction against the use of these crops was so strong in the UK because of the enormous effect and consequences of BSE (Mad Cow disease). BSE was regarded as being the result of science and technology 'interfering in nature' and creating devastating disease, including the human form (Human Variant CJD) caught by some people who ate infected meat – and with some scientists predicting that CJD could develop to epidemic proportions. However, it is highly likely that we have all at some time eaten GM food in some form – a lot of tinned tomatoes and many cereals and biscuits, for example. In 1999 over 100 million acres of land were growing genetically modified crops around the world. Seventy-two per cent of these crops are grown in the United States where there has been little consumer opposition.

Opponents of GM crops on the whole are not calling for an all-out ban, but fear that developments are so rapid that their effects cannot be monitored, and that the strict 'science and safety' approach adopted by its proponents is too narrow (such an approach looks only at the immediate outcome of a specific experiment). There are concerns that the huge multinational biotech companies that are pushing GM crops, such as Monsanto and Dow Chemicals, are buying up conventional seed companies in developing countries, and that they are taking advantage of places where there is little or no control by regulations. The companies say they work within existing laws and in some cases have helped draft bio-safety legislation.

Who has been involved in the controversy in the UK?

To emphasise the complexity of the arguments and the range of perspectives, think about the array of groups and individuals who have been caught up in the debate:

The fact that so many diverse groups have an interest makes GM foods a topic ripe for an exam question.

- scientists
- the popular press
- consumers
- traders
- international bureaucrats
- politicians
- academics
- lawyers
- ethicists in universities
- consumer and environmental groups.
- industrial corporations
- food companies
- farmers

The attitudes of other countries

Try to balance your thinking – will GM food help end world starvation, or could it be an environmental disaster?

- The United States has 72% of the world's total GM acreage – more than 30 crops, including more than half of the total soya crop.
- Argentina is the world's second largest producer of GM soya.
- Canada is third in the world's GM ranking – mainly oil seed rape, maize and soya.
- China is the fourth largest producer – mainly cotton and tobacco, and moving towards GM foods. Labelling laws are being introduced.
- Australia has 250 000 acres of GM cotton under cultivation.
- Japan is witnessing a growing consumer backlash, but is the world's leading importer of GM crops. Labelling laws have been introduced.
- New Zealand has set up a Royal Commission and a voluntary moratorium on GM imports has been established.
- Thailand has imposed a ban on GM imports, but GM companies are knocking at the government's door.
- Europe is the leading sceptic in the world, with strong consumer opposition. There have been small GM field trials in the UK – some of which have been destroyed in high publicity raids led, for example, by Greenpeace. Small-scale commercial crops are grown in Germany, France, Spain and Portugal. Ten varieties of crops are grown, including oil seed rape, maize and tobacco.

The companies who are leading the development of genetically modified crops are, on the whole, huge transglobal concerns. The annual turnover of a company like Monsanto, the leading GM firm in Britain, will be larger than the total budgets of some of the world's developing countries. There is therefore an economic, as well as a scientific, side to this issue. How do the governments of the world's poorest nations try to resist the power and influence of some of the world's richest and most powerful companies? Where do developing countries draw the line between, for example, receiving huge amounts of financial support from GM companies that would enable them to undertake projects to help develop their country, and the risk of losing sovereignty and control of their lands to foreign companies who could up and go at any time if their boards of directors, based thousands of miles away, decide that investment would be better made elsewhere?

> **KEY POINT**
>
> The four areas chosen for this section are representative of a range of topics that reflect the growing importance of science and technology in our daily lives. Science must not be seen as something 'out there', or as subjects that are merely studied for A Level exams. It has helped transform the way we live and affected in a dramatic and direct manner the basis of our standard of living. In doing this, science also affects the way we think about the world and the cultures of the world. General Studies should help you to think about this broad picture and to put scientific development into a human context.

Progress check

1. What was the estimated number of teleworkers in the world in 2000?
2. What percentage of 15-year-olds use CD-Rom and the internet to look up information?
3. The publication of what academic work led to huge controversy about evolution and the development of the world?
4. Which are the three largest producers of genetically modified crops?
5. Which pressure group led a co-ordinated destruction of a field-trial of a genetically modified crop in England?

1 10 million. 2 58%. 3 Charles Darwin's 'On The Origin of Species'. 4 United States; Argentina; Canada. 5 Greenpeace.

Sample question and model answer

1

How are computers affecting our working and domestic lives?

Step 1
Introduction.

Provide a brief and concise introduction noting:
- the hugely increased access to computers
- the use of computers for both industrial production and administration
- the opportunities for many to work from home
- the rise of e-commerce, e-mail and the internet.

Step 2
Take each of these areas and analyse the effects they have had.

- Access to computers – miniaturisation/portability
  – hugely reduced costs
  – creation of the computer industry

Remember to try to support your points with examples.

- Use of computers
  In traditional industry – automation
  – data storage
  – administration
  – specialist tasks, e.g. computer-assisted design
  In teleworking – opening up opportunities for working at home
  – linked to work colleagues through modem and e-mail
  In domestic life – shopping and banking on-line
  – communication by e-mail
  – use of the internet for information
  etc.

Step 3
Conclusion.

- It would be easy to become distracted and roam into areas of irrelevance, as there are so many aspects to the technological revolution – so take care to stay focused.
- Briefly try to sum up the huge changes that have affected our work and domestic arrangements over little more than a decade.
- You could conclude that this amounts to an 'IT revolution' from which there will be no going back.

Practice examination questions

Short answer questions

1 How might you summarise the differences in the natures of scientific and religious beliefs?

2 What are the three main forms for recording music, with an advantage for each type?

3 Why do different perceptions of the nature of a foetus lie at the heart of the moral debate over abortion?

Essay question

4 In what ways have technological developments changed patterns of popular entertainment over the past 100 years?

Chapter 10

Synoptic assessment

What is the synoptic module in General Studies?

AQA A	M6
AQA B	M6
EDEXCEL	M6
OCR	M6

Module 6 of each exam board specification attempts to pull the others together. You will be tested on your understanding of the connections between the different elements of the subject. The aim is to test your grasp of 'the big picture', and all A Level specifications, whatever the subject, will include a minimum of 20% synoptic assessment.

The purpose of the synoptic module is therefore 'to develop candidates' abilities to integrate knowledge and skills from a range of disciplines in order to show appreciation of how they relate to one another and how each may contribute to the understanding of the issues being studied' (AQA General Studies Teachers' Guide).

How each Awarding Body examines the synoptic element

AQA A	M6
AQA B	M6
EDEXCEL	M6
OCR	M6

AQA A

- Based on the study of Society, Politics and the Economy.
- Providing opportunities for the integration of all other aspects of the course, including use of number and date.
- Main focus will be around key current affairs, social developments and 'perennial and contemporary issues'.
- There will be:
  - a case study, which will be issued up to two weeks before the exam, with short and extended written responses.

AQA B

- One compulsory essay section, the question being based on a variety of source materials covering elements of all aspects of the course.
- A second essay, from a choice of two.
- The module as a whole which is the synoptic theme is based around 'Space and Time'.
- The questions will include elements of the use of number and data.

Edexcel

- It is expected that candidates will make a range of links between the areas studied, and will be able to demonstrate the use of number and data in answering two structured pieces of extended writing from a choice of four.

OCR

- Questions will be based on the module 'Culture, Science and Society'.
- There will be two compulsory questions – one essay and one based on stimulus material.

What does the synoptic element seek to examine?

AQA A ▶ M6
AQA B ▶ M6
EDEXCEL ▶ M6
OCR ▶ M6

Whichever of the General Studies specifications you have followed, the key to effective responses is the ability to show knowledge, understanding and the skills you will have developed.

The examiners will be looking for:

- a readiness to question assumptions
- an awareness of the differences between fact, belief and opinion
- an understanding of the 'softness' or 'hardness' of evidence – just how conclusive it is.

At the heart of this is the ability to ask appropriate questions and not to take everything at face value. The best exam answers will be those that:

- show ability to inter-relate issues in different contexts
- reflect a range of knowledge and understanding (with appropriate terminology)
- understand relationships between relevant concepts and ideas
- use information from within and beyond the resources provided in a question, where this is appropriate
- reflect good structure and balance
- distinguish between fact and opinion, and implicit and explicit values
- come to valid and thoughtful conclusions.

Different types of synoptic questions

AQA A ▶ M6
AQA B ▶ M6
EDEXCEL ▶ M6
OCR ▶ M6

Make sure you are prepared for the types of questions you will face.

Each of the different specifications tackles the synoptic paper in slightly different ways. However, we can look at them as falling into two types of questions.

Comprehension (AQA A; AQA B; OCR)

If you are taking the AQA A paper you will be given the series of passages on which the questions will be set two weeks before the exam – they call these documents a 'Case Study'. The other two papers using this type of approach will give the documents to you together with the questions when you go into the exam room.

There will be time to read the material if you haven't seen it in advance – ensure that you do this.

Since one of the requirements of the General Studies specifications (whichever one you have studied) is to test your ability to use number and data, part of the source material you will be asked to read will contain some element of this. It might be graphs, or tables of numerical information, for example, and you will be expected to refer to this at some point in your answer. It is important to do this if you want to obtain a very good mark for this paper, since it is a skill that the Awarding Bodies who set the papers have to test – it will therefore have to feature in some form at some point in the synoptic paper.

Essays

All of the different specifications will ask you to write essays – if you sit the Edexcel paper it will be entirely based on essays. Although the essays could well be based around one specific area of the specification (AQA A essays will focus on 'society, politics and the economy', for example) remember that Unit Six is synoptic. Credit will therefore be given for answers that draw on knowledge, understanding and skills you have gained throughout the course. AQA B essays are also based on resource material that will be given to you along with the questions.

Practice examination questions

Comprehension

(This example is a specimen produced for the AQA B Unit 6 paper).
Read the source material below and then answer the following question.

Figure 1

Objective A – promote changes in travel behaviour

Target A1   To initiate a travel awareness campaign in 1996.

Objective B – reduce the need to travel by private car and encourage the use of alternative means of transport

Target B1   To increase the proportion of major developments that are located within existing urban area at sites well served by public transport and other non-car means of travel.

Target B2   To develop a 'Company Transport Plan' for County Hall and other main County Offices, to reduce the proportion of staff travelling to work, particularly by car, and to encourage other employers to do the same.

Target B3   To limit average road traffic growth within the County to 13% above the 1995 level by the year 2011, compared with the constrained growth forecast of 26% and the demand growth forecast of 46%, and to plan County Council transport schemes accordingly.

Target B4   To stabilise the proportion of journeys to work by the following means of travel at 1991 levels by the year 2001, and to increase the proportion by the year 2011:

	1991	2001	2011
Bus & Train	12%	12%	15%
Bicycle	3%	3%	6%
Walking	8%	8%	11%

Target B5   To stabilise the number of school children and students travelling to and from schools and colleges by means other than private motor vehicles at 1996 levels by the year 2001 and to increase the proportion by 10% by 2006.

Growth rate in motor vehicle traffic

Mode of journeys to work

Source: New Transport Plan for Surrey County Council, 1996

1   **Surrey County Council faces a problem. It will have based its assessment of the problem on a number of different kinds of evidence:**
   • historical   • social   • political   • economic.
   In what respects might each of these kinds of evidence have offered only a limited view of the problem and the County's solution to it?

Essay

Here is a specimen essay question which is based on source material, the sort you will find in the AQA B paper. Read the source material (in Figures 2 and 3) and then answer the following question

2   **How far do the 'facts', such as those in Figures 2 and 3, tell us the 'truth' about the family in the Western world; and what light do they throw on what we call 'family values'?**

Practice examination questions (continued)

Figure 2

HOLDING TOGETHER BETTER THAN MOST

The American family is going to hell in a handcart, as everyone knows, with high rates of divorce, rotten kids and neglected old folks. True, the American family unit breaks up and reassembles itself with unfortunate velocity, but in other ways the picture is positively heart-warming. Here are a few examples:

Staying together. When youngsters finish school, they are increasingly likely to settle back with their folks. In 1980, 48% of the 18-to-24-year-olds lived at home; by 1995, that had risen to 53%. Among 25–34-year-olds, the percentage increased from 8% to 12%. Economic reasons play a part in these decisions, of course; it is clear, however, that for young Americans home remains the place where, when you have to go there, they have to take you in.

Attitudes. Contrary to conventional wisdom, teenagers see eye-to-eye with their parents on most things. According to a Department of Education survey, 73% agree with their parents on what to do with their lives; 87% agree on the value of education; 73% on women's roles; 70% on religion, 66% on racial issues;

and 63% on how to dress. The one area without much sign of youthful dutifulness – what is permitted on a date – has probably been a matter of dispute since the days of cave families.

The elderly. About 15% of America's elderly people live with their children, a higher proportion than most North European countries (though lower than in 1962, when 28% did). The increase in older people living alone is not a sign of abandonment but of greater choice. Surveys show that people prefer to live independently if they can. Anyway, out of sight does not mean out of mind; up to three-quarters of elderly parents have at least one child they see every week; a third see a child daily.

Nor is it true that Americans pop their grannies into nursing homes with unseemly haste. Eight out of ten disabled elderly people live outside institutions; 70% of these rely on their families, particularly their daughters. Only 5.4% of over 50s live in an institution, fewer than a decade ago. Most rich countries put away a larger proportion than that...

Source: The Economist, London, 22 February 1997

Figure 3

FACTS AND VALUES

When we seek to know the facts, the questions which we ask, and therefore the answers which we obtain, are prompted by our system of values. Our picture of the facts of our environment is moulded by our values, i.e. by the categories through which we approach the facts; and this picture is one of the important facts which we have to take into account. Values enter into the facts and are an essential part of them. Our values are an essential part of our equipment as human beings. It is through our values that we have that capacity to adapt ourselves to our environment, and to adapt our environment to ourselves, to acquire that mastery over our environment which has made history a record of progress. But do not, in dramatising the struggle of man with his environment, set up a false antithesis and a false separation between facts and values. Progress in history is achieved through the interdependence and interaction of facts and values. The objective historian is the historian who penetrates most deeply into this reciprocal process.

A clue to this problem of facts and values is provided by our ordinary use of the word 'truth' – a word which straddles the

world of fact and the world of value, and is made up of elements of both. Nor is this an idiosyncrasy of the English language. The words for truth in the Latin languages, the German *Wahrheit*, the Russian *pravda*, all possess this dual character. Every language appears to require this word for a truth which is not merely a statement of fact and not merely a value judgement, but embraces both elements. It may be a fact that I went to London last week. But you would not ordinarily call it a truth; it is devoid of any value content. On the other hand, when the Founding Fathers of the United States in the Declaration of Independence referred to the self-evident truth that all men are created equal, you may feel that the value content of the statement predominates over the factual content, and may on that account challenge its right to be regarded as a truth. Somewhere between these two poles – the north pole of valueless facts and the south pole of value judgements still struggling to transform themselves into facts – lies the realm of historical truth.

Source: E H Carr, What is History?, Macmillan, 1961

These two examples are specimen essays from the synoptic papers produced by AQA A and by Edexcel.

3 What do you understand by 'equality of opportunity'? Why is it a concept that has received so much attention in Britain during the last 30–40 years? What measures have been taken to eliminate discrimination and how effective do you consider them to have been? What further needs to be done?

(Assessment and Qualifications Alliance A Specimen)

4 'Society should be grateful that science, through genetically modified foods, has provided the means to solve the world's food shortage.' Critically evaluate this statement from the perspectives of science, society and morality.

(Edexcel)

Practice examination answers

Chapter 1 Modern society

1   *Points to cover in your answer include the following:*
    Political correctness is needed to:
- regulate extremists in society
- help to eliminate discrimination and remove unjustified unfairness from society
- challenge us to consider the reality of our feelings – which can lead to promotion of fairness in society.

    Political correctness will not lead to a fairer society because:
- many examples are trivial and have no impact on society
- it is now seen as being rather passé
- it leads to petty regulations
- the time and money involved would be better spent promoting a fair society in other ways.

2   *A good answer on Equality of Opportunity would cover such areas as:*
- wealth, class, gender, race, sexuality and disability
- the growth of the Welfare State, which has been an important step in creating a platform for greater equality over the past 30–40 years.
    Measures taken include:
- legislation to deal with unfair discrimination in society on the basis of race, gender, sexuality and disability, particularly relating to employment.
    Effectiveness:
- more will be perceived to have been achieved on some fronts than on others, e.g. gender rather than race. Various high-profile cases can be quoted here.

3   *This answer gives no factual response to the question set; rather it aims to set out the formula and process to be able to handle a piece of coursework. This is an individual project that is part of the OCR coursework question. To do it successfully you must complete the following three sections:*
- background planning – recognise, explore and describe the question. Plan for and search to obtain information relevant to the question
- option generation and decision-making – generate and compare two ideas related to the issue and justify the one you choose to take forward
- use two examples of study-based learning methods to understand the issues, plan and implement a chosen solution and review progress
- monitoring, evaluation and reporting – agree methods to check whether the problem has been solved and describe your results, review your activity against agreed objectives and agree actions for improving performance. Present an individual report on your findings, including an IT-generated graph and a report for publication including a reflective evaluation of your project.

4   *A good answer to this will distinguish between 'fact' and 'opinion' and acknowledge bias and prejudice. There should be a broad approach to the issue, with a challenging of the statement. A very good answer will acknowledge that the statement does not necessarily relate to the present situation but rather to an ideal which has, by implication, been lost and ought to be aimed for.*

Chapter 2 Politics: continuity and change

1   *The notion of 'right' and 'wrong' is decided by a range of factors:*
- codes adopted by societies or groups
- the relationship between these and the legal code
- roles played by parents, families and the peer group
- the education system
- views expressed by politicians, media, etc.
    Differences of opinion are tolerated because of acceptance of certain freedoms, e.g.
- freedom of speech, movement and assembly
- fair trial and presumption of innocence
- privacy, withdrawal of labour and protection of personal property.

2   *This is a similar piece of coursework to that discussed in Question 3 in Chapter 1. This, however, is a group project. As with Question 3 in Chapter 1 there are three sections which must be completed:*
- background planning – recognise, explore and describe the problem, agree responsibilities and working arrangements, make clear and relevant contributions to group discussions
- option generation and decision-making. In your group, generate and compare options and justify the options for taking forward. Plan and implement the chosen solution

and review progress. Make a clear presentation of your view of the options to your group
- monitoring, evaluating and reporting – agree methods to check if the problem has been solved and describe results and agree actions for improving performance.

3   *This is a Unit 6 synoptic question. Hence high-quality answers are those that bring together information from different areas of the specification. The question examines the issues relating to the actions of those objecting to the building of the runway. These concern freedom of expression within a democracy. Various points could be touched upon.*
- Breaking the law is one way of getting publicity. However, is it right to break the law in any circumstance? Can violence ever be condoned?
- Should there be limitations on the ways in which people can exercise their freedom?
- Were Swampy's actions in defiance of democracy or an extension of it?
- What is the role and significance of pressure groups like Friends of the Earth?
- What is it about the environment that it is particularly important to protect?

Chapter 2 Politics: continuity and change (continued)

4 *Young people are less interested in politics because:*
- there is little to make them want to defend democracy as an ideal
- the political system fails to address their needs
- the young are often passionate about politics, but have a wider perspective than Westminster
- single-issue policies are more likely to appeal to them
- pop music and the fashion industry have a higher profile, politics is seen as old-fashioned
- of the generation gap

- sleaze, etc. creates a cynical view of the political world
- money and commerce are now seen as the primary forces for change in society.

However,
- the vast majority of young people are still on the electoral role and vote at General Elections.
- young people are often the most passionate campaigners for Friends of the Earth, Greenpeace, etc.
- their disinterest in mainstream polices is compounded by a doubt about political parties' ability to make change.

Chapter 3 The economy today

1 Attractions of designer gear:
- It projects an image that one wishes to promote by making a social statement.
- It confers status amongst one's peers.
- It makes one 'belong' to a particular minority group.
- It suggests that one can afford the best.
- It associates one with famous names.
- It adds style and panache to a drab world.
- It provides employment for millions.
  Objections to designer gear:
- Much of it is beyond the means of those who buy it.
- It is uneconomical and unnecessary.
- It is ephemeral, becoming quickly obsolete.
- It encourages snobbery, vanity and materialism.
- It is socially divisive.
- It is morally corrosive and is symptomatic of a decadent Western society.

2
- A balanced diet should contain sufficient carbohydrates and fats to meet energy needs.
- Integration of diet and exercise is necessary because:
  - this leads to better cardio-vascular fitness, a reduction in heart disease and a reduction of high blood pressure, etc.
  - It helps with stress management
  - It produces greater physical flexibility and muscular strength, etc.

- Quality of life is in the eye of the beholder. Generally speaking, however, there is a link between an energetic and active life and an enhanced sense of well-being. The extent to which high levels of physical fitness contribute to high levels of mental, social and emotional fitness can also be mentioned.

3 *In answering this question you need to do the following:*
- define 'ability' e.g. David Beckham, Tony Blair, Eminem.
- discuss the fact that it comes down to supply and demand, i.e. if the 'ability' is in short supply and the demand is there, then higher rates of pay will occur.
- in discussing the Maximum Wage make the arguments for and against:
  for: stops ludicrous sums being paid to certain media personalities, etc., and could mean more money for a wider group of people.
  against: stifles flair and initiative and hard work ethic (i.e. Protestant Work Ethic, much favoured by Thatcher's Conservative Government).
- Discuss the overall principles as follows:
  - 'A fair day's wage for a fair day's work'.
  - What does this mean in reality?
  - Is it a supply and demand concept only?
  - What about the caring professions? What value does/should society place on these?
  - Should the chief executive of a public utility company receive 15 times the salary of the sewer maintenance staff they employ?

Chapter 4 Belief, non-belief and values

1 Iran, Afghanistan and Pakistan are those mentioned in the text.
2 Catholic, Protestant, Orthodox.
3 Atheism/Agnosticism/Materialism/Humanism/Hedonism.
4 Introduction should acknowledge that some form of religious belief has marked every recorded society.
- Even if you hold religious views yourself, you will have to acknowledge that there has been a dramatic decline in Christian observance in the UK, and that this has not been seen to the same extent in other religions.
- You could look at different explanations for this including:

  - there is now a more personal view of religion – formal attendance at a church is not seen as so important.
  - the view that traditional religious observance is seen as lacking relevance.
  - religion has been seen as a conservative and reactionary force that has not kept abreast of scientific and technological progress, but if it could do so, religion might regain some of its status.
- You can then look at whether future trends will lead to a continued decline in religious belief. Give reasons why, not just your own opinion.

Chapter 5 Artistic and social developments

1 Post and lintel.

2 The example provided here is that of the Impressionists, but you could choose any school with which you are familiar. You should mention the following points:
- formed following the collaboration of Monet and Renoir in 1869
- completed smaller, more intimate works on site, not in a studio
- set a style in which the impression, or the atmosphere created was as important as the objects being painted
- used primary colours and their derivatives – no black in the palettes of many of the Impressionists
- exhibited from 1874 to 1896
- prominent members included Monet, Renoir, Pissaro, Degas and Cézanne.

3 The sculptor creates a central core in the rough shape of the casting. This is covered in wax to the exact thickness and shape required of the final metal. This is then covered in plaster, and the whole thing is baked. The wax melts and runs off through tubes inserted into it prior to firing. The molten metal is then poured into the space left behind by the melted wax to create the casting. The inner and outer cores are chipped away to reveal the completed object.

4 Film and cinema can be divided into several eras:
- The silent movies of the first part of the century, with stars like Charlie Chaplin, Mary Pickford and Rudolf Valentino.
- The 'talkies' developed quickly from the late 1920s – the 'Jazz Singer' (1927) containing snippets of sound. By the early 1930s all films had full sound, so scripts and plots could become more complex.
- Colour began to develop in the later 1930s, but was very expensive. However, from the 1950s virtually all films were made in colour. One notable exception in the 1990s was Steven Spielburg's 'Schindler's List', which was abut the Holocaust and which was made in black and white to highlight the bleakness of its content.
- Audiences peaked in the late 1940s, by which time many in Britain were going to the cinema twice a week. The arrival of the television age saw steep declines in cinema audiences in the 1950s and 60s.
- Today the industry tends to concentrate on block-busters like 'Jurassic Park', or the 'Star Wars' films, which attract huge audiences and make large profits.

Chapter 6 Art, culture and society

1 Marx's view was that art was an expression of the underlying economic relations in its society – either before, or after, the Revolution that would inevitably bring about workers' control at some point. Art could only be seen as 'great' when it was progressive, i.e.
- it helps to inspire, and bring forward the eventual victory of the working class in pre-revolutionary societies
- it strengthens the values of society in revolutionary communities.

2 In Medieval Europe, where there was no paper, artists used wood panels, plaster walls, stained glass and parchment. Also the fine woollen rugs made from the wool of their animals by nomadic Asian herdsmen.

3 The Arts Councils in each of the constituent countries of the UK provide direct government subsidies to help fund opera, dance and drama; touring and experimental groups; orchestras and festivals.
- The National Lottery provides 'one-off' funding for specific projects, which might be for a small grant to help some small community project to get off the ground, up to the multi-million-pound support controversially provided to assist the rebuilding of the Covent Garden Opera House.

4 *Your answer should include reference to the following:*
- the acquisition of collections that can be seen by the public
- education, both in the gallery/museum itself, or by mounting a travelling exhibition, or loans to other institutes
- preservation and development of national, regional or local culture
- display of the best of the works currently available, either in permanent form, or by mounting specific exhibitions on a theme
- creating centres of expertise that can be available to experts through lectures, visits, libraries, archives,etc.

Chapter 7 Scientific and technological progress

1 Through the air; through contamination; through direct contact; by sexual transmission; through blood; from animals.

2 Distribution of data and information; fostering conservation; promoting financial credit for agriculture; developing soil and water resources; arranging international exchange of new strains of plants; working to control diseases of plants and animals; providing technical and specialist assistance.

3 Fortran, Algol and Cobol.

4 *For:*
- The need to maximise food production in a world with a growing population.
- Pests destroy 35% of the world's crops.
- The cost of cereal crops lost to pests is estimated at £300 million.
- Modern chemicals break down quickly and don't persist in soil.
- The savings in terms of crops saved far outweighs the cost of buying the chemicals.

Against:
- The risk of residues of powerful chemicals in the soil.
- There has been a serious loss of wildlife caused by chemical sprays – e.g. decline of Peregrine Falcons and Golden Eagles.
- Some chemicals have been found to poison humans.
- The lesson of DDT pollution shows the powerful and abiding consequences of the use of this chemical.

Chapter 8 Controversies in science and technology

1   Answers should cover:
- the extent to which the right to life is guaranteed by the European Convention on Human Rights
- whether medical staff might be accused of murder
- the extent to which medical staff are bound to preserve life as part of their professional code
- the extent to which the wishes of the family should sway medical opinion
- whether the final decision should rest with the courts, medical opinion or the wishes of the family.

2   The main – albeit inadequate – steps that have been taken are:
- to control exhaust emissions and introduce more efficient engines in vehicles powered by internal combustion engines
- to reduce the number of coal-powered electricity-generating stations (although gas – a frequent alternative – is also a fossil fuel)
- statutory controls on emissions from factory chimneys and many domestic fires.

3   Work into human fertility, miscarriage and congenital disease.

4 • Your answer should acknowledge that there are ethical as well as medical dimensions to this question, which should be the basis of your introduction.
- You might think that there are times when it is not acceptable to terminate life, but that is not what the question is asking, unless you take the view that it is never acceptable.
- Be objective – consider the areas that some people feel do provide reasonable grounds, e.g.:
  – when people are in a permanent vegetative state
  – when people are in the final stages of terminal illness
  – perhaps when the State has decreed a form of capital punishment involving lethal injection?
- Try to be objective in weighing up the strength of arguments for and against.
- If you think trying to compare medicine and religion is similar to comparing chalk and cheese, try to discuss why this is the case, and how this complicates thinking. Discuss the role of ethics and philosophy in coming to a decision
- Draw a conclusion that seeks to acknowledge different perspectives before coming to a personal view.

Chapter 9 Science and culture

1   Scientific belief – based on mathematical models, laws, hypothesis, experiment and verification.
Religious belief – based on faith and personal experience.

2   (i)   Vinyl discs – one advantage: the music can be started at any point, 'mixing' in clubs
(ii) Audio cassettes – one advantage: very light and portable
(iii) Compact discs – one advantage: quality of sound, difficult to damage.

3   Opponents of abortion see the foetus as a human life, an unborn child. They argue that since there is no single moment when the bundle of cells turns into a viable human being it has to be said that life begins with conception.
Supporters of abortion see the foetus as having potential for life, in the same way that an acorn has the potential to become an oak tree, or an egg to become a chicken. However, it does not, and cannot, exist as a separate 'being' and is therefore an appendage of the mother with no life of its own.

4   Answers should briefly touch on the 'pre-electric' world – e.g. no recordings, no amplification, no microphones, etc. You should then set out and consider separately where there have been major developments in entertainment, and the role of technology in these:
- radio, TV and video recording – television in particular has become the major source of leisure and relaxation
- music – the development of recorded music from the first cylinders to today's CDs and DVDs, the quality of sound getting better at each stage
- film – from the first flickering images to the computer-assisted technology of today's cinema.
Your answer should draw some conclusion about the enormity of the developments, but remember that the question is primarily about the *technology*, not the entertainment itself. Do not end up describing your favourite programmes, or entertainers, as this would be irrelevant and gain no marks.

Chapter 10 Synoptic assessment

The following answers come from the relevant Awarding Bodies.

1   The Council will have considered evidence setting limits to understanding the problem and to solving it, of the following sort:
(a) (i)   the historical evidence it will have considered will be reports and recollections of travel-to-work patterns of past; of a town well-served by trains and trolley-buses; of employees living near their work, and of cycling and walking to offices.
(ii) such historical views may tempt the planner to believe that he might recapture such a 'golden age'. So much has changed since the days when a minority of households owned cars, and public transport satisfied needs.
(b) (i)   Social surveys might well have been done to find out where people live in relation to their work; the patterns of their commuting, and their attitudes towards it; and the sociology and psychology of car-use might have been investigated.
(ii) Such findings might well have encouraged the Council either to overestimate, or to underestimate the extent to which people THINK they have become dependent upon their cars, and the extent to which a change of 'lifestyle' is possible.
(c) (i)   The Council will have taken account of the policies of

the Conservative governments where the encouragement of consumer choice, road-building, and the deregulation and privatisation of public transport systems were concerned; and they will have taken note of the ambitions of New Labour to build an integrated transport system and reduce urban pollution.

(ii) The Council might have misjudged how far either set of policies is popular with either the national or local electorates. In particular, it might have overestimated the extent to which the public has been persuaded by its 'travel awareness campaign' that what needs to be done is not 'anti-car'.

(d) (i) The Council will have conducted cost-benefit analyses of each of the growth rates in the table; it will have established what the costs are of doing nothing, and of what the economic implications are of its targets.

(ii) It might not have factored in the costs to employees of rearranging their lives to make public transport use possible. On the other hand it might have underestimated the costs – because they may be fundamentally incalculable – of allowing traffic growth over 13% by the year 2011, never mind the higher rates referred to.

2

(a) it is unlikely that the American data will be very different from data from the UK, or Europe. If there are good economic reasons for young people to 'settle back with their folks' in the USA, it is certain that these reasons will occur elsewhere – though it may be that the average home in the USA is more accommodating than the average home in the UK;

(b) it may be that we should treat these 'facts' with some caution: we know nothing about the sample for this survey – though we might trust *The Economist* not to peddle dubious data;

(c) the researcher(s) who conducted the survey probably did have an 'agenda' – one hypothesis is chosen from among others for one quite human reason or another. We have to be sure that we know what is meant by 'settle back' – did the interviewees understand by it what the researcher(s) understood? And what is meant by 'agree with', in the context of religion, say, might it have meant an absence of argument on the subject, or something more? Was the researcher looking for agreement?

(d) economic reasons for behaviour will certainly detract from the case for closer family ties. Still, young people will not live with their parents if it is intolerable to them to do so. The researcher admits (in the case of the elderly) that 'people prefer to live independently if they can';

(e) if our values give us the capacity to adapt ourselves to our environment, as Carr suggests, then values are **prior** to behaviour. Yet they will really only be **revealed** in behaviour. Figure 3 data would suggest that we continue to value family ties, and that rights and duties in the family context are taken seriously. This will only surprise us if we are so unthinking as to join 'everyone' in the 'knowledge' that the family 'is going to hell in a handcart'.

3 This is a demanding question with a substantial number of dimensions. The first part asks for a definition or demonstration of understanding of a range of issues; the second knowledge of how and why awareness and concern have grown; the third specific knowledge of steps taken in law and social practice; evaluation of progress made; and finally solutions or proposals for further action.

The breadth and depth of analysis required for the first part should provide evidence of AO4 in terms of discussion about the desirability of EO as an ideal objective for society, but hardly likely ever to be achieved in any absolute sense. An answer which approaches a comprehensive treatment of the topic might be expected to cover such areas as wealth, class, gender, race, sexuality and (dis)ability. (AO1) Well-informed and aware candidates will be able to refer to the development of the Welfare State (access to free education, health care, housing, employment and a minimum standard of living for all) as important steps forward in creating a platform for greater equality, but only that perhaps. (AO1, 3 and 4) Wider educational and employment opportunities, leading to increases in individual and social mobility, coupled with the growth of communications have probably created greater awareness and the potential for changing attitudes and behaviour. In turn this has led to legislation to deal with unfair discrimination solely on the basis of race, gender, sexuality and disability, particularly relating to employment and other social situations. We should not expect too much here in terms of detailed knowledge of various Acts passed in the 1960s and 70s, but general awareness of their existence, intentions and effects, in relation to race and sex might be the minimum contribution to a good answer. (All the AOs)

We may encounter both pessimism and optimism, depending on candidates' views and experiences, and we should acknowledge that the question of discrimination might well be a personal and emotive issue for some candidates requiring a sensitive response on the part of the examiner. Perhaps more will be perceived to have been achieved on some fronts than others (e.g. gender rather than race?). Also, various individual high profile cases or incidents might be seen to distort or undermine what has been achieved on a broader front. As always in General Studies, it will be down to the individual case which the candidate presents and the extent to which it is successfully argued, supported and illustrated. (All AOs)

It would perhaps be unreasonable to expect dramatic solutions to the last part of the question, given the range and intractability of the problems. General awareness of how attitudes and behaviour are best changed, perhaps through a combination of education and legislation, is perhaps as much as we should require here. The best answers will most likely aim to cover all aspects of the question with a degree of balance, objectivity and realism in the arguments advanced. (All AOs)

(NB References are to the overall Assessment Objectives;
AO1 – knowledge and understanding applied to a range of issues
AO2 – clear and accurate communication in a concise, logical and relevant way
AO3 – marshalling evidence and drawing conclusions, using information.)

4 Candidates should explain how GM foods could solve the world's food crisis by looking at the scientific arguments in favour of GM foods. The scientific worries about GM foods should be addressed and the moral and social arguments for and against should be evaluated.
Candidates should balance the relative merits of the various arguments showing awareness of their limitations, to reach a balanced, justified conclusion.

Index